SENSING THE SCRIPTURES

Sensing the Scriptures

Aminadab's Chariot and the
Predicament of Biblical Interpretation

Karlfried Froehlich

With the collaboration of
Mark S. Burrows

WILLIAM B. EERDMANS PUBLISHING COMPANY
GRAND RAPIDS, MICHIGAN / CAMBRIDGE, U.K.

Published 2014 by
Wm. B. Eerdmans Publishing Co.
2140 Oak Industrial Drive N.E., Grand Rapids, Michigan 49505 /
P.O. Box 163, Cambridge CB3 9PU U.K.
www.eerdmans.com

Printed in the United States of America

19 18 17 16 15 14   7 6 5 4 3 2 1

Library of Congress Cataloging-in-Publication Data

Froehlich, Karlfried.
Sensing the scriptures: Aminadab's chariot and the predicament of biblical interpretation /
Karlfried Froehlich, with the collaboration of Mark S. Burrows.
pages   cm
Includes bibliographical references.
ISBN 978-0-8028-7080-3 (pbk.: alk. paper)
1. Bible — Hermeneutics.   I. Title.

BS476.F745   2014
220.601 — dc23

2014013044

A version of Chapter 1 in this volume was published as
"'Aminadab's Chariot': The Predicament of Biblical Interpretation," in *The Princeton Seminary Bulletin* 18 (1997): 262-78, and appears in revised form with permission.

Contents

Preface

This book is based on the set of six Warfield lectures that I was privileged to deliver at Princeton Theological Seminary in the spring and fall of 1997. When I accepted the invitation extended by President Thomas W. Gillespie at the suggestion of the then Charles Hodge Professor of Systematic Theology, E. David Willis, whose task it was to nominate the Warfield lecturer for the year, it was clear to me that the topic would have to deal with the history of biblical interpretation, a field that had been at the center of my scholarly interest from the beginning of my academic career. In fact, it was the experience of the need to expand one's vision of the exegetical endeavor in New Testament scholarship beyond the concern for the actual shape and the pre-history of a biblical text to include its post-history in order to arrive at a proper understanding that suggested to me the importance of serious work on the history of biblical interpretation.

The Basel of Karl Barth and Oscar Cullmann in the 1950s where I spent most of my years of graduate study was a perfect testing ground for the ideas of a fuller form of New Testament scholarship that were swirling through my head. In Karl Barth's lectures, which presented the future chapters of his *Church Dogmatics*, I, like many of my student colleagues, waited eagerly for the exegetical excursions, later reduced to smaller print in the familiar white volumes, in which the master demonstrated the art of exacting historical-critical analysis of specific biblical passages or verses in order to undergird his systematic argument. More than once in the course of unearthing such exciting treasure troves by digging to unexpected depths, Barth would reach out into the interpretation of the church fathers, the Reformers, the great biblical scholars of the nineteenth century. Everyone loved it and profited by the exercise. Oscar Cullmann held the chair once occupied by Franz Overbeck that combined the teaching of the New Testament with that of early and medieval church history. Until his death Cullmann regretted that this fruitful combination was abandoned when the faculty chose his successor. Under Cullmann's supervision, a number of dissertations tracing the interpretive history of biblical texts were written, and together with other far-sighted scholars such as Hans von Campenhausen and Ernst Käsemann he founded two series of publications, the "Studien zur Geschichte der neutestamentlichen Exegese" and the "Studien zur biblischen Hermeneutik," which solicited manuscripts on the history of biblical interpretation. For decades, the renowned publishing house of Mohr-Siebeck in Tübingen kept these series in its program and in this way encouraged a trend among biblical scholars that by now has become universal.

When I began teaching at Drew University in the early 1960s, I was allowed to continue the Cullmann-Overbeck tradition of combining New Testament studies and early church history in my teaching assignment. Already during those early years I developed a course, "History of Biblical Interpretation," which I also taught regularly at Princeton. It is still my conviction that such a course offers students a particularly compelling and comprehensive introduction to the theological aspects of church history, following Gerhard Ebeling's thesis that "church history is the history of biblical interpretation." As I was getting ready to work on the Warfield lectures, I decided it was time to pull together the strands of all my various research projects over the years that had fed into the revised versions of that course, and to attempt a synthesis of what I had learned over the years from my study of the sources, from the interaction with students and colleagues, and from the ongoing discussion in the literature. In the meantime, Beryl Smalley's magisterial *Study of the Bible in the Middle Ages* had appeared in its third edition and had spawned the formation of "SSBMA," the small but very active "Society for the Study of the Bible in the Middle Ages," which gathers a devoted band of enthusiasts every year during the Congress of Medieval Studies at Kalamazoo, Michigan. At the same time plans were taking shape to translate the incredibly rich but forbidding volumes of Henri de Lubac's *Exégèse Médiévale: Les quatre sens de l'Ecriture* into English, a massive project that still remains incomplete. I have learned a great deal from both of these masters of the field. Smalley and especially de Lubac are my constant reference and discussion partners in these lectures.

The lecture format was also an invitation to present the material without the burden of an extensive apparatus as a fairly simple argument, which can be followed easily yet turns out to be more involved and challenging when it comes to its implications. This may have led to oversimplification at certain points. I have tried, however, not to compromise scholarly integrity and to present at least basic documentation for the numerous auxiliary subjects and details on which I touch in the dense formulations of my paragraphs. The extensive subject index is an attempt to provide some access to the wide range of issues that presented themselves for consideration in the course of my basic outline. "Aminadab's Chariot" as the enigmatic but entirely appropriate title for the lectures was a delightful discovery that occurred to me when I was sorting through the many biblical images used by medieval authors who were trying to illustrate their vision of the standard fourfold sense. It was an exciting moment when I first saw this chariot pictured in the intriguing stained glass panel of Abbot Suger's ambulatory in the basilica of St. Denis during one of my study periods at Paris in 1955. It fascinated me as it has fascinated and puzzled art historians for decades, and its analysis is part of my final argument here. The insight that it had a parallel in Prudence's heaven-storming chariot of the bodily senses described so boldly in Alan of Lille's *Anticlaudianus* was triggered by the work of my colleague John Fleming of Princeton University, who taught me to pay attention to the non-theological literature of the Middle Ages, in Latin and in the early vernacular languages of Europe, as examples of biblical interpretation reflecting the theological trends of their time.

The fact that the lectures were delivered at Princeton Seminary, the place where I taught several generations of students, should also explain the obvious local coloring of my text, which would perhaps be out of place in a strictly literary publication. Addressing a Princeton audience, I used the occasion to refer to locally prominent figures, first of all Benjamin Breckenridge Warfield, whose named chair I held, but also to close friends and colleagues at Princeton Seminary such as Bernhard W. Anderson, Ellen Charry, Edward A. Dowey, Ulrich Mauser, Kathleen McVey, and E. David Willis. Another deliberate decision was to draw attention to the work of my doctoral students over the years to whom I feel I owe a considerable debt of gratitude. Witnessing their scholarly endeavors during the dissertation stage and following their careers afterwards have greatly enriched my own scholarship, and it has been a joy to mention some of their names: Robert Bernard, Bart Ehrmann, Paul Rorem. Of course, there were others, but one of them has contributed more than anyone else to the hatching of this book: Mark S. Burrows.

Preface

Mark Burrows wrote his dissertation on Jean Gerson, a major fifteenth-century theologian during the age of conciliarism, a movement in which I was keenly interested myself. He served as my teaching assistant in the history of exegesis course and has remained a close friend and esteemed colleague both professionally and personally ever since. When I was lacking the energy to return to the lectures and prepare their publication, Mark Burrows encouraged me and offered tangible help. With a careful and skilled hand he shaped my rough prose into readable chapters, and sometimes even did more. Being a gifted poet himself, he added the gentle touch of the characteristic beauty of his native tongue, and in the sections discussing Bernard of Clairvaux he contributed significantly to my own conclusions, based on his own intensive study of Bernard's Sermons on the Song of Songs. If the book reads well, it owes this quality to Mark Burrows's labor of love. His collaboration made the difference, and I am deeply grateful to him.

Karlfried Froehlich
Pentecost 2014
Princeton, N.J.

CHAPTER ONE

Principles and Rules: Smelling the Issues

These are hard times for biblical interpretation. Not only that, they are hard times for the Bible itself. Recent reports of Bible societies in the West reveal that the sales of Bibles in Western languages are dramatically down in recent years, except in Eastern Europe. One might be tempted to answer that the market is simply saturated. Obviously we are only scratching the surface with this answer. It may, however, have a bearing on the problems biblical interpretation is experiencing. What one finds for sale almost exclusively are translations, and translations of course are interpretations. The multiplication of English translations in print in recent decades, if it is not exhilarating, has reached frightening dimensions, and most of these translations claim some official authority and support. This is true not only for the old favorites like the King James (or "Authorized") Version, but for new ones as well — such as the New Revised Standard Version, the New International Version, the New Jerusalem Bible, Today's English Version, The New English Bible, the Good News Bible, the Ecumenical Version, and a host of others; a comprehensive list would fill a small and ever-expanding volume of its own! A major problem, then, is the very existence and thus the rivalry of multiple authoritative interpretations.

In this situation, the integrity of the biblical word itself seems to be dissolving in the experience of our generation. We read our daily devotions or the text for a congregational Bible study in one translation and then in another, and we hardly recognize that it is the same passage. We want to memorize a verse and are faced with an embarrassing range of possible wording, right down to such basic texts as the Lord's Prayer and the Twenty-third Psalm. We want to buy a searchable Bible for our computer, but which should we choose when we don't know for sure what words to search for? It is no wonder that people are opting for the King James Version again; at least one knows what one will find there! Again, however, the problem with translations only scratches the surface. How much more serious must be the problems with biblical interpretation in general when we dig deeper?

Not that long ago, the future of biblical interpretation looked bright. In the wake of the Second World War, the "biblical theology" movement was sweeping the international scene, and American scholars played a leading part in its development. Teachers like James Muilenberg, G. Ernest Wright, and Bernhard W. Anderson inspired an entire generation with their focus on a theology of the "Mighty Acts of God," as witnessed in the literature of the Old Israel and the New — but also as experienced in the contemporary upheavals and triumphs of the postwar era. This was the time when form criticism and tradition history illumined biblical texts in amazingly new ways. It was an age when the German Old Testament scholar Gerhard von Rad could make a compelling academic argument for an inner dynamic of the Old Testament tradition as leading logically — and, in a way, inevitably — to the New Testament, and Hartmut Gese could argue for the canon of the Septuagint as the normative one for Protestant theologians who "can never endorse the Masoretic canon, for it obscures in significant measure the continuity [of the Old] with the New Testament."[1] The biblical theology movement had an immense influence on theological trends in the past four decades, not only in terms of its impact on social ethics and social action, on confessional and ecumenical theology, and on interdisciplinary efforts within the theological curriculum, but also in terms of its shaping power in the rapid growth of American evangelicalism.

Times have changed. The early enthusiasm for this movement has been dampened by a good deal of perspectival reorientation, in part through the increased intensity of Jewish/Christian dialogue and Holocaust studies. It has also been influenced by new forms of scientific investigation in anthropology, sociology, and social psychology. Postmodern hermeneutics in general have moved from a central interest in author, genre, and textual transmission to even more fundamental questions — such as that of the nature of a text, the process of the emergence of meaning, and the "reader response" to the Word. For biblical interpretation, this has opened a whole new can of worms. For people in the churches where the concern for the use of the Bible has

---

1. Hartmut Gese, "Erwägungen zur Einheit der biblischen Theologie," *Zeitschrift für Theologie und Kirche* 67 (1970): 423.

its natural place, this has meant an unprecedented invasion of unsettling forces: perspectival pluralism, subjective relativism, textual competition, and a whole new measure of confusion at the realization that there is no clear authority anywhere that could adjudicate between the sides being taken. David Tracy, a Roman Catholic theologian, has described the situation as "the once stable text having now been replaced by the unstable reader," while Robert Jenson, a concerned Lutheran scholar and churchman, has repeatedly characterized the intellectual trends of late modernity as driven by a "nihilist hermeneutics."[2]

These are harsh words, perhaps too harsh. The "text" never was that stable. Bart Ehrman has demonstrated that doctrinal "corrections" of New Testament passages were accepted into the received text as late as the fourth and fifth centuries,[3] and the work of the so-called Paris Bible "correctories" tried to establish a stable text of the Vulgate in the thirteenth century when the confusion of rival versions was becoming intolerable. What of the "unstable reader"? This, of course, was the charge leveled against Protestant exegesis in general by Catholic controversialists of the sixteenth and seventeenth centuries; for them, Protestant biblical interpretation was the epitome of unbridled subjectivity — and what later came to be ridiculed and lamented as the "principle of private judgment." Nothing new here either.

One thing is clear: however stable the text and however unstable the reader, neither has ever existed outside a community of faith. It was a church council and a pope who finally created a stable Vulgate by endorsing the post-Tridentine *Clementina*. It was Protestant churches in which such "unstable" readers found themselves united under the common confessional commitment to the Scriptures as their sole norm and rule.

One natural reaction to the insecurity about the authority, integrity, and normativity of the Bible has been the phenomenal growth of fundamentalist groups in the United States and elsewhere, and their enormous influence on public life and opinion. A fundamentalist approach to Scripture is often the answer of well-meaning people who, facing the personal and societal ambiguities of biblical pluralism, are unprepared or unwill-

---

2. David Tracy, *Plurality and Ambiguity: Hermeneutics, Religion, Hope* (Chicago: University of Chicago Press, 1994), 12; Robert Jenson, "How the World Lost Its Story," *First Things* 36 (1993): 19-24; Robert Jenson, "Can a Text Defend Itself? An Essay *De Inspiratione Scripturae*," *Dialogue* 28, no. 4 (1989): 251-53.

3. Bart Ehrman, "The Text of Mark in the Hands of the Orthodox," in *Biblical Hermeneutics in Historical Perspective: Studies in Honor of Karlfried Froehlich on His Sixtieth Birthday*, ed. Mark S. Burrows and Paul Rorem (Grand Rapids: Eerdmans, 1991), 19-31.

ing to accept the measure of required relativism — in part because they have only one life to live and prefer clear authority structures consonant with their religious experience, and in part because of their honest search for a better society. But such an attitude joins them to a longstanding anti-intellectual undercurrent in American culture, one that finds intellectually demanding debate unnecessary and sophisticated argument repulsive.

Of course, not all fundamentalism is anti-intellectual. If we look for the trend in the mainline churches of the United States, at least, it is frequently part of a strong tradition of confessionalism, and such a commitment tends by its very nature to be decidedly intellectual. Confessionalists have to be willing to think, and think hard, as anyone who has ever studied a confessional document of the sixteenth century knows. One of the most conservative branches of American Lutheranism, the Lutheran Church–Missouri Synod, used to prepare its future ministers in a secondary school system which offered a thorough and comprehensive liberal arts education from a young age on, the benefits of which are still remembered with gratitude by scholars such as Jaroslav Pelikan and Martin Marty, whose historical work dominated the landscape of twentieth-century theological scholarship. One of the towering figures of the Reformed tradition, Benjamin Breckinridge Warfield (d. 1921), was a solid biblical fundamentalist if there ever was one, a scholar with a formidable mind and an apologist par excellence for the doctrine of the plenary verbal inspiration of the Bible, Old and New Testament alike. Like his colleagues at Princeton Theological Seminary at the time, Warfield regarded the Bible as the one and only repository of saving doctrines which God had provided for humankind, to be teased out of the progressive revelations contained in the Scriptures into a perfect synthesis. This, Warfield argued, was the work of the church's theologians, past and present, and he thus called this enterprise "biblical theology." The doctrine of biblical inspiration and inerrancy was only one of these doctrines. For Warfield, as David Kelsey has observed, this doctrine was not indispensable logically; indeed, no other Bible doctrine depended on it.[4] But it was methodologically necessary, once it had been established. While Warfield claimed that he could prove his thesis, his interest must be seen primarily as part of his confessional commitment, his admiration for the Westminster Confession and its central place in the unfolding of Bible doctrines. As he put it:

4. David Kelsey, *The Uses of Scripture in Recent Theology* (Philadelphia: Fortress Press, 1975), 21.

It is our special felicity that, as Reformed Christians and heirs of the richest and fullest formulation of Reformed thought, we possess in that precious heritage, the Westminster Confession, the most complete, the most admirable, the most perfect statement of the essential Christian doctrine of Holy Scripture which has ever been formed by man.[5]

Warfield obviously did not worry about a "predicament" facing practitioners of biblical interpretation. The task of quarrying the Bible for doctrine was a joy and a challenge worth devoting one's life to. If there was any predicament, it probably was his cross of having to fight a host of adversaries, detractors, and wrongheaded thinkers — not only outside the church, but within its own ranks. With regard to the Bible itself, only one point was a source of frustration for him: not errors of fact or contradictions, which dissolved easily as adjustable difficulties, but rather the hazards of the transmission of the text. Warfield realized that neither in the English Bible nor in the best Hebrew and Greek texts available to him in print did he have the absolutely inerrant Bible for which he fought so hard. His response to the difficulty was simple: "The Bible we declare to be 'of infallible truth' is the Bible that God gave us, not the corruptions and slips which scribes and printers have given us, some of which are in every copy."[6] Only the supposedly lost autographs were truly "inspired." From Warfield's insistence on the autographs one might infer his opinion about the role of the biblical languages in the seminary curriculum: here was a scholar's scholar, one who insisted that the proper study of scripture in its "original" languages was the work of engaging the text authentically and faithfully. The ancient humanist quest to return *ad fontes,* "to the sources," meant the close study of the text in Hebrew and in Greek, a task for which no translation could be properly substituted.

This is the point where "Aminadab's chariot" comes in. Do we know who Aminadab is? Of course we do not, at least in terms of the figure who appears under this name in the biblical narrative. When we look him up in a dictionary of the Bible (or Google him), we quickly discover that the quest is a complicated one indeed. The Hebrew Bible, and thus the King James Version and the NRSV alike, know of two persons by this name, though it is spelled

---

5. See his *The Inspiration and Authority of the Bible* (Philadelphia: The Presbyterian and Reformed Publishing Company, 1948), 111.

6. B. B. Warfield, "The Inerrancy of the Original Autographs," in *Selected Shorter Writings of B. B. Warfield,* vol. 2, ed. John E. Meeter (Nutley, NJ: The Presbyterian and Reformed Publishing Company, 1973), 582-83.

with double "m" and an ayin in Hebrew. One of the two is prominent enough to appear in the New Testament genealogies of Jesus as the great-grandfather of Boaz, the husband of Ruth (see Matt. 1:4 and Luke 3:33). The Hebrew Bible also mentions three people with a very similar name, Abinadab, the most important of whom is the worthy who kept the ark at Gibeah after the Philistines had returned it — on a chariot! — before David took it to Jerusalem (see 1 Sam. 7:1 and 2 Sam. 6:3). The Greek translation of the Old Testament, the Septuagint, calls all of these persons "Aminadab," as in this book's title, and adds two more: the natural father of Esther (whose name is not mentioned in the Hebrew book of Esther; Mordecai was Esther's foster father), and an enigmatic Aminadab who is connected with "chariots" *(harmata),* according to a verse in the Song of Songs (6:12).[7] In this verse, the Latin Vulgate follows the Greek and reads "propter quadrigas Aminadab" ("on account of the *quadriga* of Aminadab"); the Latin plural designates a chariot with a team of four. This finally provides the Aminadab from whom the title of this book derives, because for centuries during the Middle Ages, this "Aminadab's chariot" with its four horses was among the common biblical images suggesting the one Bible (chariot) with its fourfold interpretation (the four horses).

Unfortunately, the Hebrew verse in question — Song of Songs 6:12 — presents us with an absolute conundrum. Marvin Pope in the Anchor Bible calls it "the most difficult verse in the Canticle," a verse which "continues to vex translators and commentators."[8] First of all, while the original Hebrew does speak of chariots *(markevot),* there seems to be no name connected with it; the Hebrew reads *"markevot ammi-nadib,"* "chariots of my people — my noble, princely people" (from *nadib,* "prince"). The rest of the sentence is of no help. It seems to say: "I did not know — my soul — it set me — chariots of my princely people." Now, what are we to do with a verse like this? Can we just leave it out or replace it with an ellipsis (. . .)? No version of the Bible has dared to do this. All of them attempt a translation — which is to say, an interpretation. We have to interpret, even though — or perhaps precisely because — there is no clear meaning to be found in the words themselves. And herein lies the predicament: interpretation is necessary because the Bi-

---

7. The Vulgate text, which has this as the eleventh verse of chapter six, reads as follows: "Nescivi: anima mea conturbavit me, propter quadrigas Aminadab." The text in this Latin version is what shaped medieval readings in the West. And, we should note, it is itself — like the Septuagint version of this verse — a rendering that eliminates ambiguities in the original Hebrew text.

8. Marvin Pope, *The Song of Songs: A New Translation with Introduction and Commentary,* The Anchor Bible 7C (Garden City, NY: Doubleday, 1977), 584.

ble comes in the form of human language, and language forces the reader to construct meaning in the reading and then ponder what it may have to do with the Word of God. In a case like this verse from the Song of Songs, what else can we do but construct a meaning that is not only possible but plausible?

In the nine pages that Marvin Pope devotes to this impossible verse, we come to recognize with amazement the variety of options interpreters — Jewish, Christian, and modern literary critics alike — have put forward.[9] They have tried to emend the text, to postulate insertions, to transpose or reinterpret particular words, to construct a possible syntax, to infer from the context. The results are dangerously speculative; every interpreter goes out on a limb, and each interpretation is vulnerable to criticism. But danger can also be both fascinating and attractive. It is amazing to watch the logic: the more intractable the textual problem, the greater the zeal and creativity applied to it. After all, biblical interpretation means and always has meant exercising one's imagination. We sometimes forget this simple truth. The goal of interpretation is not to remove dangers, but to face them squarely — and then to go out daringly on a limb.

Concerning this problematic verse from the Song of Songs, there has been much daring indeed among translators. A sampling of versions makes this abundantly clear: "Before I knew, my desire hurled me on the chariots of my people, as their prince"; "I did not know myself; she made me feel more than a prince reigning over the myriads of his people"; "Before I knew it, my heart had made me the blessed one of my kinswomen"; "Before I realized it, I was stricken with a terrible homesickness and wanted to be back among my own people." These are only a few of the many modern versions available in English, and what is clear from the variety is that all these attempts seem to be groping in the dark. There are many more. Two millennia is a long time for imaginative attempts to put this small piece into the mosaic of the whole, that "vast maze of coherence which a life with and under the biblical word . . . has created in the soul and mind of Christian people." Aminadab's chariot, by scribal accident and then by the pure power of the image — and not perhaps, one might argue, without divine providence — has appropriated a place for itself at the heart of the history of biblical interpretation in the West.

In this and so many other instances, the Bible reveals itself to be an utterly fascinating book, with its strange and remarkable stories, images, puzzles, and projections. It was this fascination that first lured me and

9. See Pope, *Song of Songs,* 584-93.

many others to the study of theology. As a teenager, I belonged to a group of Sunday school assistants whose job it was to tell Bible stories to younger children. During the Thursday training sessions offered by our pastor, I annoyed him with so many questions about what was behind those texts that he said one night, "When you're out of school, why don't you study theology? I promise you that you'll get more answers than you ever bargained for." He was right. Moreover, ever since my seminary years in the early 1950s, I have been much impressed by Gerhard Ebeling's thesis, formulated in the title of his inaugural lecture at the University of Tübingen in February 1947, that "church history is the history of the interpretation of Scripture."[10] It seems utterly right for a church historian to attempt a "history of biblical interpretation" as a task that introduces what "theologizing" could and perhaps should mean today.

There are a few standard "histories of interpretation" one might consult, although only a few of these are in English. Invariably, they present the material in chronological order, organizing it by periods. But there is a problem with any periodization: it suggests linear development and is tied to the idea of progress, a progress that comes to reflect the particular agenda of the author. This danger is nowhere more apparent than in the old standard work in English, Frederick W. Farrar's *History of Interpretation*, a volume continuously available in print since its first publication in 1886.[11] Farrar was a progressive Anglican educator and churchman in his day, well known as a teacher and preacher, and Dean of Canterbury Cathedral from 1895 until his death in 1903. He delivered the substance of this book as the Bampton Lectures at St. Mary's Church, Oxford, in 1885. In these lectures, Farrar defined his agenda as an apologetic endeavor, that of "defending the cause of Christianity by furthering the truth." Looking at "the truth" concerning the history of biblical interpretation, however, his summary judgment is that "the task before us is a melancholy one" because, on the whole, "past methods of interpretation were erroneous," "systematizing the art of misinterpretation" rather than furthering interpretation.[12] Going through

---

10. See Gerhard Ebeling, *The Word of God and Tradition: Historical Studies Interpreting the Divisions of Christianity,* trans. S. H. Hooke (Philadelphia: Fortress Press, 1968), 11-31. The title in the English version is slightly at variance with the German. It should read, "Church History *as* the History of the Interpretation of Scripture" ("Kirchengeschichte *als* Auslegungsgeschichte der Heiligen Schrift").

11. Frederick W. Farrar, *History of Interpretation* (1886; Grand Rapids: Baker Book House, 1961).

12. Farrar, *History of Interpretation,* 8-9, and xi.

his seven periods, Farrar sees system after system of these "age-long misapprehensions" being "condemned each in turn by the widening knowledge of mankind."[13] Obviously, he takes his stand enthusiastically with critical post-Enlightenment scholarship with its belief in "progress," though with some Anglican caution and the optimistic conviction that the divine truth enshrined in the Bible, whatever it may be, will in the end stand vindicated.[14] No apologetic strategies can be more directly serviceable to this end, he feels, than "the removal of false methods of interpretation by which divine authority has been impaired."[15]

This triumphalist scientism disregards in an embarrassing way the ever-continuing predicament of biblical interpretation. There will never be a time when all problematic passages are satisfactorily explained, as both Farrar and Warfield seem to expect. History-writing looks at the past for the sake of the present and the future, but the path it traces can never be seen simply as a transition from darkness to light. History must give us perspective, and today we must stress the plural and speak of perspectives, insights into the various options of looking at a vast enterprise such as biblical interpretation as these have been exercised in the past and have come to have their own effects — with all the dangers, promises, and limits these involved. History is never fully past, and if its questions are not acknowledged they will continue as a gnawing burden into the present.

This new probing of the history of biblical interpretation finds a structure not based on chronology but rather on a topical approach suggested by the traditional fourfold sense of Scripture as this came to dominate medieval hermeneutics from the time of Augustine to the Reformation. Schoolchildren memorized its elements through a simple mnemonic verse probably composed by a thirteenth-century schoolmaster:

> Littera gesta docet,
> Quid credas allegoria,
> Moralis quid agas,
> Quo tendas anagogia.[16]

13. For Farrar's discussion of these presumed "periods," see *History of Interpretation,* 12-13. His approach presupposes a "progressive revelation" (4, 6, 9) that reflects his view of history as always improving — and, as he felt, leaving behind the confusions of the past.

14. Farrar, *History of Interpretation,* xvii.

15. Farrar, *History of Interpretation,* 18.

16. The ditty has been traced back to the *Rotulus pugillaris* of the Dominican Provincial Augustine of Dacia (d. 1285). See Angelus Walz, "Augustini de Dacia O.P.: 'Rotulus pugil-

I have rendered this little jingle in rhyming English as follows:

> The letter teaches the deeds of the past,
> Allegory that which to believe thou hast,
> The moral sense what thou must do,
> Anagogy the upward path to pursue.

In suggesting this approach, I am well aware of the wholesale rejection of the fourfold sense among Protestants almost from the beginning. Martin Luther, who had used the system in his early exegetical work, began criticizing it as early as 1516 as a useless diversion, typical of the formalism of scholastic theologians who had nothing better to do than play word games.[17] Post-Enlightenment biblical scholarship almost without exception saw the fourfold sense as a hopeless antique from the horror chest of the dark ages. Farrar raises this concern when he speaks of the "pure fiction of the *multiplex intelligentia* or fourfold sense" which "vitiates the popular compendiums of five hundred years."[18] Many more recent evaluations are no less disparaging.

I am also conscious, however, of its recent revival, inaugurated by the historical studies of the Jesuit theologian and later Cardinal Henri de Lubac, who published four volumes on medieval biblical interpretation from 1959 to 1964 under the title *Exégèse médiévale: Les quatre sens de l'écriture.*[19] De Lubac was a major representative of the French "nouvelle théologie," which, though initially censured by the authorities of his order and in Vatican circles before the Second Vatican Council, attempted to break old molds of what he considered to be the stale pre-modern theological attitudes that had long prevailed in the Roman Church. On this basis, de Lubac and others in this progressive theological movement hoped to make room for a new spirituality, one based on the notion of a *ressourcement,* a retrieval that looked back to the pre-Thomist sources of Catholic doctrine.

---

laris' examinatus atque editus," *Angelicum* 6 (1929): 256. On the history of this jingle, see also Henri de Lubac, *Medieval Exegesis: The Four Senses of Scripture,* vol. 1, trans. Mark Sebanc (Grand Rapids: Eerdmans, 1998), 1-9, 271-77.

17. For more on Luther's criticism, see below, pp. 24-27 and 59.

18. Farrar, *History of Interpretation,* 26.

19. To date, three of Henri de Lubac's four volumes have appeared in English translation. The first, published by Eerdmans in 1998, is translated by Mark Sebanc; the second and third, published by Eerdmans in 2000 and 2009, are translated by E. M. Macierowski. The fourth and final volume of this series has not yet been translated into English.

There have been Protestant voices among this renewal movement as well. David Steinmetz published an article as startling as it was compelling in *Theology Today* in April 1980, whose provocative thesis threw down the gauntlet in the face of modern biblical criticism: "The medieval theory of levels of meaning in the biblical text, with all its admitted defects, flourished because it is true, while the modern theory of a single meaning, with all its demonstrable virtues, is false."[20] Steinmetz's central point about the multiple meaning of the biblical text certainly has the sympathy of the "postmodern" hermeneutics of recent years, reckoning as it does with the polysemous nature of texts and with multiple levels of understanding which incorporate a variety of perspectives. For Steinmetz, and others following his lead, a text deserves to be read in terms of its "afterlife," the accumulation of meanings attributed to it by later readers. Texts have histories, and any exegetical treatment of a passage points to this wider horizon of understandings. Texts have a *Wirkungsgeschichte,* a history of "effects," and this tradition of (re)readings reminds us of their power as well as their "instability," as it were. This is also a measure of their creativity, resilience, and power, as we shall see.

Thanks to the enigmatic Aminadab of Song of Songs 6:12, one of the common designations of the fourfold method throughout the long Middle Ages has been the "quadriga," the chariot drawn by four horses. Other biblical images were also used for this purpose. They have in common that they depict moving fours: the four flowing rivers of paradise — or, more precisely, the one river dividing into four streams; the four-wheeled trolleys in Solomon's temple; and especially the throne wagon of Ezekiel's vision, the *merkavah* (Ezek. 1; 10), with its four living creatures and four wheels. All these images imply that the fourfold sense is something both complex and dynamic, a movement full of energy and vitality — and one that has a future. The *merkavah* was also frequently used as a symbol of the unity and diversity of the four Gospels; thus, an early and resilient tradition of Christian art depicts the four living creatures whose faces Ezekiel describes as the symbols of the four evangelists — a man for Matthew, a lion for Mark, an ox for Luke, and an eagle for John. They could move freely in all directions, with their wheels within wheels, a magnificent sight, and this is exactly what the evangelists did: "Their voice has gone out into all the earth and

---

20. "The Superiority of Pre-Critical Exegesis," *Theology Today* 37, no. 1 (1980): 27-38; here 38. This article has been recently republished in David Steinmetz, *Taking the Long View: Christian Theology in Historical Perspective* (New York: Oxford University Press, 2011), 3-14.

their words to the ends of the earth" (Ps. 19:4) — all four corners of it. The "four corners" may explain why a fourfold division of scriptural senses, not a threefold or a fivefold one, emerged as the norm: four is the number of the inhabited world, the *oikoumene,* the region for which the scriptural word is destined. Aminadab's swift chariot, the quadriga of scriptural senses, comes with four horses in the medieval world of symbolic reality. It did not have to be this way, but the Vulgate clearly speaks of a quadriga in Song of Songs 6:12. And since these four lead this chariot, it "makes sense."

In what follows, I combine this tradition of the fourfold sense of Scripture with the system of the five bodily senses. Aristotle taught that there are five senses, not four or six: seeing, hearing, smelling, tasting, and touching.[21] These serve as a rhetorical device to organize our approach to the task of biblical interpretation, but it is not without a certain logic that fits each of these so-called "senses." In the moral tradition, where they were not seen as neutral but as gates for the temptations of the flesh, they became popular ever since Augustine described his own conversions as a fight with the allurements of the five senses in his *Confessions.* The literature of the seventeenth and eighteenth centuries is full of titillating allegories of the senses, where it often remains unclear whether the authors are more interested in rejecting the sensual pleasures or reveling in their descriptions of them!

A major reason for combining the two in organizing this book is the peculiar ambivalence of the term itself: we call both the forms of scriptural understanding and the forms of physical perception "senses." The entry in the *Oxford English Dictionary* shows that the word-field in English covers the five bodily senses as well as several psychological activities in the vicinity of feeling, but a large area of use concerns words and language: sense is "the meaning or signification of a word or phrase."[22] The situation is similar in Latin, though with a different distribution of weight: the largest area of usage here is perception, awareness, and feeling, while *sensus* as the mean-

21. For Aristotle's discussion of the senses, see his treatise *De Anima,* trans. William David Ross (Oxford: Clarendon Press, 1961); cf. also Richard Sorabji, "Aristotle on Demarcating the Five Senses," *The Philosophical Review* 80 (1971): 55-79. For a general discussion of the five senses in literature, including a review of Aristotle's approach, see Louise Vinge, *The Five Senses: Studies in a Literary Tradition,* Acta Regiae Societatis Humaniorum Litterarum Lundensis 82 (Lund: Liber Läromedel, 1975), esp. 48-53. See also Martha C. Nussbaum and Amélie Oksenberg Rorty, eds., *Essays on Aristotle's De Anima* (Oxford: Clarendon Press, 1999). For further discussion, see chapter 5 below.

22. *The Oxford English Dictionary,* ed. J. A. Simpson and E. S. C. Weiner (New York: Oxford University Press, 1971), 457-61.

ing of a word or phrase constitutes a small and relatively late group under the heading, "that which occurs to the mind." In Greek, the mind would be the *nous,* and there is no terminological bridge to the senses, *aisthētēria.* "Sense" as the "meaning of a word or phrase" would have to be related to *nous;* thus, the composite noun *hyponoia* could be rendered as the "subsense" of the classical texts which the later allegorists attempted to spell out. The bodily senses *(aisthētēria),* on the other hand, belong in the discussion of human perception, the relation of the self to the outside world — or more broadly to reality itself. As such, they were considered to be activities of the soul *(psyche),* which at that time was seen as the constitutive part of the self.

The classical tradition reckoned with a wide variety of ways of perceiving. Plato's psychology did not distinguish between the five senses, but rather focused on the contrasting feelings of hot and cold as well as pleasure and discomfort or fear. Aristotle, however, introduced a new biological perspective: body and soul together constitute the self. Thus, not only the soul perceives, but also the body. "Sensation is produced in the soul by way of the body"[23] — a general truth that Thomas Aquinas, centuries later, formulated succinctly in his claim that "What is in our intellect, has been in our senses before."[24] In fact, Aristotle's orientation, helped along by Aquinas's loyalty, dominates the theological discussion as well as aesthetics and the understanding of art during the Middle Ages, as we shall see throughout this study.[25] Returning to English and Latin again, we see what happened in the English usage, and probably in later Latin as well: there was a strong shift of emphasis in the word field of "sense" and "senses." The importance of language as an access to reality has increased tremendously. This change implies at the very least that hermeneutics as the theory of interpretation, and aesthetics as the theory of perception, belong closely together in the Western tradition.[26] In terms of our topic, then, the four senses of Scripture and the five bodily senses make a good pair. Our approach is a "doubling," then, of the notion of the "senses," inviting us to consider how it is that interpretation might be understood as a "sensing" of the Scriptures.

23. Aristotle, *De Sensu et Sensibilibus* 1.436.b1. *De Sensu* is part of the *Parva Naturalia,* ed. William David Ross (Oxford: Clarendon Press, 1955). See also *De Anima* 1 and 2.

24. Thomas Aquinas, *De Veritate* 2.3.19.

25. On the role of the five senses in the art and visual culture of medieval Europe, see Carl Nordenfalk, "Les cinq sens dans l'art du moyen-âge," *Revue de l'art* 34 (1976): 17-28.

26. Hans-Georg Gadamer explores the connection between hermeneutics and aesthetics in considerable detail in his writings; see especially *Truth and Method,* trans. Joel Weinsheimer and Donald Marshall (London: Continuum, 1989).

It should be no surprise, therefore, that Aminadab's hermeneutical chariot has a counterpart in a chariot of the physical senses. One of the earliest allegorical poems in the Middle Ages, Alan of Lille's *Anticlaudianus,* tells the story of Prudence, who invites the seven liberal arts to construct a chariot on which she, together with Wisdom, will ride to heaven in order to ask God for the archetype of a perfect soul, to fashion a new human being who would overcome the imperfection of the old, the original work of nature.[27] The five senses are the team and Reason is the charioteer. The party does reach the Empyrean, but Reason can go no further. Theology appears and counsels Prudence to leave the chariot behind and mount a single horse, Hearing. This advice is followed and the mission succeeds. Alan is quite aware of possible criticism of his artifice, which C. S. Lewis has called "nearly worthless" — viz., "a book of the melancholy kind that claims our attention solely as influences."[28] Alan defends himself by drawing heavily on the precedent of the hermeneutical quadriga: "Let those not show disdain for this work who are still wailing in the cradles of the nurses and are being suckled at the breasts of the lower arts. . . . For in this work, the sweetness of the literal sense will soothe the ears of boys, the moral instruction will inspire the mind on the road to perfection, the sharp subtlety of allegory will whet the advanced intellect."[29] The chariot is a conveyance, a means of trans/portation — or of "transfer," to recall the word's etymology. It suggests dramatic movement. But in what direction? We were not quite sure in the case of the "quadriga Aminadab," but here we are told in no uncertain terms: it is a movement upward, an *anagōgé,* a journey to God, like the sweep of the chariot that took Elijah into heaven, or if one prefers, like the winged chariot of Plato's *Phaedrus.*

Here, then, we already begin to "smell" what is at stake, an appropriate beginning since Aristotle assigns to the sense of smell a central position.[30] Mathematically, the number five allows for a center, and this is where smell belongs: on one side are the two senses dependent on a medium such as air and transparency (seeing and hearing), and on the other, the two that

---

27. Alan of Lille, *Anticlaudianus, or The Good and Perfect Man,* trans. James J. Sheridan (Toronto: Pontifical Institute of Medieval Studies, 1973). The five horses are described in Book 4 (121-26).

28. C. S. Lewis, *The Allegory of Love: A Study of a Medieval Tradition* (New York: Oxford University Press, 1985), 98, 100.

29. *Anticlaudianus,* 40-41.

30. Aristotle treats smell in *De Anima* 2.9; see also Thomas K. Johansen, "Aristotle on the Sense of Smell," *Phronesis: A Journal for Ancient Philosophy* 41 (1996): 1-19.

are independent (taste and touch); in the human face, eyes and ears are located above, tongue and touch — which alone of the senses is distributed throughout the body — below the nose. But Aristotle also knew that our sense of smell was "less discriminating and in general inferior to that of many species of animals," admitting that we "have a poor sense of smell and our apprehension of its proper objects is inseparably bound up with and so confused by pleasure and pain, which shows that in us the organ is inaccurate."[31] That said, smell is the "middle" sense that Aristotle relates to taste — we both taste and smell "flavors" as either sweet or bitter — and taste for him represents a particular form of touch. Fragrances ignite something deep within us, in our experience and in our memory, which also carries a strong sense of anticipation: we long for certain aromas we have known in the past and found pleasurable.

When we look beyond Aristotle to the research being conducted by neuroscientists today, an altogether different picture emerges.[32] We now know that the sense of smell — or olfaction — is the most primitive sense in the human body, located in the same part of our brain that effects emotions, memory, and creativity — and this is a strong triad, indeed! Of course, Aristotle assumed that smell was the exclusive domain of the nose. We now know better, since smell is facilitated by breathing, but it actually "happens" through the agency of a small patch of neurons in the upper nasal passage and the ways these communicate with the limbic system of the brain. The sense of smell, according to studies of this part of the brain, is vital in enabling us to identify foods, seek mates, and sense danger. The etymological root of "scent" — from the Latin *sentire*, "to feel" — reminds us of this. By means of smell we experience great sensual pleasure, as when we notice the delicate fragrance of perfumes or the natural aroma of flowers. Certain scents can also jolt our minds, causing us to become immediately alert, as the use of "smelling salts" reminds us. Sharp fragrances "wake" us to danger, as we experience when exposed to the acrid smell of smoke; pleasant fragrances lure us, as interior designers of the large "magnet" stores found in shopping malls know, causing them to require customers to enter through a maze of perfume stations. We also now recognize that 80 percent of what

31. Aristotle, *De Anima* 2.9.

32. For a recent discussion of "smell" drawing on a wide range of research in the field of olfactory studies, see Avery N. Gilbert, *What the Nose Knows: The Science of Scent in Everyday Life* (New York: Random House, 2008). Gilbert prefaces his account of this work with an epigraph from Alexander Graham Bell, who suggested in 1914 that "if you are ambitious to found a new science, measure a smell."

we taste depends on our sense of smell, and our brain recognizes more than 10,000 different odor molecules. Smell matters, and smelling is a means of avoiding pain and finding pleasure! Smell may be "less discriminating" in humans than in some other animals, but its ability to orient us in our world is powerful and vitally significant. And orientation is what we are after here, as we "smell" what is at stake in interpreting the Bible.

What, then, are the issues involved in the never-ending predicament of biblical interpretation? What are we to make of the necessity of constantly having to construct a meaning, though there is seldom just one correct answer to problems found in scriptural texts? How might we evaluate the "orientation" within which these texts found and expressed meaning? How are we to respond to such challenges creatively and imaginatively? It seems simple enough. Without further ado, we roll up our sleeves and go to work in "smelling" and solving the problem — yes, the *problem,* because that is what we assume it to be. We begin this task by comparing textual evidence, establishing the meaning of words, emending the text or proposing an alternative syntax, consulting the context and, finally, attempting a translation — which is to say, we wager an interpretation. When it comes to this strange verse from the Song of Songs, we may end up siding with the editors of the New Revised Standard Version, who render it this way: "Before I was aware, my fancy set me in a chariot beside my prince," and then add a footnote: "The meaning of the Hebrew is uncertain." Undoubtedly, this offers one solution to an apparently intractable textual problem. But is the challenge of this verse — and, indeed, that presented by any biblical text we might read — exhausted by being treated as a problem?

The steps we normally take in addressing such predicaments belong to the world of methods and rules, an extremely useful category of things when it comes to problem-solving, like the mechanical arts of Aristotle's cosmos of knowledge. But they are only tools designed to ease the predicament of having to find explanations to problems that have no obvious solutions. And, in point of fact, the history of biblical interpretation where it has been sketched or described has generally been approached as a history of tools, of rules applied and methods utilized in the attempt to solve the questions texts raise. This is clearly the case in Farrar's Bampton Lectures. Of course, since Farrar takes such a dim view of all exegetical "methods" prior to the advent of modern critical studies, they all receive failing marks ranging from "deficient" to "erroneous" and "insipid," with only slight variations of mitigating qualification. For each of his pre-Reformation epochs, Farrar can even name a "definite exegetic compendium" that illustrates the arbitrary rules and methods in use at the time; for the rabbinic epoch, he mentions the seven Rules of Hillel, for the Alexandrian epoch some methodological sections from Philo, for the patristic epoch Tyconius's "Book of Rules" and Eucherius's "Formulae of Spiritual Understanding," and for the scholastic epoch what he considers to be the "fallacious" theory of a fourfold sense.[33]

I myself thought at one time that such clearly formulated textbooks of exegetical rules constituted the best sources for the history of biblical interpretation. They seemed to allow us to articulate and quantify differences, changes, and transformations from one form of interpretation to another with ease. Those rules and methods were taught and learned, and we can distill the theory behind the exegetical practices of commentaries, sermons, and treatises quite directly from the teachers' manuals, rather than having to piece it together by careful, painstaking analysis of volumes of interpretation. I even edited and published a collection of such hermeneutical texts. But in working on this project, I soon realized that the situation was far more complicated than I had initially presumed. For one thing, most of the rules were not original to the context of interpreting the Bible; they were borrowed from the surrounding culture. David Daube has shown that Hillel's Rules originated in Hellenistic law-court oratory,[34] Philo's hermeneutical keys had their precedent in the classical methods of Homeric interpretation, and John Cassian's formulation of the fourfold sense goes back to an Augustinian model which was borrowed from late-classical rhetoric. The texts themselves taught me that knowing methods and rules did not suffice for a full understanding of what was going on in the theory and practice of biblical interpretation. The knowledge of methods and rules may make an exegete, but does not yet make an interpreter.

Let me unpack this last sentence a bit. "Exegesis" was part of the Hellenistic educational system, which, according to Henri-Irénée Marrou, moved in three stages, all of them focused on classical texts like Homer and Hesiod.[35] The first stage inculcated the basic skills of reading and writing. The second stage familiarized the student with the literary heritage in several steps (*merē,* parts): there was first the *meros diorthōtikon* — we would say textual criticism — in which the text would be established, dictated,

---

33. Farrar, *History of Interpretation,* 18-27.

34. "Rabbinic Methods of Interpretation and Hellenistic Rhetoric," *Hebrew Union College Annual* (1949): 239-64.

35. See Henri-Irénée Marrou, *A History of Education in Antiquity,* trans. George Lamb (New York: Sheed & Ward, 1956).

copied, and corrected. It was followed by the *meros anagnōstikon,* where memorization as well as reading and declamation, complete with contests and prizes, were central, and finally by the *meros exegētikon,* "exegesis" proper, which took the most time and effort. In "exegesis," the teacher, called *grammatikos* or "grammarian," explained the texts in terms of their language form: he would dwell on the meaning of words, many of which were archaic, the derivation and etymology of names, inflection, and syntax. Then the content was discussed: the stories behind the text according to place, time, event, and persons. This gave students a basic knowledge of classical mythology. Once all this work was done, however, a final step of interpretation was envisaged: the *meros kritikon,* taught in the schools of rhetoricians and philosophers rather than by the grammarians. Here, the leading question was no longer how the classics should be studied, but why — for example, why Homer was important. At this stage, the young minds were introduced to the ruling *ethos* of Greek society, the values, the norms, and the heroic models which that society embraced and drew from these texts.

To accomplish this, methods and rules were not enough since they were nothing more than the shared tools for fixing the obvious problems of language and its written expression, literature, but did not reveal what this language expressed, how it functioned in the minds of people whose value system was nourished by it. We need that which the *meros kritikon* was supposed to provide: that is, an understanding of the "why," an expectation of what the text was ultimately going to do, of the wider frame of reference, the governing ethos. Since Homer as well as the Bible had become "sacred" texts for the communities in which they had authority, we need a grasp of the religious goal of interpretation, the theological parameter into which the interpretation is supposed to move the text in the mind of the hearer and reader.

In order to mark the distinction, I have called this frame "principles," reflecting the Latin and Greek equivalents, *principia* and *archai,* rather than the meaning we commonly associate with the modern English word. These "principles" are close to but not identical with the concept of *mentalité,* which is the object of an exciting branch of recent historiography, the "history of mentalities" or "attitudes" — which is to say, those underlying sensibilities, feelings, presuppositions, unarticulated and often unconscious assumptions of an age, which color everything we do and think, but for this reason are dazzlingly difficult to pin down. The "principles" are the tip of this immense iceberg, that part of it that sticks out of the water because it has risen to the surface of the interpreter's consciousness. Paying attention to the "principles" of biblical interpretation means taking into account the articulated faith and hope of the interpreters as well as of the communities they served.

What should be clear is that I am not here calling "principles" of biblical interpretation what many people today might expect under this heading: biblical inspiration, the canon, creedal or confessional identity, and an authoritative teaching ministry. For me, these topics do not belong under principles but are formal presuppositions shared by the people and communities who are part of the history of biblical interpretation in all ages. Like Warfield's doctrine of inspiration, they are indispensable methodologically, but not logically. To understand the dynamics of the history of interpretation at any point, something else is needed. Together with the methods and rules, we must understand the specific form which the expectation took of how the Word of God would be conveyed and received through the biblical text in that particular situation.

A striking example demonstrating that rules cannot be separated from underlying principles, and principles cannot be discussed without rules, is found in Augustine's famous handbook *On Christian Doctrine.*[36] Augustine composed it as a guide to the interpretation and use of the Scriptures in the church. Having taught as a professional rhetorician himself, he suggests a wealth of methods and rules on how to handle and even manipulate the language of Scripture. The second book in this volume develops his famous theory of signs as a theory of language signs, and books three and four spell out the specifics of dealing with "unknown," "obscure," "literal," and "figurative" language signs. On an initial reading, the argument of the first book seems to have nothing to do with this technical linguistic discussion. It speaks of "things to be used" and "things to be enjoyed," of the life of Christian witness, and of the double love of God and neighbor as commanded by Christ. What Augustine spells out here are not methods and rules for the analysis of language, but rather the principle for the sake of which the Bible exists — that is, the theological parameter into which all interpretation should move the hearer or reader. It is this principle which allows him to declare even the Bible to be dispensable: "There are people," he notes, "who do not need the Bible except for teaching others because

---

36. My favorite translation of Augustine's *De doctrina christiana* is *On Christian Doctrine* by D. W. Robertson Jr. (Indianapolis: Bobbs-Merrill, 1958). It was republished by Macmillan in 1994 and reprinted by Dover in 2009.

they [already] have a firm hold on faith, hope, and love."[37] This also allows him to formulate the rule that any interpretation of a biblical passage is "correct" if it serves to promote the double love of God and neighbor.

Obviously, Augustine's specific formulation of the principle was not operative for all other interpreters. For the rabbis, the interpretive parameter was given by Israel's faith in the covenant and the gracious gift of Torah as the norm of Jewish life; in the Qumran sect, this Torah was understood as the Torah of the end time interpreted by the message of the prophets. The principles of Origen's exegesis had to do with the Alexandrian's fervent interest in the fate of the human soul and his hope that this fate was determined by the saving providence of the one God, the God of Israel and of Jesus Christ. In the history of Christian interpretation, the principles always included the conviction that God's action in the historical person of Jesus Christ was central to God's plan of salvation, God's *oikonomia*. Beyond that, they could show immense variation in scope, emphasis, and vital concerns.

"Aminadab's chariot" as a reading of a perhaps confused — and certainly confusing — passage from the Song of Songs (6:12) suggests that earlier generations of Christian interpreters did not regard their work simply as a task of solving problems, as a bind or predicament in which Bible users found themselves. Rather, they saw it as an opportunity. As a child, I still grew up with the legend that Martin Luther rediscovered the Bible when he found the unknown book chained in the library at Erfurt and began to read it with flaming cheeks. It may have been literally chained; there are some surviving chained libraries, and I wish theological libraries with huge book losses could have them today! But figuratively, nothing is farther from the truth. The Middle Ages, particularly the late Middle Ages, were a period of unmitigated Bible enthusiasm, when people of all sorts took delight in any opportunity to interpret Scripture, finding with amazement ever new levels of meaning. John the Scot, writing in the ninth century, had compared the multiplicity of scriptural senses to the feathers of a peacock. The *Biblia pauperum* of the fourteenth century paired scenes from the New Testament with prefigurations from the Old Testament, two at a time. Its later imitations featured more — three, even five such prefigurative scenes. Living in the world of the Bible meant living in a richly symbolic universe, and this meant unlimited opportunities for discovery.

Discovery, of course, cannot happen without exploration, and exploration presumes the hope at least of discovery — even if what is eventually

---

37. *On Christian Doctrine* 39.43.

found is quite different from what one set out to find. Thus, Christopher Columbus saw himself as an amateur exegete who interpreted his discovery of the westward passage to the Orient as nothing less than a Spirit-guided act of biblical interpretation, as the implementation of a prophetic charge given to no one else but him, a humble child of Franciscan piety. These are the crucial events as Columbus himself describes them: in the night of Christmas Eve, 1492, working out of the bowels of a stranded ship named *Santa Maria,* grounded because a boy had accidentally taken the rudder, he was forced to leave some people behind on a paradisiacal island, thus establishing Navidad, the first Christian settlement in the New World, among a most beautiful people, "people of love without venality." For Columbus, no doubt was possible: what had happened was clearly providential, the ordained fulfillment of a biblical vision of the end time. What else could it be? In interpreting this incident, John Fleming suggests that

> We may put the question somewhat crudely and ask whether this account of the founding of the first, doomed European settlement in America is "history." Did all this happen *in reality,* as our typical vocabulary rather pretentiously might put it? Was there in fact a village named Navidad, and did it find its strange birth in the manner described? The answer to the first question — did Navidad exist? — is almost certainly yes; but the answer to the second question will depend, as so much in medieval exegesis depended, upon whether one speaks *literaliter* or *spiritualiter.*[38]

How biblical interpreters over the centuries perceived the Bible speaking both literally and spiritually, and of things clear and obscure, is the concern of this book. It will also beckon us as contemporary readers to take up this task ourselves — an exploration that we will pursue facing difficulties and in the hope of unexpected discoveries.

---

38. John Fleming, "Christopher Columbus as a Scriptural Exegete," in Burrows and Rorem, eds., *Biblical Hermeneutics in Historical Perspective,* 173-83.

CHAPTER TWO

Littera: Touching the Ground

The necessity of interpretation is a bind in which we find ourselves as soon as we open the Bible. It is a constant, unavoidable, never-ending necessity, whether we like it or not. An impossible verse makes this clear: in Song of Songs 6:12, we hear the strange and apparently nonsensical words, "I did not know — my soul — it set me — chariots of my princely people." We have to do something with this verse, one way or another; we cannot just let it stand uninterpreted. We began our consideration of the history of biblical interpretation with "Aminadab's chariot," the Latin Bible's guesswork interpretation of the last phrase of the jumble "*merkevot ammi-nadib,*" in which medieval biblical scholars saw a symbol of the quadriga, the fourfold sense of Scripture: literal, allegorical, moral, and anagogical: "propter quadrigas Aminadab." We also exercised our medieval creativity once more and combined Aminadab's chariot with the heaven-storming chariot of Prudence and its team of five senses: sight, hearing, smell, taste, and touch, the story Alan of Lille told in the late twelfth century.

Now let us consider two horses, one from each team, that seem to be somehow of the same color: *littera,* the literal sense, and the sense of touch. Touch is a strange phenomenon among the five senses. In Aristotle's hierarchy, it is the lowest, even below taste, but he meant this as a way of speaking of its foundational place in our perception: "The primary form of sense," he insists, "is touch, which belongs to all animals."[1] When the moralists spoke

---

1. *De Anima* 2.2. On this point, see also Cynthia Freeland, "Aristotle on the Sense of Touch," in *Essays on Aristotle's* De Anima, ed. Martha C. Nussbaum and Amélie Oksenberg Rorty (Oxford: Clarendon Press, 1999), 227-48.

of the temptation of the senses, the sensual delight of touch was always considered the most dangerous. Yet there is a universal quality to touch which distinguishes it from the other senses. Aristotle observed that touch does not have a particular location in the body; it is diffused throughout. More than that, this apparently lowliest sense is the primary perception common to all animals. At the end of his treatise *De Anima,* he submits that touch is the only sense animals cannot live without.[2] They have the sense of touch for the sake of "being" itself, all other senses for the sake of "*well*-being." Touching the ground is a lowly scenario, but one that is entirely essential and absolutely foundational and necessary for all the other senses — and vital, of course, for the basic matter of nutrition and sustenance. This broad sense of "touch" is what Christian interpreters were talking about when they spoke of the literal sense of Scripture.

It is this down-to-earth quality which makes the literal sense so exclusively appealing and normative in our demythologized, detheologized secular world. We make a distinction between scientific and applied interpretation and allow some higher sense, some flights of fancy or intuitive and freely associative excursions in the latter genre. Critical exegesis, however, investigates one sense only: the literal. Farrar puts it this way: "By exegesis I always mean the explanation of the immediate and primary sense of the sacred writings."[3] He goes on to suggest that "[w]e may therefore assume that all exegesis must be unsound which is not based on the literal, grammatical, historical, contextual sense of the sacred writers."[4] The restrictions implied in these quotations are quite specific: historical-critical exegesis concentrates on the writings, the texts, their words, and their immediate content; it focuses on the intention of the human authors; and, finally, it tries to ascertain the original intention of both.

Today, critical exegesis has modified — or, more precisely, expanded — this list: to the words of the text, we have added concern for context, social location, and tradition history. To the intention of the human authors we have added the phenomenon of reception, the side of the hearer. And to the text's original intention we have added an interest in its self-life, its post-history, and the effects of its impact — or what in German is called its *Wirkungsgeschichte,* or history of effects. As suggested in the last chapter,

---

2. Aristotle, *De Anima* 3.13.

3. Frederick W. Farrar, *History of Interpretation* (1886; Grand Rapids: Baker Book House, 1961), vii.

4. Farrar, *History of Interpretation,* xxv.

postmodern hermeneutics is building new bridges to traditional concepts and concerns in this and many other ways.

Frederick Farrar and many Protestants after him have been convinced that their engagement of the interpretive task is rooted in the Reformation of the sixteenth century. The rejection of the fourfold sense and the determined shift to a focus on the literal sense only, as they understand it, is a hallmark of that period, and is often especially credited to Martin Luther. Yet Luther by his own admission embraced the fourfold interpretation without hesitation in his younger years, and the first Psalms commentary of 1513-15 is an eloquent witness to this effect. His criticism of this traditional method, however, began as early as 1516, and a quotation dating to the autumn of 1517 expresses it deftly and sharply:

> Holy Scripture wants to be treated with fear and humility and studied with devout prayer rather than with a clever mind. It is therefore impossible that no harm is done to themselves and others whom they teach by those who, relying on their blank minds, jump right into it with their unwashed feet like pigs, as if this was just another human science; they wallow in it without any respect and discrimination. This is why we have so many candidates ready to teach, who after they have learned their grammar read theology right away without any study, saying: "Hmmm, the Bible is an easy thing." This happens most of all to those who have filled their bellies with those pods of the pigs, I mean of the philosophers. Saint Jerome already complains about them, that they pull the reluctant Scripture by their whim, and the saying has become true that Scripture has a waxen nose. This is brought about by those dull and foolish dreamers who play around with literal, allegorical, moral, and anagogical sense and call themselves scholastic doctors. Well, what an exceedingly proper and true name, for they are "scholastics," schoolboys interested in playing games and pretending to themselves and others while knowing nothing of what the letter and what the spirit is. Such Scripture study in the fourfold interpretation would have been bearable, if it were regarded as no more than a first lesson for beginners. But they now declare that this game is the apex of all learning and they never arrive at a true understanding which can never be reached without purity of heart. Yet even the most godless people drive that quadriga.[5]

5. *Decem praecepta Wittenbergensi praedicata populo,* D. Martin Luthers Werke, Weimarer Ausgabe 1, 507:25–508:4.

Luther's outburst is fairly clear in itself, but it bears some analysis in our context. First, the reformer knows all about the fourfold sense: he mentions the image of the chariot, the quadriga; he enumerates all four interpretations and clearly rejects them — not individually but as a system. He would not mind seeing it used as a training device for beginners, but in the hand of arrogant scholastic theologians it has become a manipulative tool dominating exegetical work and undergirding self-serving hypotheses of speculative theology rather than confronting readers with the existential claims of the Bible. The graphic image of the "waxen nose" which Luther will frequently use in his polemic against allegory — that is, something one can press into any shape one likes — says the same thing as the charge that the fourfold sense is being misused as an arbitrary game plan, a learnable methodology for just another field in the curriculum.

Second, Luther is clearly aware that the fourfold sense was an explication of an original twofold sense.[6] He mentions the two elements, namely, letter and spirit. Paul used this pair in 2 Corinthians 3:6, but it was known in Hellenistic Jewish circles as well: Philo of Alexandria saw in it a dynamic upward movement of interpretation in which a text in its meaning would rise from a lower level to a higher. Origen added a middle level in analogy to the trichotomy of body, soul, and spirit; and John Cassian, to whom we owe the first formulation of our standard quadriga, worked with a basic dichotomy of historical and spiritual interpretation, the second of which he subdivided into allegory, anagogy, and tropology, probably in order to conform the senses to Paul's "theological virtues" of faith, hope, and charity. Luther does not criticize this twofold sense of letter and spirit in the quotation noted above; he even seems to endorse it, and with it the basic anagogical, upward dynamics against a misused system of the four senses.

Third, Luther stresses that true understanding, the highest level, cannot be reached without purity of heart, awe, and humility. Scripture must be studied, he says, with devout prayer rather than with clever ideas. He does not speak here of exposition, but of an understanding of the Scriptures *(intelligentia scripturarum)*, because the interpretation of the Bible brought together what he called "grammatical understanding" and "soul understanding" — without, however, equating the two. The latter presupposed the former but was not automatically "triggered" by it. As he went on

6. For a detailed discussion of Luther's view of the "literal" and "spiritual" senses, see Karl Holl's classic "Luthers Bedeutung für den Fortschritt der Auslegungskunst," in *Gesammelte Aufsätze zur Kirchengeschichte*, vol. 1: *Luther* (Tübingen: J. C. B. Mohr, 1921), 414-50.

to suggest, a true understanding depends on making what he described as a new beginning in the act of interpreting. It is for the sake of this principle of understanding which requires inner conformity and personal involvement that Luther insisted increasingly on the point that there is only one sense to be looked for in biblical interpretation — the simplest, the foundational, the literal. He often called it a *sensus grammaticus,* thus revealing that he saw it as closely linked to its language form: the biblical language in its natural sense, he held, was simple, clear, unequivocal, a parallel to the manger of Bethlehem in which the incarnate God was found. Luther, of course, assumed God to be the primary author of Scripture; "the Holy Spirit says" is a frequent introduction for his citations from Scripture. But even more frequently, he makes Scripture itself the subject of the phrase: "Scripture says," as if it were a person with a living voice. The biblical word for him had a personality; Luther urged the interpreter to listen to its habits *(mos scripturae),* its way of speaking *(modus loquendi theologicus),* and its authorial intentions.

This sounds rather easygoing for a preacher who had just denounced those would-be interpreters who think the Bible is a cinch: "Hmmm, the Bible is an easy thing." But Luther speaks of "understanding," not exposition or even interpretation, and thus gestures toward the significance of an encounter. Yet he also knew that such a dynamic process could never be easy, and was surely not "automatic," because of the hardness and resistance of the reader's human heart that had to be overcome. One starts with the letter and works on the form of the language, but then one has to pray for God to reveal the truth — which is a kind of engagement, an experience of meaning. That is, the literal and spiritual senses are very closely linked for Luther, but there is no smooth, natural transition from one to the other. A big leap is required, a leap whose success cannot be programmed by following a firm set of "rules." Luther renounces rules and regulations for the interpretation of the Scriptures: "I cannot stand rules or [set] measures that presume to interpret the Scriptures," he insisted, "because the Word of God teaches in all freedom and cannot be imprisoned in such a way."[7] In terms of method, there is one sense, the *sensus litteralis.* But this one sense in its dynamic union with the spiritual sense has absorbed all the others in the quest for understanding. "Every passage of Scripture has infinite understandings," says Luther; "however much you understand, do not become

7. Martin Luther, *Sämtliche Werke,* vol. 4: *Predigten über die Evangelien,* ed. J. G. Plochman (Erlangen: Carl Heyder, 1832), 1, 49.

overly excited and do not resist other possibilities."[8] We can see from this that Luther really is not a good candidate for the role of the true ancestor for the exclusive preoccupation with the literal sense of Scripture as this has come to dominate modern biblical scholarship.

For this ancestry in the Reformation era, one would rather have to look to the humanists, especially Erasmus and his admirers, both in Luther's camp and elsewhere. The difference is unmistakable. While Luther used Erasmus's scholarship, he strongly disliked his rationalist approach to the Bible. Erasmus, he felt, was too cold, too detached, particularly for the way he treated the biblical text as a thing of the past — without allowing himself to be grasped by it. Luther resented in his humanist colleague the schoolmaster that he was, despite all the vitriolic denunciation Erasmus heaped upon the "scholastics," which agreed with Luther's own distaste.

At this juncture, it is very important to observe, however, that any insistence on the primacy of the literal sense in the Reformation era should not be understood in any sense as merely a revival of early Christian hermeneutics. Appropriating a national literature of the Jewish people which had itself only gradually been theologized, the early Christian interpretation of the Bible was anything but "literal." In fact, it could not be literal. Jesus and Paul still worked within the rabbinical framework; the principle was the horizon of Torah, but it was Torah as read in the style of Qumran — which is to say, Torah of the end-time, of the new *basileia* breaking in. Early Jewish Christians, in light of the conviction of Jesus' resurrection, sharpened this principle by focusing attention on the messianic concretization of this end-time Torah in the person of Jesus, which on the one hand gave authority to his traditioned words, while on the other hand allowing his life and death to be tied to the Jewish Scriptures under the prophetic category of promise and fulfillment. This key to reading the holy book may at first have been felt to be no more than a set of different rules applied to interpreting Torah — the Book of Hebrews and the Epistle of Barnabas demonstrate this stage. But it shifted the center of Scripture to the prophetic writings and away from Torah, and thus quickly became a new principle.

With the step beyond the Jewish matrix, scriptural interpretation in terms of promise and fulfillment proved a very effective tool of mission and apologetics; the biblical argumentation in the work of Justin Martyr and other apologists makes that clear. All these writers profited from the respect Jewish apologists had secured for their Scriptures in the culture of

8. *Scholae in Ps. 118*, D. Martin Luthers Werke, Weimarer Ausgabe 4, 318:36-39.

the Empire by emphasizing their antiquity. But this should not dissuade us from taking seriously a strong argument made years ago by Hans von Campenhausen, who reminded us that early Christianity in the Empire did not have an absolute need to retain the Old Testament.[9] Indeed, Marcion, who rejected these scriptures as the work of an inferior God, considered himself a good Christian. Anti-Marcionite Christians kept them primarily because they were too good a tool for supporting Christian apologetic strategies and missionary endeavors to discard them altogether.[10]

They also did not absolutely need the *written* New Testament. It is crucial to recall that oral culture still dominated the acceptance of authority in the strata of society in which Christianity had its greatest strength in late antiquity. When Papias collected the material for his "Exegesis of the Lord's Words" at the beginning of the second century, he searched for information on the oral teaching of the generation of "elders" who had heard the preaching of the apostles: "I assumed that what is derived from books does not profit me so much as that which is derived from a living and abiding voice."[11] Clement of Alexandria refers to traditions he credits to Pantaenus, who headed the Christian school at Alexandria and, like Jesus, did not leave a single written line as far as we know. "The presbyters did not write," says Clement.[12] It was the continued recognition of an existing written Old Testament, for Christians in the settled form of the Greek Septuagint, that led to the concept of a written New Testament as its counterpart, perhaps achieving its normative status primarily — as Irenaeus says — as the verifiable authority of the public teaching of the apostles against adversaries such as Christian Gnostics, who called on new Christian writings as well as on a secret oral tradition from these same apostles.[13]

Early Christian interpretation of the Jewish Scriptures was shaped, it seems, in the context of apologetics. The prophetic principle of promise/fulfillment used in the missionary appeal to Gentile as well as Jewish audiences belongs here as much as the Gnostic application of an ideological grid

---

9. See Hans von Campenhausen, *The Formation of the Christian Bible*, trans. J. A. Baker (Mifflintown, PA: Sigler Press, 1997), esp. ch. 3.

10. See Adolf von Harnack, *Marcion: The Gospel of the Alien God*, trans. John Steely and Lyle Bierma (Jamestown, NY: Labyrinth Press, 1990).

11. As cited by Eusebius, *History of the Church* 3.39.4.

12. Clement of Alexandria, *Eclogae propheticae* 27.1, in *Clemens Alexandrinus: Excerpta und Eclogae propheticae*, Die griechischen christlichen Schriftsteller der ersten drei Jahrhunderte 17, ed. Otto Stählin (Leipzig: Hinrich, 1909), 144.

13. Irenaeus, *Against Heresies* 3.1-2.

to Old and New Testament texts, as Elaine Pagels has described it,[14] or the attempt to make biblical texts conform to Stoic cosmology which Kathleen McVey has demonstrated for Theophilus of Antioch.[15] In all of these ways of interpreting, the "letter" or literal sense inevitably played an openly negative role. "Literalism" was the assumed characteristic of Jewish interpretation, and often meant no more than that its practitioners did not accept the messianic identity of Jesus. Paul's rhetoric of opposing letter and spirit in 2 Corinthians 3, whatever else may have to be said about the passage, claims the superiority of the latter over the former, of the Christian reading of the Scriptures "in the Spirit" over that of the synagogue. When Origen developed his threefold sense on the model of body, soul, and spirit, he did not hesitate to identify the first level with "flesh," the other negative term that Paul opposes to "spirit." The literal, bodily sense of the text is the fleshly sense, and this must be left behind in the interpretive move as quickly as possible. "The old has passed away. Behold, everything has become new" (2 Cor. 5:17).[16]

Origen is responsible for urging careful attention to the details of the text as part of his enthusiastic endorsement of classical Alexandrian philology. But the turn to the "literal sense," the lowest of all, as a positive concept is a later phenomenon. It belongs to the epochal changes of the Constantinian century, when the apologetic task changed into the task of coping with the triumph of Christianity. The first instance of this is the supposed fight between the schools of Alexandria and Antioch. That there was rivalry and controversy between the two cities is clear from the political and doctrinal history of the period. The connection of Antioch with Nestorius accounts for the loss of much of this school's literature. Modern textbook wisdom speaks of a battle over biblical interpretation in which the Antiochene fa-

14. Elaine Pagels, *The Johannine Gospel in Gnostic Exegesis* (Nashville: Abingdon Press, 1973), and *The Gnostic Paul: Gnostic Exegesis of the Pauline Letters* (Philadelphia: Fortress Press, 1975).

15. Kathleen McVey, "The Use of Stoic Cosmogony in Theophilus of Antioch's *Hexaemeron*," in *Biblical Hermeneutics in Historical Perspective: Studies in Honor of Karlfried Froehlich on His Sixtieth Birthday*, ed. Mark S. Burrows and Paul Rorem (Grand Rapids: Eerdmans, 1991), 32-58.

16. Origen attributes "literalism" as a weakness to Jewish readers of Scripture: "If anyone wishes to hear and understand these words literally he ought to gather with the Jews rather than with the Christians. But if he wishes to be a Christian and a disciple of Paul, let him hear Paul saying that 'the Law is spiritual.'" Origen, *Homilies on Genesis and Exodus* 4.1, Fathers of the Church 71, trans. Ronald Heine (Washington, DC: Catholic University Press, 1982), 121.

thers appear as the good guys, the Alexandrians as the villains. The real picture, of course, is far more complex and interesting.

First of all, we know nothing of a fight between the schools, but only of the wild polemic of one against the other. We do have knowledge of sharply polemical treatises by Antiochene exegetes against Alexandrian allegory, but nothing in kind from the other side. The background is the concept of a textual commentary, in Greek: *hypomnēma*.[17] The genre was a product of Alexandrian scholarship, and its actual creator was Aristarchos (d. 144 BCE), the fifth director of Alexandria's *mousaion,* a fabulous "institute of advanced study" associated with the greatest library in antiquity. Aristarchos was a *grammatikos* interested in the text of Homer and the revered Greek writers, and, to be more exact, in the stages of textual work leading up to *exēgēsis.* These stages included word analysis, syntax, and background mythology, but not philosophical reflection on its value and truth. In other words, his primary interest was in what Homer *said,* not what he *meant* for Hellenistic culture. It seems that the Antiochene biblical commentators regarded themselves as the true heirs of this venerable tradition.[18] They respected the Old Testament as a document of ancient Jewish history, for which they were promptly derided as "Judaizers." In the Psalter, they tried to reconstruct the original order of the Psalms using inner-biblical clues, and they considered only a few Psalms as "messianic" in the sense of predicting Christ's coming.

Still, they had no problem with the inspiration of both Old and New Testament books and with the divine lessons provided therein for the Christian life. But the means by which God taught was not *lexis,* the plain words of the text, as carefully as these should be handled. Nor was it *historia,* the narrative formed by the words, as much as its content needed precise reconstruction. Rather, it had to do with the *pragma,* or what we would call the "historical facts" reported. Interpreting Genesis 1–3, they accused the Alexandrians of denying the factual basis of the story. While acknowledging numerous rhetorical figures, similes, and metaphors in the text, they insisted that there must have been a real Adam, a real Eve, a real Serpent, and a real place where all of this happened. Otherwise God could not make his point. And what precisely does God teach? The *pragma* for the

---

17. See my essay "Bibelkommentare — Zur Krise einer Gattung," *Zeitschrift für Theologie und Kirche* 84, no. 4 (November 1987): 465-92.

18. For a discussion of Antiochene exegesis and some texts in English translation, see my book *Biblical Interpretion in the Early Church* (Philadelphia: Fortress Press, 1984), 19-23 and 82-103.

Antiochene theologians functions in the Bible as an example, a model for Christian living. We have a treatise by Diodore of Tarsus on the Pythonissa, the woman necromancer whom Saul in his distress consulted (see 1 Sam. 28). Chiding Origen for finding divine mysteries behind every word of the story, Diodore declares that the words of a psychotic king and a wicked woman are not the Word of God, but part of a *pragma* by which God warns every reader to shun such diabolical practices. The "literal sense," in this case, is what we today would call "history."

The second serious consideration of the literal sense as a positive concept belongs in the controversy over the Latin Bible translation in the fourth and early fifth centuries. The loss of bilingualism in the Empire falls into this period. Cicero and Tertullian could still write Greek, but not Augustine. We must remember that the Septuagint, the basis for the Latin versions of the Old Testament, was not regarded by Christians as a translation of an inspired Hebrew text, but as a different book with its own, superior inspiration, and this is what lent it a superior authority. Augustine still regarded it as the normative text against which Latin translations should be checked. Jerome, however, fought for the "Hebrew truth," arguing from the analogy of a river's water being purer near the source.[19] We do not know the exact meaning of his phrase "Hebrew truth." How can truth be Hebrew or Greek? It may be deliberate hyperbole to draw attention to his claims of having mastered the source.

Indeed, such claims are not uncommon in this period. Jerome tells of his toil in trying to learn Hebrew and Aramaic, the sweat it took to translate, his consultations with a Jewish acquaintance *("Hebraeus meus")* who came to him by night for fear of the Jews. Yet most of this storytelling seems to be hyperbole, if not outright fabrication. Pierre Nautin voiced the suspicion two decades ago, and subsequent studies tend to confirm it: Jerome really did not know Hebrew.[20] He certainly learned Greek well during his first stay at Antioch, where grammatical concepts, textbooks, and teachers were available for this purpose. But nothing like this existed for Hebrew. Jerome could not learn, and thus "know," Hebrew, as we define the term "knowing

19. "Multo purior manare credenda sit fontis unda quam rivi." Jerome, *Against Helvidius* 8, Patrologia Latina 23, ed. J.-P. Migne, 191B.

20. Pierre Nautin, *Origène: Sa vie et son oeuvre* (Paris: Beauchesne, 1977), 214-19, 284-92, 326-61; also in the article "Hieronymus," in *Theologische Realenzyklopädie,* vol. 15 (Berlin: Walter de Gruyter, 1986), 309-10. The judgment of Michael Graves is far less radical: *Jerome's Hebrew Philology: A Study Based on His Commentary on Jeremiah,* Vigiliae Christianae Supplements 90 (Leiden: Brill, 2007). On pp. 3-9, Graves reviews the various opinions.

a language" — that is, as having a grasp of the system of forms as well as syntax — except by living in a linguistic community where learning would happen through use. Like Aristarchos, he was a gifted philologist, curious about the meaning of words, and could certainly decipher text written in Hebrew letters. He knew numerous words and phrases, and could ask about etymologies and name lore. But could one call this dilettantism "knowing Hebrew"? The few sections of the Vulgate that can be attributed to Jerome's own labors are revisions of existing translations, done by comparing one or more Greek translations, and constantly consulting Origen and Eusebius.[21] His introductions to biblical books and his treatise on the etymology of Hebrew names, which formed part of practically every medieval Bible, were compiled from the same sources and are a dubious contribution to the comprehension of the real literal sense of the Hebrew Scriptures. This does not mean that Jerome's philological passion had no positive influence on the appreciation of the literal sense among future generations. It does suggest, however, that Jerome himself misled generation after generation into vastly overrating his expertise.

Beryl Smalley, one of the foremost experts on medieval biblical interpretation in an earlier generation, did not suspect that anything was wrong with Jerome's self-proclaimed identity as a "man of three languages" *(vir trilinguis),* but she notes quite correctly that enormous progress was later made in this area, particularly in the twelfth and thirteenth centuries. The objective of her book *The Study of the Bible in the Middle Ages* was to trace the contribution of medieval Christian Hebraists, as she put it, as the story "of a stage in the secularization of medieval thought."[22] This is one way of looking at this matter, and one that is much in line with Farrar's assumptions about the progress of scientific exegesis. But there are other ways as well. One of Smalley's discoveries, Andrew of St. Victor, knew far more Hebrew than Jerome and wrote commentaries on most books of the Old Testament, restricting his exposition doggedly to the literal sense.[23] He did so, he writes, not because he preferred the literal

21. For a discussion of Jerome's role in assembling the Vulgate, see D. C. Parker, "Vulgate," in *The Anchor Yale Bible Dictionary,* vol. 6, ed. David Noel Freedman (New York: Doubleday, 1992), 860-62.

22. Beryl Smalley, *The Study of the Bible in the Middle Ages* (Oxford: Blackwell, 1952), 372. See also her "Preface to the Third Edition," published by Blackwell in 1983 (vii).

23. See Beryl Smalley, "Andrew of St. Victor, Abbot of Wigmore: A Twelfth-Century Hebraist," *Recherches de théologie ancienne et médiévale* 10 (1938): 358-73. See also Frans A. van Liere, "Andrew of St. Victor: Scholar between Cloister and School," in *Centres of Learn-*

over the spiritual senses, but because his practice was an ascetic feat, an exercise in humility, like the discipline of cutting out sweets during Lent.

The decisive establishment of the positive appreciation of the literal sense, however, did not come with Jerome. It came, paradoxically, with Augustine. His earlier professional position as a rhetorician made it natural for him to be interested in good language. At that time, he considered biblical language as substandard, precisely in its literal sense: *ad litteram*, "as the words sound or read," it was poor form, and as *historia*, "the story they tell," it was poor content.[24] When he joined the Manicheans, he aligned himself with a religion which insisted on a literal interpretation of the Old Testament precisely in order to reject it. By his own account, he was freed from this logic by listening to Ambrose preaching the Old Testament "allegorically," demonstrating that the unsavory language was there for a reason and could be moved into higher levels of meaning hidden behind it. The way he explains what happened seems to suggest that he embraced even more fervently than others the traditional negative evaluation of the literal sense: "I was delighted to hear Ambrose in his sermons to the people saying, as if he were most carefully enunciating a principle of exegesis: 'The letter kills, the spirit gives life' (2 Cor. 3:6). Those texts which, taken literally, seemed to contain perverse teaching he would expound spiritually, removing the mystical veil."[25] He goes on to explain the role that the Bible's simple and sometimes crude form played as "a means of coming to faith in [God] and a means of seeking to know [God]":

> Already the absurdity which used to offend me in those books, after I had heard many passages being given persuasive expositions, I understood to be significant of the profundity of their mysteries. The authority of the Bible seemed the more to be venerated and more worthy of a holy faith on the ground that it was open to everyone to read, while keeping the dignity of its secret meaning for a profounder interpretation.[26]

This passage offers a fascinating and important insight into Augustine's view of Scripture for several reasons. It suggests how much impor-

---

ing: Learning and Location in Premodern Europe and the Near East, ed. Hendrik Jan Willem Drijvers and Alasdair A. MacDonald (Leiden: Brill, 1997), 187-95.

24. Augustine tells this story more fully in *Confessions* 6.4.5-6. Among the many recent translations of this classic work, my choice is *Confessions,* trans. Henry Chadwick (New York: Oxford University Press, 1992).

25. *Confessions* 6.4.6 (Chadwick, 94).

26. *Confessions* 6.6.8 (Chadwick, 96).

tance he attributed to the work of interpretation, particularly in the face of "absurd" or "crude" texts; these were there for a purpose, after all, and that was in part so that it was "open," as he puts it, to all readers, the simple as well as the sophisticated. He also came to view the Bible as concealing its "mysteries," so as to allure readers, to entice them to work hard at seeking to know the hidden meaning available by means of "a profounder interpretation." And this meant that a life devoted to seeking God took shape in and through reading such texts. This required hard work, but it also depended on desire.

We see how this same emphasis emerges in his treatment of the senses, above all because of their power of attraction. The "temptations of the lust of the flesh" *(temptationes concupiscentiae carnis)* belonged to all the senses, with sexual temptation as focused most particularly on the sense of touch.[27] This approach reminds us of Aristotle's view of the body's role in perception, or *aisthēsis,* which we examined earlier.[28] In his *Confessions,* Augustine describes his love of God in terms of a mode of engaging the five senses — and thus, a means of encountering God through these forms of experience:

> But when I love you, what do I love? It is not physical beauty nor temporal glory nor the brightness of light dear to earthly eyes, nor the sweet melodies of all kinds of songs, nor the gentle odor of flowers and ointments and perfumes, nor manna or honey, nor limbs welcoming embraces of the flesh; it is not these I love when I love my God. Yet there is a light I love, and a food, and a kind of embrace when I love my God — a light, voice, odor, food, embrace of my inner man, where my soul is floodlit by light which space cannot contain, where there is sound that time cannot seize, where there is a perfume which no breeze disperses, where there is a taste for food no amount of eating can lessen, and where there is a bond of union that no satiety can part. This is what I love when I love my God.[29]

When Augustine turned his attention to biblical interpretation, he articulated an approach that was remarkably congruent with this: it involved

---

27. See *Confessions* 10.34.51-52 (Chadwick, 209-10), where he focuses on "sight" as a way in which we experience the "touch" that stirred and disturbed him.

28. See above, p. 13.

29. See *Confessions* 10.6.8 (Chadwick, 183).

work, and hard work as we shall see, but the guiding direction of that work was a matter of properly ordered desire. As we mentioned earlier, the first book of his hermeneutical treatise, *On Christian Doctrine,* formulated the basic argument in terms of the distinction between "use" and "enjoyment." This was a necessary prologue — the statement of the fundamental principle — to any treatment of the rules involved in the practice of interpretation.

Augustine's later life story stands as an illustration of how he began to work out this insight. Because Genesis 1–3 had been the crucial testing ground for the Manicheans, Augustine devoted himself to writing three commentaries on these chapters — and if we count the discussion in his *Confessions,* four — as if in rebuttal.[30] In retrospect, he admits that in the first one he had tried hard to beat the Manichean interpretation by its own rules. The effort was unsuccessful. He ended up doing exactly what Ambrose had done, which is to say, he offered a figurative interpretation. He did not give up, though; in the preface to the third commentary, which he entitled *On Genesis ad litteram,* he lists three groups of interpreters: literalists, allegorists, and those who recognize both a literal and a figurative sense.[31] He placed himself in the third category, because he finally realized that *ad litteram* means two things: first, it has to do with what the story says *(secundum historiam),* but this entails, second, its prophetic implications *(secundum prophetiam).* The surprise here was Augustine's discovery of the actual power of the literal sense, not its supposed weakness.

This is even clearer in his treatise *On Christian Doctrine.* Here, his famous sign-theory explains what happens in language communication: voiced or "lettered" words signify things (that is, they have a referent), and these things in turn can signify other things (that is, they may have a second referent). Animals always make good examples: an ox means a real ox, but that real ox can also mean an apostle, according to 1 Corinthians 9:9: "Thou shalt not muzzle the ox that treadeth out the corn."[32] There are problems with word signs: they may be unknown — do we, for example, know what "cumin" is when we read in Matthew's Gospel "You pay tithe of mint and cumin" (23:23)? Words may also be ambiguous: thus, a "page" could be a part of a book or a person at the door. Augustine devotes two entire parts

30. *Confessions* 11-12.

31. See Augustine, *On Genesis: A Refutation of the Manichees, Unfinished Literal Commentary on Genesis, The Literal Meaning of Genesis,* trans. Edmund Hill (New York: New City Press, 2002).

32. See *On Christian Doctrine* 2.10.15.

of the treatise to offering "remedies" for such problems.[33] And these involve the study of languages and of the liberal arts — that is, grammar, logic, dialectic — as well as all useful knowledge of "things" in the world. But if in studying the Bible one follows the series of signs pointing to things pointing to other things and so on, the final "thing" is always God. All words, all signs, all things finally lead to God, the creator, who is the source and the comprehensive parameter of all that is. What Augustine marvels at is that the entire journey of the signs begins with nothing more than a humble sound *(flatus vocis)* or a simple lettered word *(littera)*.[34]

In exploring this discussion, Samuel Preus has suggested that two levels of the "literal sense" are operative in Augustine: the first is an edifying level that teaches faith, hope, and charity directly, while a second is what he calls an "unedifying" level, one that needs to be lifted up into the other.[35] His argument is not convincing, because for Augustine the *littera,* or literal sense, does not elicit just one level of understanding. As Augustine puts it,

> When, from a single scriptural passage not one but two or more meanings are elicited . . . there is no danger if any of the meanings may be seen to be congruous with the truth taught in other passages. . . . For the author himself may have seen the same meaning in the words we seek to understand. And certainly the Spirit of God, who works through that author, undoubtedly foresaw that this meaning would occur to the reader or listener.[36]

This argument shows that Augustine links the literal sense to the intention of the author, but it also suggests that the human author is of no great interest for him. What is important, however, is that language as such through which truth is expressed is a human phenomenon, even a human convention, and for God to use it becomes an act of amazing condescension which should spur us on to ever greater love for him.

This conviction was the place from which the epochal turn to a full, positive consideration of the literal sense in the Middle Ages began. Abe-

33. *On Christian Doctrine* 2.10.15–3.4.8.

34. For a discussion of the *flatus vocis* in Augustine's *Confessions,* see Marcia Colish, *The Mirror of Language: A Study in the Medieval Theory of Language* (Lincoln: University of Nebraska Press, 1968), 38-39.

35. See James Samuel Preus, *From Shadow to Promise: Old Testament Interpretation from Augustine to the Young Luther* (Cambridge, MA: Belknap Press, 1969), 9-16.

36. See *On Christian Doctrine* 3.27.38.

lard's interpretation of the Tower of Babel makes this clear (Gen. 11:1-9).[37] The traditional understanding was that in the beginning there existed but a single language, Hebrew, which perhaps God himself gave to Adam and Eve; following this view, the diversification at Babel was an act of divine punishment. Abelard thought otherwise. He observed that, according to the second Genesis creation story (Gen. 2:19-20), God left the "naming" of creatures to Adam; Adam had to invent language in paradise, and this took effort and time. The first couple must have spent several years at the task. Abelard points out that the Genesis account (Gen. 10:5, 20, 31) suggests that different languages existed before Babel in the various divisions of humanity, the result of the ingenuity of humans in expressing their thoughts since thought was a reference level shared by all. At Babel, God only confused the existing languages. Putting them together again, the task of learning languages, therefore, is a proper exercise of human reason and its power over a human phenomenon. Abelard urged the nuns of Héloise's convent to study Greek and Hebrew as part of their ascetic exercises. In this way, they could imitate God's restorative miracle at Pentecost, an event which Abelard understood as different languages being spoken and not just heard. Pentecost, when God once more unified what had been rationally developed by humans and then confused through human sin, was the culmination of the history of language, the apex of the feasts of the church year, a claim that one finds reflected in the name of Héloise's convent, "The Paraclete."

In Abelard's time, the quadriga, the system of the fourfold sense of Scripture, was firmly established as a precious legacy of the early Christian age. But these senses no longer conveyed the simple idea of an ascent, which as Augustine had suggested exploded from the literal level into a multiplicity of spiritual meanings — with all signs in the series from sign to thing pointing ultimately to God. The senses now were ordered. As illustrative of this point, the form of teaching and learning that emerged in this period, scholasticism, emphasized the importance of the schools as places that facilitated all such learning, the locus for the proper ordering of intellectual subject matter. The Middle Ages was a period devoted to the love of learning, and fascinated by schematic tables, outlines, and visual aids that might help in the clarification and memorization of subjects of knowledge.

The most common organizing principle for the system of the four

---

37. See Arno Borst, *Der Turmbau von Babel: Geschichte der Meinungen über Ursprung und Vielfalt der Sprachen und Völker,* vol. 2, part 2 (Stuttgart: Anton Hiersemann, 1959), 631-35.

scriptural senses was the metaphor of a building.[38] Jerome already spoke of the literal sense as a "foundation," and Gregory the Great expanded the metaphor: first, the foundation is laid *(littera)*, then the walls are erected *(allegoria)*, then the house is decorated with paint *(tropologia,* the other word for moral interpretation).[39] Medieval authors mention a fourth step: the roof is put on: namely, anagogy *(anagogia)*. Aminadab's chariot, to return to an image we explored in the previous chapter, suggested the application of the fourfold sense as a dynamic sweep upward. The building analogy does the same: a house is built from the bottom up, but in strict sequence. Hugh of St. Victor used the building analogy throughout his work to explain the structure of his understanding of biblical interpretation.[40] Time and again he returns to the importance of the literal sense, which constitutes the building's foundation. Like the sense of touch, it has two aspects: on the one hand, it must have absolute priority, since there is and will be no building without a foundation; on the other hand, it is the lowliest part of the building. A foundation consists of rough stones and rocks thrown down into the pit without refinement — that is, raw material for the real work, the careful construction of the superstructure.

What is this foundational, literal sense in the Bible? Hugh identified it with the historical sense: *sensus litteralis seu historicus.* With this equation, he followed a patristic tradition which took up the terminology of the Antiochene theologians but differed from their conclusions: "The letter is the narration of things done"[41] — not the things, the *pragmata,* themselves, but their narration. In ancient historiography, "things" narrated required an eyewitness: one wrote "history" if one had been there or had information

38. See Henri de Lubac, "Symboles architecturaux," in *Exégèse médiévale: Les quatre sens de l'Ecriture,* vol. 2, part 2 (Paris: Aubier, 1964), 41-60.

39. *The Letters of Gregory the Great* 5.53a, trans. John R. C. Martyn, Medieval Sources in Translation 40 (Toronto: Pontifical Institute of Medieval Studies, 2004), 382. This letter has often been printed as a preface to the edition of Gregory's *Moralia,* e.g., in Patrologia Latina 75, 509-16.

40. For a discussion of Hugh's biblical hermeneutics, see Part 1 of Paul Rorem, *Hugh of St. Victor* (New York: Oxford University Press, 2009). Apart from Hugh's main works, *De sacramentis* and *Didascalicon,* two small treatises are of importance here: *Chronicon, vel de tribus maximis circumstantiis gestorum,* translated into English in *The Medieval Craft of Memory: An Anthology of Texts and Pictures,* ed. Mary Carruthers and Jan Ziolkowski (Philadelphia: University of Pennsylvania Press, 2002), 32-40; and *De scripturis et scriptoribus sacris,* Patrologia Latina 175, ed. J.-P. Migne, 9-28.

41. "Historia est rerum gestarum narratio," in Hugh of St. Victor, *De sacramentis, prologus,* Patrologia Latina 176, ed. J.-P. Migne, 184C.

from someone else who had. In this sense, imaginary or fictional narration was not history but story or "fable." For Latin Christians, *fabula* referred to a non-event, *historia* to a real event. There was, of course, no "fable" — as they understood it — in the Bible; its literal sense was historical because it was "the narration of true events of the past," a past that extended from the Creation through the time of the early church. This literal or historical sense of the Bible fitted together into a clear factual outline, something that everyone could grasp. Thus, Hugh was very interested in having the *realia,* the down-to-earth features of the stories, expounded: times, places, persons, circumstances, events. One reason was that he actually was a schoolmaster. He taught boys, teenage aspirants, and young clerics, at the school of St. Victor. His pupils could learn and memorize these details: the series of the kings of Israel and Judah, the sequence of the life of Jesus, or the stations of Paul's missionary journeys. Peter Comestor's *Historia Scholastica,* a bestselling textbook of the High Middle Ages, presented a narrative outline of biblical history with some world history interspersed, in Hugh's terms a "compendium of the literal sense."[42]

In light of this new emphasis on the letter as history, Hugh also reflected more deeply on Augustine's model of the nature of language. Beyond sign and thing, such a story required a storyteller, and thus relied on the intentions of an author to hold the two together. Hugh added a middle term he called *"sensus,"* between the letter (Augustine's sign) and its higher meaning (Augustine's thing). This "sense" was the word's immediate — or, as Hugh put it, its "primary" — signification on the level of human convention, what the word first of all says when the author chooses it to express his or her intention. It is the "inside" to the "outside" of the word. Following Hugh, Thomas Aquinas in the thirteenth century used this clarification, sharpened its implications, and thus gave another boost to the growing preference for the foundational role of the literal sense in the quadriga. Letter and immediate signification together form the literal sense of all language: one word has, first of all, one meaning. The explosion into multiple meanings regulated in biblical interpretation by the three spiritual senses can occur only after this first literal meaning has been established. Thomas's formula for this model is, "All spiritual senses are founded on the literal."[43]

42. See Mark John Clark, *A Study of Peter Comestor's Method in the Historia Genesis,* Ph.D. diss., Columbia University, 2002.

43. The basic source here is Thomas Aquinas, *Summa theologiae* 1a.1.9-10. Two other important Aquinas texts are *Quodlibetum* 7.6.14-16 and *Lectura* c. 4, *lectio* 7 of the Galatians Commentary.

Thomas drew a number of conclusions from this. First, only from the literal sense can any argument be constructed; language needs an objective referent for a verbal exchange to allow a rational solution. People talking to each other acknowledge a common platform by using a common language. They must be able to trust it; otherwise, why talk? Second, metaphor is a part of the convention of human language. It can therefore be reckoned as belonging to the literal sense, because when people use this convention, they intend the metaphor. Third, the role of the intention of the author is thus of utmost importance for the literal sense. Thomas already uses a new thirteenth-century definition: "The literal sense is what the author intends." In relation to the Bible, this is an eminently theological statement since God, according to Thomas, is the true author of Scripture.

Even in Thomas, however, the human authors of Scripture come to be appreciated more and more, and the trend soon became universal. The rediscovery of Aristotle among Christian scholars during this period was a major factor in this development.[44] By drawing on Aristotle's general teaching on causality, they found a way of distinguishing between God as the primary and the human writers as secondary, instrumental authors. The specific notion of a fourfold causality, when applied to the books of the Bible, naturally directed attention to the activity of the human authors: the material cause, drawing on Aristotle's terminology, would be the substance of the story to be told or the argument to be unfolded, while the efficient cause, the author, came to be seen as both God and the human writer; the formal cause was the method of treatment, while the final cause, God's will to save, was what we have called the "principle." Discussing these "causes" gave considerable freedom to look at any book of the scriptural canon as a literary work, and literary analysis — including grammar, style, logical progression, rhetorical structure, etc. — flourished in the interpretation of the literal sense of the Bible at the same time when the vernacular literatures began to cut out their own independent niche.

This assumption of a "double authorship," together with the definition of the literal sense as authorial intention, raised new difficulties. Can non-biblical literature have more than an entertainment value? Can it teach "truth"? And, as a related issue: Can it be understood to have a spiritual

---

44. For more on this see two pertinent sections in my chapter "Interpretation of the Old Testament in the High Middle Ages," in *Hebrew Bible/Old Testament: The History of Its Interpretation,* vol. 1: *From the Beginnings to the Middle Ages (Until 1300),* part 2: *The Middle Ages,* ed. Magne Sæbø (Göttingen: Vandenhoeck & Ruprecht, 2000), 496-558; here 519-22 ("The Impact of the Reception of Aristotle") and 538-46 ("Thomas Aquinas").

sense? Many authors during this period began to think so, and many readers did as well. But theologians frequently objected. The Bible alone, they insisted, could have spiritual senses because only God as the primary author can make both word-signs as well as the things signified into "signs" that point to higher levels of spiritual meaning. While the culture in the fifteenth century seemed ready to read other books besides the Bible, and to treat the Bible more freely as a work of literature, some saw the gulf between the Bible and all other books widening ever more. If one had to read authorial intention in order to find the literal sense of a book, then any human author as a sinful being was suspect by definition, and so was the literal sense of his or her work; the Bible alone as an authoritative text that reflected God's eternal intention, they argued, could be considered as supremely trustworthy.[45]

With this distrust of human words, based on an undergirding distrust of human intentions, the firm basis of Aquinas's literal sense as "one word, one meaning" collapsed, even in terms of interpreting the Bible. The result of this development was significant. In the fifteenth century, confusion if not chaos reigned in what people meant by the "literal sense" of Scripture. A striking example of this is the nomenclature that emerged during this period concerning the so-called "double literal sense" *(duplex sensus litteralis)*. Scholars have long been aware of the presence of this term in Nicholas of Lyra, the great advocate of the literal sense of the Old Testament in the fourteenth century.[46] He used the expression for prophetic utterances which have a double fulfillment, e.g., 2 Samuel 7:14-15: "I will be a father to him, and he will be a son to me." This verse stood as a prediction concerning Solomon; Hebrews 1:5, however, applies it to Christ. Because of this Nicholas of Lyra begins to call both of these senses "literal" — and he could have said "historical" as we have discussed it here — in order to protect the historical integrity of both Solomon and Christ.[47] In his interpretation of the two witnesses of Revelation 11, he again finds a "double literal sense": this

---

45. For an extensive discussion of authorial intention of non-biblical literature, see A. J. Minnis, *Medieval Theory of Authorship: Scholastic Literary Attitudes in the Later Middle Ages,* 2nd ed. (Philadelphia: University of Pennsylvania Press, 2010), 160-210.

46. See the introduction to *Nicholas of Lyra: The Senses of Scripture,* ed. Philip Krey and Lesley Smith (Leiden: Brill, 2000), 15-18, and several of its essays, esp. Teresa Gross-Diaz, "What Is a Good Soldier to Do? Scholarship and Revelation in the Postils on the Psalms," 111-28.

47. Frans A. van Liere, "The Literal Sense of the Books Samuel and Kings: From Andrew of St. Victor to Nicholas of Lyra," in Krey and Smith, eds., *Nicholas of Lyra,* 59-82.

prophecy, he says, was first fulfilled in Pope Silverius and Patriarch Menas of Constantinople, two defenders of the Council of Chalcedon in the sixth century, but the more complete fulfillment will come in the future, when Enoch and Elijah will return to preach against the Antichrist.[48]

Alexander Minorita, another Franciscan commentator on the Apocalypse, however, while calling the first fulfillment *historia,* refuses to equate this "history" with the "letter," because it is the fulfillment of a prophecy and therefore part of the spiritual sense.[49] James Perez of Valencia divided the double literal sense of prophecies into the sense the words make and the sense in which they are uttered.[50] Thus, the words quoted by Nicholas of Lyra may be heard as referring to Solomon or David, but the intention — the vision of the prophet — covers both the reference to Solomon and to Christ. One can even find in the documents of the Council of Constance a sophistic theory of a "double literal sense," one that distinguishes a "mere grammatical, untrue, potentially deceptive literal sense" of words — the gobbledygook of mere words, or "senseless language" — from the "true literal sense" which conveys what the author wants to say.[51] With such a claim, the bottom has dropped out of the chariot. The lowest "sense" is declared to be no sense at all, and this can only mean "nonsense."

Luther's positing of a single literal sense, which is at the same time *sensus grammaticus* and *sensus theologicus,* is different from all these tortured answers to the predicament of assuming a dual authorship while defining the literal sense as pointing to authorial intention. His approach abandons the entire system of the quadriga, but he accomplishes this by redefining the single literal sense as including rather than excluding the dynamics of the spiritual ascent in its scope — that is, he joins this late-medieval tendency to widen the notion of the "literal," though for entirely new reasons. According to Luther, God is at the beginning of the interpretive procedure and gives the words as they are written; God also stands at its end as the one who has to give

48. See Philip Krey, "The Apocalypse Commentary of 1329: Problems in Church History," in Krey and Smith, eds., *Nicholas of Lyra,* 267-89.

49. Alexander Minorita, *Expositio in Apocalypsim,* ed. Alois Wachtel, Monumenta Germaniae Historica: Quellen zur Geistesgeschichte des Mittelalters 1 (Weimar: Böhlau, 1955), 230-32.

50. See Preus, *From Shadow to Promise,* 109-10.

51. See my essay "'Always to Keep the Literal Sense in Holy Scripture Means to Kill One's Soul': The State of Biblical Hermeneutics in the Beginning of the Fifteenth Century," in *Literary Uses of Typology from the Late Middle Ages to the Present,* ed. Earl Miner (Princeton, NJ: Princeton University Press, 1977), 20-48.

the reader-as-interpreter true understanding — certainly not without serious work on text and grammar, but also against the works-righteousness and pride that seem often to accompany it. In a way, the logic of the breakthrough in the High Middle Ages is reversed. There the new insight was that, despite God's authorship, the rights of the human authors have to be respected. In Luther, the new logic is that, despite the rights of human authors and interpreters, God remains the sovereign Lord over his Word.

Post-Enlightenment hermeneutics in its historical-critical mode has changed the principle of biblical interpretation once more. Since the Enlightenment, it is the parameter of autonomous reason into which our scientific methods are designed to move the text. For this, we have to keep God out of the picture. We are dealing with human authors and human authors alone. This is a decided advantage. Gone are the days when one had to worry about dual authorship. We are among ourselves, so to speak, humans investigating humans. Biblical scholarship can be taught and learned; its methods do uncover the literal sense, helping us ask, "What did the text say in its original setting?" There is still plenty to uncover, it seems; the future of biblical scholarship in this mode appears to be bright. But does this approach bring with it any disadvantages? Not only fundamentalists today think this to be the case. Thomas Merriam makes this point, arguing in 1978 that "[t]he literalism of a scrupulously scientific Biblical Scholarship is a fundament of spiritual boredom."[52] And Eugen Drewermann, a controversial German Catholic theologian, raises this question from the vantage point of a depth-psychological reading of Scripture, when he asks,

> What is the point of an interpretation of the Bible which does not contain a single authentic feeling, one single deeper insight, anything truly significant? Or an interpretation of Holy Scripture which actually forbids one to bring along any of one's own feelings or sensibilities, inner tensions and personal questions? How is it possible to hear something of God when the required methodological condition is that one must be concerned exclusively with the genesis of certain religious opinions among certain social constellations of the distant past instead of with God and one's own person? When such an exegesis accompanies the reading of Holy Scripture, it leads a person neither to God nor to him- or herself.[53]

---

52. Thomas Merriam, "Dissociation and the Literal Interpretation of the Bible," *Downside Review* 96 (1978): 84.

53. See Eugen Drewermann, *Tiefenpsychologie und Exegese*, vol. 1: *Die Wahrheit der*

The principle of autonomous reason apparently is no longer the only option. Drewermann himself is interested in the parameter of the deeper self and its experience. But God enters the picture as well. Now, what are the options? Can we, should we expand the horizon of biblical interpretation again after we have deliberately restricted it for so long? Here, the question is not simply that of the nature of the "literal" sense. Here we now turn to consider the three "spiritual" senses of the quadriga, giving us room to ponder the issue in its deeper dimensions.

Formen: Traum, Mythos, Märchen, Sage, und Legende (Olten: Walter-Verlag, 1984), 25. The quote occurs in a section entitled "Vom religiösen Irrweg der historisch-kritischen Methode," 23-28. See also his memoir, *Was Ich Denke* (Munich: Goldmann Verlag, 1994), esp. 60-64.

CHAPTER THREE

Allegoria: Seeing the Beauty

It is a remarkable fact of cultural history that the Reformation of the sixteenth century constitutes a watershed in regard to the role of sense experience in the life of the churches. The Catholic Middle Ages were an age of seeing, while the churches of the Reformation elevated hearing to the highest rank among the senses. The medieval Roman Church offered to the believer a host of sight experiences, not to mention smell and touch, as accompaniment to the biblical word in all its forms. As its central act of worship, the Mass was a beautiful visual spectacle, a drama which, since the thirteenth century, had its high point in the elevation of the elements, the demonstration to the eyes of believers that Christ was "really, truly, and substantially" present.[1] In contrast, the Reformed churches in particular developed a polemical concentration on hearing the Word against what they considered to be the exuberance of visual phenomena; they emphasized a visual plainness, which expressed itself from the architecture of church buildings to the way they furnished their houses of worship.

It must be said, of course, that not all images were destroyed in Zurich and Geneva; Zwingli, for example, expressly exempted stained glass windows from the "war on idols."[2] What this suggests, however, is that polemics is not a suitable basis for a holistic integration of the Bible's riches within the life of our churches. The biblical message, we say, is addressed to the whole

---

1. See Gerard G. Grant, "The Elevation of the Host: A Reaction to Twelfth-Century Heresy," *Theological Studies* 1, no. 3 (1940): 228-50. Late medieval manuscript illuminations depicting the Mass invariably show this moment.

2. Zwingli, *De vera et falsa religione,* ed. Emil Egli and Georg Finsler, Sämtliche Werke 3, Corpus Reformatorum 90 (Leipzig, 1914), 905.

person, and the whole person's perception employs all of the senses: hearing needs seeing, and seeing needs hearing. In today's churches, banners, art exhibits, and Christmas pageants are a common sight even in Presbyterian and Reformed churches, while many Roman Catholic churches — guided by the reforms of the Second Vatican Council — have reduced the abundance of visual images in their interiors, while the liturgy celebrated there now elevates the place of the sermon.

Of course, we have come to assume as modern people that beauty is something perceived primarily in seeing. Aristotle had a different view, holding a much broader appreciation of the senses generally: while he did not denigrate sight, as we shall see, he situates his discussion of the senses generally as a matter of *aisthēsis,* or perception. That is, all of the senses enable us to "perceive" our world and our place in it, an insight that marks a decisive development in the West. Because of his view that every sense contributes to perception, Aristotle explores the nature of the "soul" from a biological angle, seeing its role as related to the body in all its senses. One might well say that this marks the beginning of "scientific" psychology.[3]

As we earlier noted, Aristotle ranked vision without question as the highest and most decisive of the senses. After all, the microcosm as represented by the human figure elevates the eyes above the ears, the nose, and the mouth. An earlier tradition had also regarded the sense of sight as paired with fire, the highest element of the macrocosm. Aristotle was not so sure about that. He coordinated fire with smell — fire gives off smoke, and smoke smells — and water with sight, since, he noted, there seems to be a great deal of water in the eyes. Thomas Aquinas defined sight not only as the highest of the senses but also as the most spiritual, most perfect, and most universal sense, because in contrast to the others it operates without "natural imputation" either of the sense organ or of the object seen.[4]

The assumed "spiritual" nature of the sense of sight had a strange consequence. Already in antiquity, blindness was not considered a very great evil. According to Aristotle, only touch is indispensable for life. The other senses are there for a person's well-being, and had nothing to do with their essential "being." Loss of physical sight was regarded as intensifying the spiritual quality of seeing. The poet Tiresias was deprived of his physical sight by the wrath of Hera, but Zeus compensated the loss by bestowing

---

3. See here Louise Vinge, *The Five Senses: Studies in a Literary Tradition,* Acta Regiae Societatis Humaniorum Litterarum Lundensis 82 (Lund: Liber Läromedel, 1975), 15ff.

4. Thomas Aquinas, *Summa theologiae* 1a.78.3.

on him the gift of "seeing the future things to come," or prophetic vision. Among the few details reported by the tradition about the bard and poet Homer is the assertion that he was blind — a blind seer who communicated his inner visions in immortal words! What did Homer see? Greek culture was convinced that Homer's vision encompassed the entire cosmos, its deep mysteries, its origin, and its future course. It was all there in the text of his epics, and this, of course, is where "hearing" or reading has its necessary place for this kind of vision. Words and texts are indispensable; indeed, they are foundational for human experience in its personal and social forms. Seeing and hearing belong together.

It is the same with allegory in biblical interpretation. Allegory has to do with seeing, but in this case it points to an inner vision of what has first to be read in the text. Aminadab's chariot has to start somewhere on its sweeping journey upward, and while the literal basis is very slim in this case — recall the predicament we spoke of earlier in interpreting the vagaries of Song of Songs 6:12 — the chariot has its home base in a verse and its words. Indeed, the very word "allegory" itself makes the point that seeing and hearing belong together. It is a late word in the Greek vocabulary, not in use before the second century BCE, and it is an artificial word creation: *alla-agoreuein,* which means "to say/something else," something beyond the word that is said — which is to say, word *and* vision.

A great deal of confusion arises in the contemporary hermeneutical discussion because many people do not realize that there are two kinds of activity to which the word "allegory" has been applied — that is, both in its nominal form (*allēgoria, allēgorikos*) and as a verb (*allēgoreuein* or *allēgorein*). The rhetorical tradition in which the term was apparently coined and first used classified allegory as a trope, an intentional word figure that a speaker used to enhance the intellectual appeal of an argument. It pointed to how words "say" something different from what they otherwise seem to suggest, although not without some mental bridge of similarity or likeness. Quintilian connected allegory with the concept of "metaphor," giving it the precise definition of extended metaphorical speech: *"Allegoria est metaphora continuata,"* or "allegory is a sustained metaphor,"[5] recalling that the noun "metaphor" derives from a verb *(metapherein)* meaning "to carry/beyond." We might call this a "rhetorical allegory."

The second use concerned an interpretive procedure which was applied to the normative texts of Hellenistic culture, Homer and the ancient poets, in

---

5. Quintilian, *Institutio Oratoria* 8.6.44.

the schools of the later philosophers. We might call this an "interpretive allegory." The procedure goes back to Homeric scholarship in the Hellenistic age, or the fourth and third centuries BCE. We spoke of Aristarchos of Alexandria in the preceding chapter as the prototype of an exegete whose sole concern was the text of Homer and its explanation, but one who was uninterested in the "truth" of Homer's poems, the "why" of their foundational importance for society's ethos, which was the concern of the final step in the interpretive process, the *meros kritikon,* or "criticism"; an ethos requires a philosophy.

In the case of Homeric scholarship, the philosophy behind the enterprise came from Alexandria's competition, the school of Pergamum in Asia Minor.[6] Here, the Stoic philosopher Krates of Mallos developed the framework of interpretive allegory, calling himself proudly *kritikos* rather than *grammatikos.* For Aristarchos as an exegete, Homer was to be interpreted as an author of texts to be cherished, and as such he was a human being, admirable yet fallible. For Krates and his followers, the *kritikoi,* Homer was a divinely inspired proclaimer of mysteries — the tradition of the "blind seer" had its main supporters in these circles. Homer saw the truth and communicated it in his sacred poetry as the *hyponoia,* or "sub-sense," which it was the critic's task to "uncover."

Earlier Stoics had used this supposed sub-sense to boost their own philosophical theses: if Homer could be made to say it, even if in veiled form, it must be true. Following from this, Krates and other later Stoics used the authority of their own rational system to interpret Homer: if the scientific truth of Stoicism established an important doctrine, then this had to constitute the sub-sense of Homer's language which one was interpreting. Homer was seen as a kind of oracle, like that of Delphi, thus employing a certain manner of speaking, a rhetorical mode — which, they argued, was "metaphorical" throughout. It should hardly come as a surprise, therefore, that the old terminology of seeking the *hyponoia* in Homer's epics slowly disappeared, being eventually replaced by the rhetorical terminology of *allēgoria* when the word appeared sometime in the second century BCE. When this development occurred, the two uses — rhetorical and interpretive allegory — came to be closely related, even though they were not identical and should be distinguished. In this sense, speaking or writing allegorically is not the same as interpreting allegorically — which is to say that one who interprets allegorically is not necessarily interpreting an allegory.

---

6. Rudolf Pfeiffer, *History of Classical Scholarship from the Beginning to the End of the Hellenistic Age* (Oxford: Clarendon Press, 1968), 234-51.

The first major writer to apply interpretive allegory to the inspired text of the Bible was Philo of Alexandria. We know so much about this thoroughly Jewish thinker because later Christians assumed with Eusebius of Caesarea that Philo was a Christian; the legendary account Eusebius remembers claims that Philo met Peter in Rome and was converted there by the Apostle.[7] Philo's principle of interpretation, the horizon into which he wanted to move the biblical texts, was the same as that of other contemporary rabbis: that is, the context of Jewish life under the Torah. Of course, Philo never thought that allegory made the literal observation of the law unnecessary. But his eclectic Hellenistic philosophy explained for him the "sub-sense" of the biblical texts in the cosmological and ethical categories of contemporary scientific thinking. Jewish compatriots in the Hellenistic world as well as their non-Jewish neighbors thus could be made to see the superior value of this ancient divine literature. Philo's intention in allegorizing was clearly apologetic.

Philo's precedent was forcefully followed in the world of Hellenistic Christianity by Origen, likewise of Alexandria.[8] Origen made full use of Alexandrian philological exegesis in his textual work on the Bible, but as a Christian philosopher and teacher his deeper interest was in the tasks of the *meros kritikon.* His principle of interpretation was no longer life shaped by the Torah or the consonance of the Jewish scriptures and Hellenistic philosophy, but rather the common Christian conviction about God's *oikonomia* and God's universal will to save. But what was it that God wished to save? According to Origen, this had to do with the fate of souls. His treatise on biblical hermeneutics came as the fourth part of a much longer work he entitled *On First Principles;* the first three parts of this text explore his understanding of the nature of souls under Divine Providence in answer to questions that the Christian baptismal creed did not directly treat.[9] Origen's apology for the Bible at this point is not defensive but rather missionary:

7. Eusebius, *History of the Church* 2.17.

8. See here Gerald Bostock, "Allegory and the Interpretation of the Bible in Origen," *Journal of Literature and Theology* 1, no. 1 (1987): 39-53; Karen J. Torjesen, *Hermeneutical Procedure and Theological Method in Origen's Exegesis,* Patristische Texte und Studien 28 (Berlin: Walter de Gruyter, 1985); and Henri de Lubac, *History and Spirit: The Understanding of Scripture According to Origen,* trans. Anne Englund Nash (San Francisco: Ignatius Press, 2007).

9. See Origen, *On First Principles* 4. For an English translation of this section, see *Biblical Interpretation in the Early Church,* ed. and trans. Karlfried Froehlich (Philadelphia: Fortress Press, 1984), 48-78. A full translation of the entire treatise is found in *Origen: On First Principles,* ed. and trans. George W. Butterworth (New York: Harper & Row, 1966).

he addresses himself to everyone, at least all who were willing to listen, because he was convinced that the biblical writings expressed the supreme truth.

This fourth section on hermeneutics opens with a theory of inspiration that extends both to the Septuagint and to the New Testament, offering a more complete formulation than any before or after. It includes every detail, even the history of the textual tradition and any mistakes scribes may have made; the entire phenomenon of the Christian Bible, according to Origen, was to be understood as part of the *oikonomia* of Divine Providence. For proof, he appealed to experience, pointing to such "evidence" as the success of Christianity in the Empire, the amazing fulfillment of prophecy, and the personal experience of readers like himself. On this basis he concluded that an "inspired" text had to be read "spiritually." As he went on to conclude, all of Scripture had a spiritual sense, even if not all of it had a bodily sense as well — even though he felt that most passages did.[10] As he put it, God's aim is "to hide [secret mysteries] in texts which on the surface seem to offer a plain narrative of events."[11]

Origen addressed a wide audience of his contemporaries, including but not limited to those within the Christian communities, because he was convinced that God had given the Bible to all people. It was to be read and interpreted as a tool for human education generally. The threefold interpretation according to which each text was interpreted to have a body, a soul, and a spirit had its parallel, he reasoned, in three classes of hearers: the simple, the advanced, and the perfect.[12] Its purpose was always to lead upward, to help in the soul's ascent, which he understood as the very essence of salvation. Origen had no difficulty finding scriptural warrant for his three stages of interpretation; he pointed to the image of the Passover lamb in Exodus 12:9, where the admonition to "eat the head" established the spiritual sense, while the call to "eat the feet" established the literal sense and "eat the entrails" suggested the food of life which doctors produced from the ugly parts left over after this had been chewed and sufficiently ruminated.[13] The text also warns against "eat[ing] the flesh raw," which Origen interprets as a reference to Jewish literalism, while the call not to "eat it boiled" pointed to

10. See Origen, *On First Principles* 4.2.5 (Froehlich, 58-59).
11. Origen, *On First Principles* 4.2.8 (Froehlich, 61).
12. Origen, *On First Principles* 4.2.4 (Froehlich, 57-58).
13. For Origen's treatment of this passage from Exodus, see his commentary on the Gospel of John in *Origen: Commentary on the Gospel of John,* trans. Ronald E. Heine, Fathers of the Church 80 (Washington, DC: Catholic University of America Press, 1989), 276-79.

the dilutions of the "water" of Gnostic speculations, and the insistence on eating only what had been "roasted in the fire" suggested the Holy Spirit. He analyzed the Levitical rule about the preparation of a sacrificial animal (Lev. 1:6) in a similar manner: "first skin it" meant to liberate the important core from the literal sense; "then cut it up progressively into pieces" suggested the distinction of the law, the prophets, and the Gospel, which implied a manner of adapting these biblical portions for beginners, advanced, and perfect "hearers."[14]

As in Philo's allegory, Origen's procedure of allegorical interpretation was strictly rational, based on analogy as well as verbal association. Each phrase might hide a new mystery. This assumption demanded careful attention to every detail of a text. It also tended toward an atomistic approach, however, one that often blurred or obscured altogether the matter of context — a point that his critics among the Antiochene theologians duly noted. For Origen, unity did not reside in the story, but rather in God's mind. God seeks attentive readers for every aspect of his text. Thus, Origen could find hints that pointed to the need for allegorical interpretation everywhere in Scripture: choice of words, word order, etymology, and numerology — all of these held intended clues. Even more importantly, logical problems, sudden transitions, impossibilities, and anthropomorphic expressions for God were there to alert the reader to the need for an allegorical interpretation. Origen treats these discoveries as stumbling blocks that Divine Providence had put into the text for the purpose of exercising the mind.[15] His examples are not only from the Old Testament, but also from the New. The following excerpts illustrate this point:

> The devil led Jesus up to a high mountain in order to show him from there all the kingdoms of the world. Now who but the most superficial reader of such a story would not laugh at those who think that the kingdoms of the Persians, the Scythians, the Indians, and the Parthians can all be seen with the eye of the flesh which requires elevation in order to perceive things located down below?[16]

and

---

14. See *Origen: Homilies on Leviticus 1–16*, trans. Gary Wayne Barkley, Fathers of the Church 83 (Washington, DC: Catholic University of America Press, 1990), 35-36.

15. Origen, *On First Principles* 4.2.9 (Froehlich, 62).

16. Origen, *On First Principles* 4.3.1 (Froehlich, 64).

The saying about the right cheek being struck (Matt. 5:39) is also most unlikely, for anyone who strikes would strike the left cheek with the right hand unless he happened to suffer from an unnatural condition.[17]

While it is easy to assume that Origen found the model for his allegorizing in the allegorical interpretation of texts from Homer or in Philo, he himself suggests otherwise. He claims that he found it exemplified, and thus authorized, in the letters of the Apostle Paul, whom he admired. He has a point. In Galatians 4, Paul recalls the scriptural account of Abraham's two sons and their mothers, Sarah and Hagar. Here the Apostle first mentions briefly the few relevant details, then continues with the crucial sentence in v. 24: "These things are *allēgoroumena*. The women are two covenants." Paul's use of the relatively recent technical term here is surprising. It appears to be based on the rhetorical meaning, "these things are said allegorically," but it implies the interpretive use as well which might be rendered as follows: "the scriptural words have a sub-sense: the women have to be read as two covenants." Paul's attempted etymology for Hagar, "Hagar is Mount Sinai in Arabia," speaks for this reading. The word *allēgoria* or any of its derivatives does not appear elsewhere in Paul, but the procedure of spelling out the sub-sense of a biblical text does recur in his writings: the text that comes immediately to mind is 1 Corinthians 9:10, where the "sub-sense" of Deuteronomy 25:4 — "You shall not muzzle the ox that treads out the grain" — is identified as the apostles' right to live by the fruits of their preaching.[18] In 1 Corinthians 10:1-12, Paul recalls scriptural and midrashic Exodus traditions — the crossing of the Red Sea, the cloud, the manna, the water from the rock, the actions of the disgruntled people — in order to point to their "sub-sense," partly in allusions, partly quite openly: "The rock was Christ" (1 Cor. 10:4).

It becomes clear that the principle governing his analogies, the horizon into which he wants to move the ancient texts, is an understanding of his own time as well as that of his Christian converts as the "end time," in line with the Qumranic version of the Torah-oriented principle and the interpretive grid of promise and fulfillment: "These things were written for our instruction, upon whom the end of the ages has come" (1 Cor. 10:10). In the entire passage, Paul does not use the term *hyponoia*, nor the terminology of *allēgoria*. Rather, a third term appears: *typos*, and its cognate *typikos*.

---

17. Origen, *On First Principles* 4.3.3 (Froehlich, 65).
18. Origen, *On First Principles* 4.2.6 (Froehlich, 59).

This word family, which had no place in the vocabulary of rhetoric or interpretation before him, offers the apostle a means of describing the way his allegorical procedure identifies a text's "sub-sense." The adjective *pneumatikos* in verses 3-4 — "spiritual food, spiritual drink, spiritual rock" — may well be another such attempt, reading the experience of the presence of Christ in the sacred meal as the sub-sense of the manna and the water from the rock. The term *typos* lent itself readily to this purpose, because its meaning of "model," usually in the sense of warning, was common in moral parlance and points to the application Paul had in mind here. His shot at a novel terminology proved relatively successful. He used it again in Romans 5:14 to describe Adam as the "type of the one to come," adding the element of contrast or heightening which is characteristic of the promise-fulfillment grid as well. 1 Peter 3:21 offers a witness to the completion of the terminology: the rescue of the Christian through baptism is here called *antitypos,* the superior sub-sense of the *typos* of Noah's rescue through the ark. In the writings of the Apostolic Fathers, the terminology is firmly established: we find fifteen instances of "types" in the *Epistle of Barnabas,* eight in the *Shepherd of Hermas,* and three in the letters of Ignatius.

Origen was aware of the usage of *typos* in the Christian interpretation of the Old Testament, but he preferred calling Paul's "types" by their scientific name, "allegories," and, as should be clear now, he was not wrong in appealing to Paul for this. There can be no doubt that in the West Augustine shared Origen's insistence that "understanding the Bible" involved a dynamic movement upward, an "ascent" from letter to spirit. In Augustine's thought, however, the dynamic movement is not only upward but also forward, exemplified by the dynamic of the movement from the Old to the New Testament that was so important for Paul's use of allegory. Augustine came close to simply equating Paul's hermeneutical divide that separated letter and spirit (2 Cor. 3:6) with the divide he construed between the two testaments. For him, the two were inextricably linked in a dialectic of old and new, hidden and open: "The Old Testament is the veiling of the New, and the New is the unveiling of the Old."[19] He found support for his conviction in numerous scriptural images. Thus, for example, his reading of the five loaves in the story of the miraculous feeding made him think of the Pentateuch, and immediately he sees what happens as these five books are

---

19. Augustine, *Sermo* 300.3, Patrologia Latina 38, ed. J.-P. Migne, 1377C; see also *Questionum in Heptateuchum Libri Septem* 2.73, Corpus Christianorum Latinorum 33 (Turnhout: Brepols, 1958), line 1277: "in Vetere Novum latet, et in Novo Vetus patet."

blessed and distributed by the Lord through the hands of his apostles: both loaves and books multiply a thousandfold.[20] What could be truer than this, he wondered!

This instance demonstrates that Augustine freely pulled all the stops of the methodological instrument of interpretive allegory. Among these, the importance ascribed to numbers bears mentioning, for the language of mathematics was for Augustine a unique kind of language: it was, he notes, "not *instituted* by humans, but *discovered.*"[21] God embedded it into the structure of Creation when he made everything "according to measure, number, and weight" (Wisdom 11:21). To consider the meaning of numbers in the Bible using simple mathematical operations and Pythagorean lore, therefore, became an exciting task for Augustine. The great sermon on the 153 fish mentioned in John 21:13, in his commentary on John,[22] and the surprising reflections on the numbers twenty-two, twenty-seven, forty-two or forty-four point to this, as John Fleming has convincingly demonstrated.[23]

Augustine uses the rules and methods of interpretive allegory throughout his writings, and in following Ambrose he clearly "allegorizes." And while it might at first appear strange to us that he rarely calls his procedure by this name, the reason is clear enough: for Augustine, "allegory" was still primarily a rhetorical term denoting a string of words applied by a speaker to say one thing and mean another. As a rhetorician, he did not consider "allegory" a proper term for the anagogical dynamics implied in all biblical interpretation. The Latin Bible he used, after all, translated Paul's alternative *typos* variously as *forma, figura,* or *exemplum,* and of these Augustine preferred the most visual image — that of *figura,* which already had a home in the rhetorical tradition. To speak *in figura* meant to employ some flowery circumlocution, to use an ornamental "figure of speech" and thus to beautify in the hearer the experience of the argument. In a justly celebrated passage Augustine spells out what figuration meant for him in terms of biblical interpretation:

20. See Augustine, *Sermo* 80, Nicene and Post-Nicene Fathers (First Series) 6 (Grand Rapids: Eerdmans, 1980), 1040-44.

21. See Augustine, *De doctrina christiana* 2.38.56.

22. Augustine, *Sermo* 122.6-9, Nicene and Post-Nicene Fathers (First Series) 7 (Grand Rapids: Eerdmans, 1986), 440-43.

23. See John Fleming, "Christopher Columbus as a Scriptural Exegete," in *Biblical Hermeneutics in Historical Perspective: Studies in Honor of Karlfried Froehlich on His Sixtieth Birthday,* ed. Mark S. Burrows and Paul Rorem (Grand Rapids: Eerdmans, 1991), 175-78.

It may be said that there are holy and perfect men with whose lives and customs as an examplar the Church of Christ is able to destroy all sorts of superstitions in those who come to it and to incorporate them into itself, men of good faith, true servants of God, who, putting aside the burden of the world, come to the holy laver of baptism and, ascending from there, conceive through the Holy Spirit and produce the fruit of a twofold love of God and their neighbor. But why is it, I ask, if anyone says this, he delights his hearers less than if he had said the same thing in expounding that place in the Song of Songs [4:2] where it is said of the Church, as she is being praised as a beautiful woman: "Thy teeth are like a flock of sheep which are shorn, which come up from the washing, all with twins, and there is none barren among them"? Does one learn anything else besides that which one learns when one hears the same thought expressed in plain words without this similitude? Nevertheless, in a strange way, I contemplate the saints more pleasantly when I envisage them as the teeth of the Church cutting off people from their errors and transferring them to her body after their hardness has been softened as if by being bitten and chewed. I recognize them most pleasantly as shorn sheep having put aside the burden of the world like so much fleece, and as ascending from the washing, which is baptism, all to create twins, which are the two precepts of love, and I see no one of them sterile of this holy fruit.[24]

The beauty of this passage is striking, and the equation of difficulty and delight important: what lies hidden requires of the interpreter a disciplined effort, and this experience is itself a thing of beauty. In fact, Augustine sees the beauty that the act of interpretation reveals everywhere in the Scriptures, for the Bible is full of the most wonderful figures once one has trained one's eye to look for them and "see" them. We should not think that Augustine was an Origenistic rationalist; his analysis of biblical language was far from this, discouraging him — unlike Origen — from what might appear to us as an "over-allegorizing," as many contemporaries of his did. His approach, in contrast, sought to maximize figuration, always ready to discover new, exciting vistas and to spot unexpected images — and these were to be seen not beyond but right in the midst of the inexhaustible landscape of the Bible's language. Robert Bernard has argued that Augustine regarded the Bible's figurative language as the expression of God's

---

24. Augustine, *De doctrina christiana* 2.6.7; see *On Christian Doctrine*, trans. D. W. Robertson Jr. (Indianapolis: Bobbs-Merrill, 1958), 37-38.

own rhetoric, one that deliberately uses flowery circumlocutions because it wants not only to move and to teach but also to delight.[25] Thus, the work of "delighting the reader," the third goal of Cicero's ideal eloquence, became part of Augustine's advice to Christian preachers in Book 4 of *On Christian Doctrine* as well.

Following this lead, Augustine's "figurative interpretation" seems to roam constantly through the entire Bible, and in this way it moves up from a literal sense which for him was not so much "useless flesh" or "mere" letter as it was language with a vibrant potential. Words for him were always pregnant with infinite possibilities — "killing" when they come as law without grace, but speaking solemn truth when they promote faith, hope, and charity, and fanning fervent love when they formulate promise. The interpretive movement upward, according to Augustine, was guided by the Spirit and thus "spiritual," but it was finally a movement toward the experience of beholding the mystery, of "seeing God." For Augustine, who refers to the series of five senses frequently, vision has a definite priority in this movement. Indeed, in the *Confessions* he privileges seeing as the primary perception in the descriptions of the soul's intellectual ascent, often citing the Psalmists' hope to "see the face of God."[26] Building on this emphasis in his later writings, he defines the final goal of the mystical ascent not as union with the divine but as "seeing God" — the *visio Dei* as a mode of existence which maintained the distance between creator and creature, but restored and exceeded the bliss of the original human creation.

As part of the quadriga, the system of the fourfold sense, *allegoria* was bound to change its meaning. It now became just one part of a highly structured triad, a sense with limited competence among three higher senses. This is an important difference to keep in mind. Allegory had been the general designation for the hermeneutics of ascent from the bodily to a spiritual level, the equivalent of the Antiochene *theoria*, or the Augustinian *figura*, but by the time of the Middle Ages this was no longer the case. *Allegoria* got one corner of the square, one slice of the pie, and one might say but one horse in the team of four pulling Aminadab's chariot. Gerhoh of Reichersberg, a twelfth-century theologian, demonstrates that the special assignment of this horse was the clarification of the relation of the Old Testament to the New:

25. Robert Bernard, "The Rhetoric of God in the Figurative Exegesis of Augustine," in Burrows and Rorem, eds., *Biblical Hermeneutics in Historical Perspective*, 88-99.

26. See, for example, *Confessions* 1.18.28 and 9.3.6. For English translations see *Confessions*, trans. Henry Chadwick (New York: Oxford University Press, 1992), 20, 159.

> In the one Gospel lesson of the Wedding Feast [at Cana, John 2:1-11] we can observe four different meanings — historical, moral, allegorical, and anagogical. The historical is what we read happened literally in Cana of Galilee. The allegorical is what happened as a universal symbol between Christ and the church when a wedding was celebrated in Cana of Galilee. "Cana of Galilee" translates "zeal of transmigration," and that is, the transmigration in Christ from the Jews to the Gentiles.[27]

The mention of Christ and the church here suggests that by the Middle Ages allegory did not just cover the relation of Old and New Testament in a simple coordination of promise and fulfillment, but it included all the "consequences" of this as well: *allegoria* dealt with the total reordering of the story of salvation in light of the two-part canon — just as the familiar jingle had it that allegory teaches "what to believe thou hast." Allegorical interpretation in the Middle Ages yielded instruction in the truths of the Christian faith; its special assignment was the illumination of Christian doctrine. It reflected, and perhaps helped to encourage, the rising emphasis on preaching during this period, a matter we will explore more fully in the following chapter.

Hugh of St. Victor described the process of biblical interpretation using the metaphor of erecting a building.[28] First, the foundation had to be laid, and these were the rough stones of raw "data"; this suggests, Hugh argued, the work of mastering the "literal or historical" sense. Then the walls go up. These consist of rows upon rows of smoothly polished stones, course upon course, in precise, beautiful order. This is *allegoria,* the work of building the system of *doctrina.* "Do you want to know what these courses are?" Hugh asks. And then he names them piece by piece: Trinity, Creation, the human creature, its fall into sin, its restoration under the law, the incarnation, the mysteries of the New Testament, and man's own resurrection. The *sensus allegoricus* here was not an artificial level of interpretation that one might or might not add on as a bonus in one's exegetical activity; rather, it was a systematic and openly Christocentric theological digestion of Old and New Testament together. *Allegoria* as the Christological *rélecture*

---

27. Quoted in Henri de Lubac, *Exégèse médiévale: Les quatre sens de l'écriture,* vol. 2, part 2 (Paris: Aubier, 1959-64), 118.

28. See above, p. 38. The application of this metaphor to allegorical interpretation is developed in *Didascalicon* 6.4; for an English translation see *The Didascalicon of Hugh of St. Victor: A Medieval Guide to the Arts,* trans. Jerome Taylor (New York: Columbia University Press, 1961), 139-44.

of Scripture opened the door for developing a comprehensive "system" of Christian doctrine, or a properly ordered form of teaching.[29]

Hugh wrote this kind of book, presenting it as the "second part of sacred rhetoric," the *lectio allegorica* of the Bible, and giving it the patristic title *De sacramentis,* "On the Sacraments." But what he meant by "sacrament" here was not identical with our term "sacrament," but rather conveyed the force of the Latin translation of the Greek term *mysterion:* his book is ultimately about the "mysteries of the Christian faith," and these were to constitute the proper subject of Christian instruction. In the preface to this treatise, in fact, Hugh describes the essence of what he is doing in the image of a magnificent vision:

> The incarnate Word is our king who came into this world to war with the devil; and all the saints who were before his coming are soldiers, as it were, going before their king, and those who have come after and who will come even to the end of the world, are soldiers following their king. And the king is in the midst of his army and proceeds protected and surrounded on all sides by his columns. And although in a multitude as vast as this, the kind of arms differ in the mysteries and observance of the peoples preceding and following, yet all are really serving the one king and following the one banner. All are pursuing the one enemy, and all are crowned by the one victory.[30]

After Hugh, a totally new literature of systematic theology, the "sentences," *enchiridia,* and *summae,* descended on a new, receptive, and growing market. No longer *sacra pagina* — "the sacred page" — but rather *sacra doctrina* — or "theology" — was where the action now was. In the next few centuries theological study of this sort had its heyday, ever expanding, ever more daring, but also ever more confusing and finally enormously complicated for the simple faith of Bible readers: "What to believe thou hast?" The complexity of *allegoria* in biblical interpretation was turning into a nightmare.

It was this kind of "allegory" that was the target of the later Protestant Reformers' critique, viewing it as they did as an oppressive system of

---

29. See here Rainer Berndt, S.J., "Das 12. Jahrhundert. Überlegungen zum Verhältnis von Exegese und Theologie in *De Sacramentis Christianae Fidei* Hugos von St. Viktor," in *Neue Richtungen in der hoch- und spätmittelalterlichen Bibelexegese,* ed. Robert Lerner, Schriften des Historischen Kollegs, Kolloquien 32 (Munich: Oldenbourg, 1996), 66-78.

30. Hugh of St. Victor, *On the Sacraments of the Christian Faith,* trans. Roy J. Deferrari (Boston: Medieval Academy of America, 1951), 2.

doctrine extracted from Scripture by scholastic theology — and thus as a dogmatic imposition on the text. Let us recall here Luther's polemic against the quadriga of the schoolmen: they had torn the seamless robe of the Lord into four pieces and kept Christ from the people, he insisted, and instead beat them over the head with the doctrines of Aristotle and the pope. He criticized sharply the "playing" and "juggling" that went on in the allegorical practices of theologians, including the church fathers, especially Origen and Jerome. His graphic indictment is clearly a judgment against scholastic theology, but not a rejection of a hermeneutics of ascent, which, as we have seen, is built right into his "single literal sense": "Allegories are empty speculations, the sewer, as it were, of Holy Scripture."[31]

Luther understood perfectly well, of course, that the original meaning of *allegoria* belonged into the definitions of metaphorical language and designated a rhetorical trope: "*Allegoria* is suggesting one thing, yet understanding it differently from what the words say. You find allegory in sentences, metaphor in words and vocabulary."[32] Such a claim echoes Quintilian's classical definition of it as "a sustained metaphor," as we earlier observed. As such, it can be part of the intention of a biblical author, and belongs to the literal or intended sense. In practice, Luther did use all kinds of figurative "sub-senses" of biblical passages in his preaching and called them regularly "allegory" under the definition above. But the rejection of a scholastic theology gone wild, which he shared with most other Reformers of his time, especially the humanists, did discredit under the name of *allegoria* once and for all anything that this method might mean.

Once again, modern Protestants feel they are the lucky heirs of the hard-won victories of the Reformers. The gut feeling among us still is that allegory in biblical interpretation has been duly tried, convicted, sentenced, and hanged, and that it remains only as an object of scorn and horror. It is easy enough to strike a moral pose like Farrar did: "Must we not deplore so fruitless an exercise of fancy, so sterile a manipulation of the Sacred Book?"[33] For Adolf von Harnack, one word said it all: he calls allegory noth-

---

31. Frederick W. Farrar, *History of Interpretation* (1886; Grand Rapids: Baker Book House, 1961), 328, presents a long list of Luther's disparaging comments, among them this quotation. Unfortunately, they are unverifiable. For a strong argument against allegorization, however, see "Sermon on Exodus 1," preached on November 13, 1524, Weimar Ausgabe 16:67-80.

32. *Luthers Werke. Kritische Gesamtausgabe. Tischreden,* vol. 2 (Weimar: Böhlau, 1913), nos. 2772a-b, 649-50.

33. Farrar, *History of Interpretation,* 23.

ing other than "biblical alchemy."[34] But the original assignment of allegory in the medieval quadriga, as in the Christian tradition from Paul's letters on, was the interpretation of how the Old Testament related to the New, as we have argued. The issue remains a burning one for us as well. If we want to keep the Old Testament as a living authority in our churches and a vital source for our theologies, we need to reflect on the guiding principle which would allow us to grasp the coherence of the two, the common parameter or principle of consistency into which the texts of both parts of our Bible must be lifted in the dynamics of "seeing" what is being said.

Of course, there seems to be a relatively comfortable way out. There is always the option of treating the Tanakh — the canon of Torah, Prophets, and Writings — simply as what it is: a Jewish book, and thus surely an object of historical and archaeological interest for Christians, but in this sense basically limited to being a source for the scholarly investigation of the religious history and literature of the Jewish people. There is good reason for considering this option, especially after the ever-tightening grip of a Christian appropriation led to ever greater distance from living Jews — and seemed to go so far as to sanction violence on the part of Christians against them. Through much of European history, in fact, denying Jews the right to their sacred books was not enough. All too often they were even denied the right to live by the same Christians, who claimed as rightfully theirs the ethics of Jesus and the apostles. Many biblical scholars in the Christian orbit today are ready to hand over — or rather to hand back to Jewish readers, often remorsefully and with deep respect for the suffering the Christian tradition has caused among them — the rights to the authentic use of the Jewish Scriptures. After all, it was among their ancestors that these scriptures originated.

Whatever course we take in negotiating the question of a reading of the so-called "Old" Testament in a way that avoids a total appropriation, we must learn at the very least to live with the recognition that there is more than one legitimate continuation of the Old Testament, and that there are and must be living Jews interpreting their Scriptures in and with their lives. This witness also belongs to them, since their very existence is a vital and continuing expression of our common God's *oikonomia*. Yet the determined separation of the two parts of the Christian Bible cannot be the real answer to the predicament of churches and theological traditions that have

---

34. Adolf von Harnack, *History of Dogma*, vol. 3, trans. J. Millar (New York: Russell & Russell, 1958), 199.

lived with their Old Testament joined to the New for as long as they have. To find a common parameter of interpretation may no longer be possible for Christians without taking into account the ongoing traditions of the legitimate "owners" of the Jewish Bible, but the search for its proper expression in the Christian camp must not be given up.

One proposal which is still widely advocated among us is the rejection of allegory but the endorsement of typology as an interpretive method. There can be little doubt that Paul's use of the terminology of *typos* suggested the name of this method as well as the content. The term, "typology," however, is not old; it was coined in the eighteenth century, probably in order to find a way of keeping Old and New Testament together without the help of the hated and despicable allegory. Patrick Fairbairn's book, *Typology of Scripture, or the Doctrine of Types,* first published in 1847 and often reprinted since, made the cause of legitimate typology popular in the English-speaking world. The crucial point is the distinction to be made between what is illicit and what is legitimate. The difference, so his argument runs, is between "fiction" and "historical" truth in the Old Testament text, with allegory representing a way of interpretation that regards the text as a fiction which deliberately says "something else" than what the words actually suggest. The danger is that this "something else" is at the whim of the interpreter. On the other hand, typology as this argument suggests accepts the text in its historical reality and compares elements of it with elements of a different historical reality. Thus, events or persons in the Old Testament are related to appropriate counterparts in the New Testament: "An allegory is a fictitious narrative, or to put it less bluntly, in an allegory the historical truth of the narrative dealt with may or may not be accepted, whereas in typology, the fulfillment of the antitype can only be understood in the light of the reality of the original type."[35]

But notice how close this argument is to the polemic of the Antiochene theologians of the fourth and fifth centuries against Alexandrian allegory: they hold that God teaches not by the words of Scripture, the *lexis,* but by the facts being talked about, the *pragma.* There must be a real Adam, a real Eve, and a real Serpent for God to make his point. But the same Antiochenes acknowledged the need for an anagogical hermeneutics, for something like Aminadab's chariot, in their spiritual *theoria,* while the Alexandrians shrugged their shoulder at the charge that they "dissolved" the truth

---

35. Charles T. Fritsch, "Principles of Biblical Typology," *Bibliotheca Sacra* 104 (1947): 214-22.

of the original narrative — and they had every right to feel that they did not do anything like this. The notion of "fiction" enters this discussion only because what we have called interpretive allegory, in our modern discussion, is often confused with rhetorical allegory; if this false notion is taken out, however, typology turns out to be nothing else but prophecy, the only difference being that prophecy predicts by means of the word while typology does so by means of "things" — institutions, events, persons.

Our own investigation has shown that Paul, at least in the texts we have considered, is describing a *hyponoia,* or "sub-sense," and thus is himself practicing interpretive allegory. One might also call it "typology," but ultimately the terminology makes little difference since the force of such a reading results in the same thing. If supporters of typology still insist that the difference in the means of prophecy warrants terminological recognition, then as is so often the case medieval theologians may have had a better solution with their careful distinction between *allegoria dicti* and *allegoria facti*: namely, an allegory — not a prophecy! — of the words, and an allegory — not a typology! — of events or deeds.

Thus, there is really nothing wrong with "allegorical interpretation" in and for the Christian Bible. Indeed, from the beginning, this has been the glue that held the two together, but note well: it accomplishes this as a method. The principle was something else altogether, and this points to the faith in God's action throughout the ages, with the center of time and meaning located in "the things about Jesus of Nazareth." This phrase, of course, is taken from the story of the two disciples on the road to Emmaus. In the remarkable conclusion to this account we hear this description of events: "Then their eyes were opened and they recognized him. And he vanished from their sight" (Luke 24:13-35). What a marvelous description this offers concerning the process of Christian allegory, which promises to open our eyes as well! For allegory is about seeing, and there should be no set limit to the interconnected wealth of images that arise out of a constant and intensive life with the Bible in our inward vision, one that encompasses the whole world of the Bible's "signs" and "things." But this wide expanse of meanings has a center to it: "They recognized him."

Our journey outward thus returns finally to its starting point, the Christ of faith: "And he vanished from their sight." The boundless vision, or what we might come to think of as the chariot ride of the imagination, is not the last thing we find in concentrating on this center. The disciples are left with their experience of having seen the Lord, but not without this experience finding a language for its expression. It is present for them in the words that he spoke: "Were not our hearts burning within us while he was talking to us on the road?" But it also does this by means of the words of witness that they carried to the others. Hearing *may* come before seeing, but it also and always has a way of taking over afterward.

CHAPTER FOUR

Tropologia: Hearing the Truth

In our probing of the history of biblical interpretation thus far we have explored the literal and allegorical senses as they came to be known in the early church, examining them as instances of "touching the ground" and "seeing the beauty," respectively. We now turn to the sense of tropology as a means of "hearing the truth," the second in the list of so-called spiritual senses. As we have seen thus far, the medieval fourfold sense of Scripture amplifies the twofold Pauline formula of "letter and spirit" in 2 Corinthians 3:6. It does so by emphasizing in the relationship between the two terms not their opposition but their sequence as a dynamic movement upward — in this case, from the grounding of the literal reading to the ascent offered by forms of spiritual interpretation.

Let us remember at the outset that this basic twofold division was constitutive of early Christian hermeneutics across the various schools, traditions, and interpretive styles. As we have already seen, Origen of Alexandria saw this movement as the journey of the soul from the material world to the world of the Spirit, God's eternal realm. The Scriptures, he argued, were the divinely given tool for this journey, challenging us time and again to leave the "carnal" understanding and "seek that which is above" (cf. Col. 3:1). The shape of the fourfold sense, as we have suggested, arose as a subdivision of this one spiritual sense into three, a development, as we shall see, that seems to have emerged primarily as a teaching device. Of course, the problem with any such teacher's aid is the false presumption that, by memorizing it and carefully following the rules, one will automatically master the craft which it teaches — in this case, the skill of biblical interpretation. The crucial part, we have suggested, is not mastering the rules, but discerning the fundamental shape and influence of the interpretive principles. Such principles create the parameter — or "interpretive horizon," to use the phrase employed by Wilhelm Dilthey and later elaborated by Hans-Georg Gadamer — into which interpretation seeks to move the text.[1] One might say that this posits the overriding goal of the entire dynamic process involved in interpreting a text like the Bible.

The problem this approach raised became quite clear when we examined the development of allegory in the last chapter. The task of sorting this out became much clearer once we distinguished, methodologically, rhetorical and interpretive allegory. Both were described in this literature simply as *allegoria*, but they are clearly not alike. The primary purpose of early Christian interpretive allegory was to establish coherence and continuity between the Old and New Testaments, to demonstrate to readers the beauty of the unified witness to God's saving work, the divine *oikonomia*, and how this unity lends a consistency to this collection of otherwise distinctive and diverse writings. When allegory became specialized as but one of the three spiritual senses, its domain was in the first instance that of doctrine, the sum total of "what to believe thou hast." Yet we also heard Luther denounce the school hermeneutics of the so-called quadriga because, as he argued, it was the very vehicle that legitimated and even promoted the oppressive doctrinal system which scholastic theology had refined — down to the last detail.

This did not mean that Luther rejected the basic dynamic of ascent in biblical interpretation, or at least the interpretive dialectic of letter and spirit. His emphasis on the one literal sense intended by the divine author embraced all parts of the spiritual sense, and it did so as a single though differentiated movement meant to understand what the text says. This experience of understanding, however, had as much to do with hearing as it did with seeing. The story of the two disciples on the way to Emmaus illustrated this in a memorable fashion, as we have suggested, suggesting the larger process and goal of Christian allegory — namely, the movement toward "seeing the beauty" of this divine *oikonomia* as it came to be found in every part and even in all the particular details of the Scriptures. This narrative as we interpret it establishes the sense of hearing over that of seeing, for

1. See Wilhelm Dilthey, "The Understanding of Other Persons and Their Manifestations of Life," in *Selected Works*, vol. 3: *The Formation of the Historical World in the Human Sciences*, trans. Rudolf Makkreel and Frithjof Rodi (Princeton, NJ: Princeton University Press, 2010), 226-40; Hans-Georg Gadamer, *Truth and Method*, trans. Joel Weinsheimer and Donald Marshall (London: Continuum, 1989), esp. 300-306.

hearing is what opened these disciples to the vision. It is also what lingers within us after what we have seen is no longer present to our eyes. "Did not our hearts burn within us while he *talked* to us on the road, while he opened to us the Scriptures?" (Luke 24:32). We concluded that the same is true for us, a point that the fourth evangelist makes in the story of Jesus' encounter with "doubting" Thomas: "Blessed are those who have not seen and yet have come to believe" (John 20:29). It is also affirmed in a text favored by Luther and the early Protestant Reformers, which linked hearing with the procla-mation of the Word in the church's preaching: "So faith comes from what is heard, and what is heard comes through the word of Christ" (Rom. 10:17).[2]

To return to antiquity, though, we have already suggested that it was Aristotle who defined an ordered system of the five senses, arranging them in what became the standard sequence: sight, hearing, smell, taste, and touch. And, in elevating seeing over all the others, he opened his treatise on metaphysics with the bold claim that

> All people by nature desire to know. An indication of this is the delight we take in our *senses;* for even apart from their usefulness they are loved for themselves; and above all others the sense of sight. For not only with a view to action, but even when we are not going to do anything, we prefer seeing (one might say) to everything else.[3]

In his systematization, Aristotle privileged sight with the highest rank among the senses, though hearing came in as a close second. He reasoned that vision was the most comprehensive among the senses, revealing at a glance both the differentiation and coherence of the world around us, thus leading the beholder to the fundamental perception of a world that was at once unified but also differentiated.

The consequences of this decision are still with us in the form of the unquestioned legacy of ocularity that Greek culture gave as an inheritance to the West. The philosopher Hans-Georg Gadamer spoke of this as devel-

2. The Vulgate text here reads "Ergo fides ex auditu, auditus autem per verbum Christi." Luther translated this text to read, "Thus faith comes from hearing, and hearing from the preaching of the word of Christ"; as it stood, this passage became one frequently cited by the early Protestant Reformers, often for polemical reasons. On Luther's use of this text, see Ernst Bizer, *Fides ex Auditu: Eine Untersuchung über die Entdeckung der Gerechtigkeit Gottes durch Martin Luther,* 3rd ed. (Neukirchen: Neukirchener Verlag, 1966).

3. Aristotle, *Metaphysics,* Book A, 980a; see *The Student's Oxford Aristotle,* vol. 4, trans. W. D. Ross (New York: Oxford University Press, 1942).

oping into what he calls "the world-historical primacy of seeing."[4] For us as modern women and men, seeing has been elevated over hearing. Thus, for example, when we understand what someone tells us, we commonly say, "Oh, I *see* what you mean." One might even say that we suffer in modernity from an "eyewitness syndrome": television news programs regularly invite viewers to call in and report the news they "see." We presume — here following Aristotle — that "seeing" things gives us a glimpse of the "totality" of the differentiated truth. In movies, the soundtrack seems to support the images, with music "backing up" and reinforcing the "picture," as it were. Jacob Grimm, one of the distinguished brothers Grimm, put it this way: "The eye is a lord, the ear a servant."[5] Gadamer also reminds us, however, of what he calls "the universe of linguisticality," since language undergirds every philosophical approach to the phenomenon of hearing. We tend to associate hearing with understanding, he reasons, because of the overwhelmingly significant role language plays in our ways of making sense of things — and communicating this understanding to others.[6] And, to return to Aristotle, while sight may be more valuable with a view to the "necessities" of life, "hearing is incidentally more conducive to knowledge," a claim that points to how language enables us to "perceive" what is "invisible" to the eye — that is, a sense of the whole, and all that is "thinkable."[7]

But we should be clear that Aristotle's sequence neither was nor is the only option. In Alan of Lille's story of Prudence's trip to heaven, for instance, the one horse that was taken along for the last leg of the journey under the guidance of theology was Hearing. Hearing carried the heroine to the throne of God.[8] Even Aristotle admitted that hearing was more conducive to knowledge than seeing, even though the latter was more powerful; obviously, what he had in mind was its necessary role in the use of language. Even when we say, "I *see* what you mean," we do so not simply with a nod of

---

4. See Hans-Georg Gadamer, "Über das Hören," in *Hermeneutische Entwürfe: Vorträge und Aufsätze,* ed. Hans Förster (Tübingen: J. C. B. Mohr [Paul Siebeck], 2000), 49-57.

5. See Jacob Grimm, "Rede über das Alter," in *Kleine Schriften,* vol. 1 (Bergheim: Dümmler Verlag, 1866), 199. Grimm also notes here that the eye is more active, while the ear is more passive; that is, one can close one's eyes, but one cannot "block" sound with one's ears.

6. See Gadamer, "Über das Hören," 198-99.

7. Aristotle, *De Sensu et Sensibilibus* 1.437a; see also Louise Vinge, *The Five Senses: Studies in a Literary Tradition,* Acta Regiae Societatis Humaniorum Litterarum Lundensis 82 (Lund: Liber Läromedel, 1975), 18.

8. See Alan of Lille, *Anticlaudianus, or The Good and Perfect Man,* trans. James J. Sheridan (Toronto: Pontifical Institute of Medieval Studies, 1973), 126; and C. S. Lewis, *The Allegory of Love: A Study of a Medieval Tradition* (New York: Oxford University Press, 1985), 98ff.

our head but with words — and thus as a gesture that is conveyed by being spoken and heard.

Today we are aware of considerably more about the complex physiology of the senses than Aristotle could possibly have known in his day. Simply considering the physical phenomenon of the ear may prod us to reconsider such traditional priorities. We now know, for example, that the central parts of the inner ear, the cochlea and labyrinth, are completely developed in the human fetus after only four and a half months — in their final, lifelong size and form. Remarkably, and some might even say inexplicably, the inner ear is active and ready to work long before birth, detecting first of all — and at a remarkably early stage — the rhythm of the mother's heartbeat. In fact, the inner ear has three times as many hair cells for detecting high frequency than low — a reminder that the child in the embryonic stage develops the capacity first to "hear" the mother's voice, and only later the father's.[9] Furthermore, just as hearing seems to be the first sense ready to function, it is also apparently the last: in the final stages of life, and during the process of dying, humans can still hear things even when all other sense perceptions have ceased. One might formulate the conclusion in this way: When we begin to hear, we "are," and when we cease to hear, we "are no more."

Joachim-Ernst Berendt, an international radio personality and a leading authority on the history of jazz, has gone so far as to amend Descartes' famous postulate to claim, "I hear, therefore I am."[10] Obviously, Berendt's point is much more subtle than a simple critique of the Cartesian maxim; he goes further, accusing the philosopher of advocating the final reduction of the soul/body reality and reaching the peak of human arrogance toward the rest of creation with his elevation of thinking above all else with his now slogan-like maxim "I think, therefore I am." Since no other creature thinks like humans, this statement translates into the laconic and ultimately absurd claim, *only I* am. Berendt's formula also stands as a critique of our visual culture. We trust our visual capacity blindly, as it were. Not what we have heard but rather what we have seen is what we often judge to be real. But in actuality, hearing as our first evolutionary sense is a far more reliable and powerful judge than seeing. Apparently, we hear more than we see, a point that led Kant to suggest that not seeing only separates us from other things,

---

9. For these details see Joachim Ernst Berendt, "Ich höre, also bin ich," in *Über das Hören: Einem Phänomen auf der Spur,* ed. Thomas Vogel (Tübingen: Attempto Verlag, 1998), 69-90.

10. See Berendt, "Ich höre." I am also indebted to Berendt for the following observations.

but not hearing separates us from other persons — a much more devastating experience. The perception of hearing also covers about ten octaves, not one, the comparative size of the light spectrum that the eye can see. Its speed in noting sequential impulses as distinct from each other is six times faster. Its precision is vastly superior, such that we can judge the identity of two simultaneous tones quite exactly, as every string player knows, but not two hues of color. Finally, the skeletal structure of the body protects hearing by sheltering the inner ear with the hardest bone in the human body, an indication that evolution has favored hearing over seeing. As a common saying in German puts it, "the eye guesses, but the ear measures."[11]

One has to admit that there is much to be said for the priority of hearing over seeing in the hierarchy of the senses. This ordering also dominates the biblical material. Against the ocularity of Greek culture, the emphasis in the Hebrew Bible is on hearing. Yahweh's relationship with Israel, the theme of Israel's Scriptures, finds its center here: *shema Israel!* or "Hear, O Israel!" (Deut. 5:1). In a fascinating passage that precedes this and seems to offer its legitimation, as it were, we are told of Moses' teaching that the people are to "take care and watch yourselves closely, so as neither to forget the things that your eyes have seen nor to let them slip from your mind all the days of your life" (Deut. 4:9). But the manner in which this continual reinforcement is to happen — structuring, among other things, the learning that was to take place in the household as each generation was to teach the *two* that followed, with the reminder of how God "spoke" to Moses at Horeb (see vv. 9-10) — is through hearing: "Assemble the people for me, and I will let them hear my words, so that they may learn from me as long as they live on the earth, and may teach their children so" (4:10). Hearing thus sets the context of teaching and learning this great tradition, which itself established Israel as God's people. It also serves as the grounding of the prophetic experience, which is often prefaced with the claim that "The Word of the Lord came to me," and it is the familiar preface to the event of the prophetic message: "Thus says the Lord." Elijah experienced the presence of God not in windstorm, earthquake, or fire, but in the sound of the "still, small voice," and he covered his head in order to hear without seeing. Only when the prophet has "heard" God's word does he dare to speak (see 1 Kings 19). One might say, following Erich Zenger, that these Old Testament texts find their *basso ostinato* in the hearing of God's word.[12]

---

11. "Das Auge schätzt, das Ohr mißt." See Berendt, "Ich höre," 75.

12. Erich Zenger, "'Gib deinem Knecht ein hörendes Herz!' Von der messianischen Kraft des rechten Hörens," in Vogel, ed., *Über das Hören*, 27-43; here 30.

When we turn to the New Testament, we find a similar situation. It would seem that the writer of John's Gospel and Epistles deliberately takes into account the Greek emphasis on seeing: "We have seen his glory" (John 1:14); "we have seen the Lord" (John 20:25); "That which we have seen with our eyes, which we have looked upon and touched with our hands" (1 John 1:1). But the *kyrios* of the other Gospels and of Paul's experience is the Lord who is heard: "Heaven and earth will pass away, but my words will not pass away" (Matt. 24:35) — hearing will outlast seeing, according to this saying of Jesus, in the final days.

In this sense, Jesus' words as the tradition handed them on were to be heard in the churches, and these were largely imperatives, commands, exhortations, and instructions for action. When the early expectation of the imminent return of the Risen Christ as triumphal victor was displaced in the apostolic age by the image of the present and future judge, Jesus quite naturally came to be regarded by his followers as the lawgiver of the new age, the end time; in this he fills a role analogous to that of Moses in Israel's foundational experience at Mount Sinai: through Moses, the people heard the "Ten Words" and were given verbal Torah as guidance for Israel's life and pilgrimage. So, too, Jesus' teaching in the Sermon on the Mount finds its punctuating rhythm in the refrain, "You have heard that it was said in ancient times . . . , but I say to you . . ." (see Matt. 5:21, 27, 31, 33, and so forth). Jesus was perceived not just as a teacher of wisdom or a proclaimer of messianic fulfillment and apocalyptic insight, but certainly also as a model and instructor of behavior and attitudes for his followers. His teachings also came to function in this familiar gospel passage as a kind of living Torah, a verbal extension of the ancient teachings that continued to be read or spoken and interpreted in the synagogues.

It comes as no surprise, therefore, that the early Christian appropriation of the Jewish Scriptures, in the attempt to move their meaning from letter to spirit — which is to say, to the spirit of the messianic age — included the dimension of law. In this case, it was an eschatological law, to be sure, one that lacked a structure of this-worldly enforcement which is the third element of the process of law alongside promulgation and crisis. This eschatological law consisted of rules and advice for living in "second-to-last times," as Philipp Vielhauer has defined the apocalyptic interim in which the earliest Christian generations found themselves struggling.[13]

13. See Philipp Vielhauer, "Introduction to Part C: Apocalypses and Related Subjects," in *New Testament Apocrypha*, vol. 2, ed. Edgar Hennecke and Wilhelm Schneemelcher, trans. R. McLeod Wilson (Louisville: Westminster John Knox Press, 1991), 544-79, esp. 574.

The author of the *Epistle of Barnabas* does employ the hermeneutical key of promise and fulfillment in the interpretation of the Old Testament texts, but he also explains the food laws of Leviticus 11 in terms of moral behavior: " 'You shall not eat swine or eagle.' . . . Moses spoke here in the spirit. This then is why he mentions the swine. You shall not associate, he means, with people who are like swine."[14] The commentators speak of his allegorizing at this point, and when we examine his text in terms of method and rules we see that he is engaging in interpretive allegory. The principle, however, the interpretive horizon into which he seeks to move the text, is not that of doctrine — as was the case with Origen, for whom allegory aimed at providing information about the destiny of souls. Rather, it is the parameter of Christian action: the morality of the dynamic movement lies in the emphasis on good behavior — and the author judged what was good by the standards of contemporary society, which is to say what was held to be so in the eyes of Jew and Gentile alike. Barnabas's interpretation is interpretive allegory turned ethical; this was a crucial move, in fact, for all early Christian apologists who had to fight the suspicions and accusations of immorality as voiced in a vigorous and sustained manner by their pagan opponents.

This aspect must be a necessary ingredient in any assessment of the controversy between Alexandria and Antioch which we referred to earlier. Of course, Origen and the Alexandrian exegetes made use of ethical allegory, especially when they dealt with prescriptive passages, while the Antiochenes, on the other hand, left room for a spiritual meaning of the letter with their concept of *theoria* — the higher vision or insight which the interpreter finds in prophetic statements of the Old Testament, and traces to their fulfillment in the Christian era, when both are contemplated together. The Antiochene insistence on the literal sense, however, carefully distinguished the times of scriptural revelation — what we would today call the historical setting — in the wider context of the periods of God's comprehensive plan for the world, which they referred to as God's *oikonomia*.

We find an illustration of this in the Antiochenes' refusal to classify more than an absolute minimum of the Psalms as messianic. According to Theodore of Mopsuestia, for example, only four Psalms — 2, 8, 40, and 110 — were in fact speaking prophetically of Christ. With regard to narrative texts, interpreters in this tradition held that God did not teach through the words *(lexis)*, or through the story *(historia)*, but rather through the actual

14. See *Epistle of Barnabas* 10:2-3.

events recorded *(pragmata)*. The real question they faced was determining what these events taught, and what they meant for "right living."

In places where the answer to this question went beyond a simple rational clarification of the historical situation, such Antiochene interpreters traced how it actualized the message in ethical terms — quite understandably so at a time when the Christianization of the Empire, and not the defense of the faith, had become the primary task of apologetics. Historical events and persons in the Bible were seen as teaching about virtues and vices, about the requirements of an appropriate Christian life — and the manner in which this actually coincided with the best of the contemporary philosophical tradition. Even the Jesus of the Gospels and the Apostles of the Book of Acts came to be presented not only as teachers and proclaimers of Christian doctrine and ethics, but as its models and examples. The opponents denounced Antiochene exegesis as "Judaizing." The real danger of its rational sobriety becomes clear, however, when one considers both the roots of Nestorianism in Antioch and the fact that the leaders of the Pelagian movement — rigorous moralists as they were — found refuge with Theodore of Mopsuestia, the greatest of the Antiochene exegetes.

On the whole, Greek patristic writers did not distinguish terminologically between doctrinal, philosophical, and ethical forms of spiritual interpretation. We have earlier discussed the Greek term *hyponoia,* the "sub-sense" of a text, and its relation to the emerging terminology of both rhetorical and interpretive allegory. "Tropology" entered the hermeneutical vocabulary from the Greek rhetorical tradition as well. The root meaning of *tropos* is "a turn" (from *trepo,* "to turn"); it signified a kind, a mode, or a way, for example a particular way of life, mode of speaking, etc. Or, in the context of rhetorical theory, this was seen to suggest a figurative "turn of the phrase." Thus, "tropology" in rhetorical parlance simply meant "figurative speech," and was synonymous with what we have called rhetorical allegory.

With the transfer of rhetorical terms to the interpretive process, Greek Christian writers could call all spiritual interpretation indiscriminately allegorical or tropological. In the Latin West, however, biblical interpreters continued to make a distinction in the framework of the standard fourfold sense: John Cassian, our first witness to the later quadriga, subdivided the teaching of the spiritual understanding of Scripture into three parts — namely, allegory, tropology, and anagogy. These three branches, as he explained the matter, corresponded to doctrinal, moral, and "celestial" interpretations, a decision he seems to have made in order to make them conform to Paul's triad of faith, hope, and love.[15] Cassian derived his notion of tropology as moral exegesis from the specific meaning of *tropos* as "way of life"; it was easy for him to equate this with the Latin *mos,* "custom" or "conduct," an important noun from which Cicero had coined a new adjective, *moralis,* as the equivalent of the Greek *ethikos.* The entire Western tradition after John Cassian defined tropology as "moral locution," or simply the "moral sense" *(sensus moralis).* In Cassian's list, tropology rather than allegory came to stand as the first or highest of the spiritual senses, probably because in the list of classical sciences ethics followed physics, which he identified with the literal sense.

That this older sequence did not remain the norm was due to Gregory the Great. Gregory wrote one of the most famous biblical commentaries of all times. It happened to be an interpretation of the Book of Job, and Gregory simply called it *Moralia in Job.* In the preface, he explained why: his students in the monastery had asked him specifically for lectures on Job, and had added the request "that I should not only work out the words of the narrative through allegorical interpretations, but should straightaway slant my allegorical interpretations towards an exercise in morality."[16] This, however, was not what they got. Like the earlier fathers, Gregory did not clearly distinguish between the spiritual senses; as he himself put it, he found both the profundity of mysteries and the edification of practical virtues in the text, and he could not avoid talking about both at once. Where he did make a distinction, the correct sequence was utterly clear to him. Allegory, the sense about Christ, must come before the sense about the Christian life. Doctrine must precede ethics, just as faith precedes love.

Gregory impressed this point upon his readers with the help of a simple image: the flower comes before the fruit. And, even more pointedly, he drew upon the building metaphor: laying the foundation and building the walls must precede adding the decoration. The literal sense lays the foundation, allegory erects the walls, but tropology is what provides the decorative coat of colored paint by which the structure is adorned.[17] But there

---

15. John Cassian, *Conferences* 14.8, trans. Colm Luibheid (New York: Paulist Press, 1985), 160-61. See James Samuel Preus, *From Shadow to Promise: Old Testament Interpretation from Augustine to the Young Luther* (Cambridge, MA: Belknap Press, 1969), 21.

16. *The Letters of Gregory the Great* 5.53a, trans. John R. C. Martyn, Medieval Sources in Translation 40 (Toronto: Pontifical Institute of Medieval Studies, 2004).

17. *The Letters of Gregory the Great* 2.382. Hugh of St. Victor echoes Gregory; see *The Didascalicon of Hugh of St. Victor: A Medieval Guide to the Arts,* trans. Jerome Taylor (New York: Columbia University Press, 1961), 135, 138.

seems to be something odd about this last step. Why did Gregory not say that tropology is the putting on of the roof? Does he really want to suggest that ethics is a nice decoration, and not of the building's essence? Doesn't Gregory regard Christian morality as the goal of life, and thus the crown of biblical interpretation? One discovers in his argument on this critical point a subtle criticism of his students, those enthusiastic monks who were altogether eager for "works," for moral prescriptions, for practical recipes. It seems to be this pressure that led Gregory to focus as he does on discerning practical advice from his reading of the literal sense in his commentary on Job. But the spiritual sense for him was in no way restricted to, or even primarily understood as, a lesson in moral behavior. It included morality, of course, but could in no way be defined by it.

Biblical interpreters in the Middle Ages could have taken a cue from him in this regard, but they chose not to do so. Very soon after Gregory, we find a definite preference for tropology as a strictly moral sense, as concrete and often quite specific guidance for ethical behavior. Gregory himself implied that treating the moral sense is relatively easy for the exegete, but he insisted that allegory required hard intellectual work. It was, he felt, an attempt to cut a path through the dense forest of dark mysteries. What a joy to leave the forest behind and step out into the open! "We have gone over the [thicket of the] allegorical senses briefly so that we can the more quickly come to the wide open space of morality."[18]

In the late eleventh century, we find a precious autobiographical passage in which Abbot Guibert of Nogent tells the story of his first exposure to the fourfold sense under Anselm of Bec:

> Although I had lost time, I began longing for things that had been taught me by several good scholars. I pored over the commentaries of Scripture; I dug more deeply into the writings of Gregory, in which the keys to the art of commentary are chiefly to be found; and finally, I closely examined in keeping with the rules of the ancient authors, the words of the prophets or of the Gospels according to their allegorical, moral, and anagogical sense. The person who encouraged me most in this enterprise was Anselm, abbot of Bec, who later became archbishop of Canterbury.[19]

18. Gregory the Great, *In evangelia homilae* 40.2-3, Patrologia Latina 76, ed. J.-P. Migne, 1303B. See also Henri de Lubac, *Medieval Exegesis: The Four Senses of Scripture,* vol. 2, trans. E. M. Macierowski (Grand Rapids: Eerdmans 2006), 155.

19. *De Vita sua* lib. 1, c. 17, Patrologia Latina 156, ed. J.-P. Migne, 874B. For an English

Drawing a conclusion from his exegetical efforts, Guibert goes on to confess that "the moral meaning is in my opinion far more important than the allegorical."[20] As an abbot, Guibert was regularly called to preach to his monastic community. In fact, it was among a new generation of preachers that the priority of the moral sense in biblical interpretation had its steepest ascendancy. By the end of the twelfth century, this tendency gained even more momentum because the education of preachers had become the main curricular concern of the scholastic masters in the new universities. Preaching was much in demand in the parishes, and students were increasingly focused on acquiring the tools for this task. Their biblical studies had to be related to the everyday life of people and the masters had to consider this need in their teaching.[21]

Peter the Chanter, a famous Paris teacher at the turn of the twelfth century, used the traditional building metaphor to describe the course of what he regarded as the professional study of the "sacred page" *(sacra pagina)* — we would simply call it the study of theology. Peter represents the new trend that emphasized preaching and elevated tropology over allegory as more relevant for the reader — or hearer, as the case might be. In his description, preaching is seen as represented by the building's roof, serving a comprehensive function at once instructional and prophylactic in terms of offering moral guidance and protection at once:

> The exercise of studying Scripture consists in three things: *lectio* (lecturing), *disputatio* (disputing), and *praedicatio* (preaching). Lecturing is, as it were, the foundation and the basement . . . ; disputation is the wall of this building of study, for nothing is fully understood or faithfully preached if it is not first split by the axe of disputation; preaching, under which the others serve, is the roof, sheltering the faithful from the heat and from the whirlwind of vices.[22]

None other than Alan of Lille, the author of our *Anticlaudianus,* provided the period's standard definition of preaching: "Preaching is the plain

---

translation see Paul J. Archambault, ed., *A Monk's Confession: The Memoirs of Guibert of Nogent* (University Park: Pennsylvania State University Press, 1996), 60-61.

20. *De Vita sua* 876AB (Archambault 64).

21. See the essay "The Glossa Ordinaria and Medieval Preaching," in my *Biblical Interpretation from the Church Fathers to the Reformation,* Variorum Collected Studies Series 951 (Farnham: Ashgate, 2010), 1-21; here 12-14.

22. See his *Verbum Abbreviatum* c. 1, Patrologia Latina 205, ed. J.-P. Migne, 25A-B.

and public instruction in morals and in faith," ranking morals before faith.[23] And tropology, as Peter Comestor went on to say, was the *sermo conversionis,* the "converting word" that "pertains more to the heart's conduct, and moves it more strongly than allegory." He went on to add that tropology was also "sweeter" than allegory, an indication of the new emphasis on morality that seemed to be shaping the church at the end of the twelfth century.[24]

A thirteenth-century handbook for preachers — representing this trend that seems to have shaped "the great majority of thirteenth century sermons," as one historian has suggested[25] — goes so far as to declare that almost all those who were Christians needed most of all not doctrine but moral guidance. And this was to be based on their status, here taking into account their personal circumstances, their use of natural reason, and their role in facing the social challenges of the day.[26] Preachers stepped out into the wide terrain of tropology with gusto. It may have been necessary as a rhetorical strategy, but it was clearly also useful — and, one might surmise, expected by their audiences, whether in monasteries or parish churches. This tendency — one might even say preference — seems to reflect as well the increasing emphasis on merit that shaped preaching and theological discourse in this period, and thus was seen as a direct pastoral response to contemporary needs. We observe this in the extant record of the thousands of sermons that have come down to us in manuscripts written during the later Middle Ages as well. Even the most cursory glance at an old library catalog reveals that sermons constitute the dominant literary genre in the surviving manuscripts of the fourteenth and fifteenth centuries. These ser-

23. Alanus de Insulis, *Summa de arte praedicatoria* c. 1, Patrologia Latina 210, ed. J.-P. Migne, 111C: "Praedicatio est manifesta et publica instructio morum et fidei, informationi hominum deserviens, ex rationum semita et auctoritatum fonte proveniens."

24. Peter Comestor, *Historia Scholastica,* Prol., Patrologia Latina 198, ed. J.-P. Migne, 1055. See also Mark John Clark, *A Study of Peter Comestor's Method in the Historia Genesis,* Ph.D. diss., Columbia University, 2002, esp. the "Textual Apparatus" in the front matter. For more references to the "sweetness" of tropology, see de Lubac, *Medieval Exegesis,* vol. 2, 176-77. The English translation renders "suavité" as "smoothness."

25. See L.-J. Bataillon, "Early Scholastic and Mendicant Preaching as Exegesis of Scripture," in *Ad Litteram: Authoritative Texts and Their Medieval Readers,* ed. Kent Emery and Mark Jordan (South Bend, IN: Notre Dame University Press, 1992), 176.

26. Thomas of Chobham, *Summa de arte praedicandi,* ed. Franco Morenzoni, Corpus Christianorum Continuatio Mediaevalis 82/1 (Turnhout: Brepols, 1988); see Hans-Joachim Schmidt, "Allegorie und Empirie: Interpretation und Normung sozialer Realität in Predigten des 13. Jahrhunderts," in *Die deutsche Predigt im Mittelalter,* ed. Volker Mertens and Hans-Jochen Schiewer (Tübingen: Max Niemeyer Verlag, 1992), 301-32, here 305-6.

mons are full of down-to-earth moral instruction — "what thou shalt do" — but often seem largely if not completely removed from the actual text at hand, and thus far removed from the exacting contextual work of biblical interpretation. In the standard format of a late-medieval sermon, for example, the fourfold sense of Scripture appears only in the *dilatatio,* the rhetorical amplification of the sermon theme where some biblical examples might be used by being converted into exhortations *ad hominem.* The sermon as a whole, however, was predominantly geared toward analyzing social issues, deploring the evils of the time, and encouraging the modification of personal behavior. The background material came from people's everyday experience *(exampla)* and served political or ecclesiastical agendas, not from a more careful and nuanced exposition of the biblical text at hand.

Among the exegetes, Erasmus was probably the person who built the logical primacy of tropology most effectively into an actual theory of biblical interpretation. Because of his satirical criticism of human behavior in church and society, he is often classified as a reformer as well as a moralist. Yet a closer look reveals that the matter is not so simple: Erasmus was a humanist, but a decidedly Christian humanist who had a deep respect for the church's tradition. Manfred Hoffmann, among recent interpreters of Erasmus's hermeneutics, suggests that with all his philological concern for the letter of the Bible, Erasmus remained keenly interested in the spiritual senses of the quadriga.[27] This humanist even gave a decisive new twist to the distinction between allegory and tropology in the interpretation of the Bible: for Erasmus, the literal sense constituted the particular meaning of a text, while the tropological sense offered a general meaning. The content of this general meaning, however, or biblical morality, was being promoted by all "good literature" — Erasmus was thinking here primarily of the secular writings of classical antiquity — and thus was not limited to the Bible. After all, morality to his mind had to do with the general order of God's universal governance, while allegory pointed to the uniquely Christian form of reading as a gesture toward a text's soteriological aspect. Thus, tropology as the teaching of "goodness" had a logical priority in biblical interpretation, but it also had an essential integrity of its own. Drawn from either the Bible or the classics, a moral reading served as a preparation for a specifically Christian understanding and as a practical guide for how to live a consciously Christian life. Erasmus's principle of interpretation, the horizon into which

---

27. See Manfred Hoffmann, *Rhetoric and Theology: The Hermeneutic of Erasmus* (Toronto: University of Toronto Press, 1994), esp. 101-6.

he wanted to move the biblical text, was the "good life" according to the God-given natural order. And while this could be described as a rhetorical goal by all "good literature," he argued, it was ultimately perfected by the ethics of Christ.

Erasmus's impact on the second generation of Reformers, from Zwingli and Melanchthon to Calvin and his successors, was enormous. These theologians had abandoned the method of the fourfold sense, with Melanchthon speaking for them all when he stated that "tropology means figuration, nothing more": "a trope is a figurative expression," he suggested, adding that as such "it may be moral in its intention; ignorance made tropology ethical teaching." Nevertheless, Erasmus's principle was widely followed in later Protestant theology and preaching, particularly after Kant approached the Bible as a guide to a moral goodness that reflected God's general providence. And, while the Königsberg philosopher insisted on its accessibility to all persons through natural reason, he also held that it was most perfectly presented as part of the specific Christian message.

It is important to realize, however, that this generalized and external understanding of tropology constitutes a tremendous reduction of its potential. Reading the Bible primarily because it teaches "goodness" may be an argument for keeping the "Good Book" in public schools along with other good books. But it in no way exhausts the rich and complex meaning of the tropological sense as this developed in the medieval quadriga. After all, the fourfold sense explicates a dynamics of ascent, as we have suggested. It ultimately gestures toward an inner movement that rises from the letter to the spirit. We also saw that in the logic of its subdivision, the literal and allegorical senses still belonged together, with allegory serving as the crucial bridge linking the Old and New Testaments. Such an approach presumed that this consistency was really nothing other than an elaboration of the *sensus de Christo* that could be found throughout the entire Bible. The tropological sense as morality, as we have pursued it thus far, was therefore the extension of this specific meaning to a universal application, a step from specific to general truth. Yet this logic obscures another aspect: the step from the literal-allegorical sense *de Christo* to the tropological sense, from *factum* to *faciendum,* is also a movement from far to near, from general truth to a specific application. That is, it moves from an objective, doctrinal reality to a subjective, personal truth — from what "was done" in the distance, as it were, of history, to what "is being done" in the immediacy of experience.

Medieval interpreters drew carefully on etymology in order to define the term *tropology.* The Greek noun *tropos* comes from *trepo,* as we earlier noted, meaning "to turn"; from this, they reasoned that tropology was *sermo conversivus,* a kind of speech that sought to "turn" or "re-aim" the hearer.[28] Tropology turns the meaning of the text toward us and our lives. If allegory applied that meaning to the head, or Christ, tropology turned it to Christ's members, the church as a whole — and, yes, to each particular soul in it as well. In this sense, tropology both personalizes and interiorizes the text's meaning. In this sense, the dynamics of ascent not only denotes upward movement and expansion. It suggests as well what we might think of as a descent into self, and thus suggests a concentration of meaning in terms of personal experience. This double direction, of course, is a distinctively Augustinian theme; thus, we find Augustine using the image of the mirror to make the point: "Let Scripture be to you as a mirror"; "look at yourselves in the mirror of Scriptures"; and so forth.[29] Scripture reveals our heart to us; it shows us who we really are in the hidden and intimate dimensions of the self. This dimension is already reflected in John Cassian's primary example for the fourfold sense, the interpretation of Jerusalem: the literal Jerusalem was the city in Judah; the allegorical one represented the church; the anagogical Jerusalem stood for our heavenly home; the tropological Jerusalem was *anima,* or the soul.[30]

Tropology as the *sensus de anima* — the sense of the soul or heart — represented a widespread assumption of medieval readers of the Bible, particularly since interpreters during this period viewed the heart as the locus of human intention and action. It was thus central for cultivating the moral life, and the need to interpret a given biblical passage morally meant searching for its specific application to the life of the human soul. This greatly facilitated a peculiar spiritual interpretation of large parts of the Old Testament. All the wars, wanderings, defeats, and triumphs reported in the historical narrative were not only those of ancient Israel, teaching lessons about warfare and travel, but spoke of the combats, vagaries, temptations, and victories of the soul in its moral struggles. Tropology "actualized" the text. What happened once long ago, "back there" in ancient times, was seen to be happening daily here and now. The work of reading the Bible morally,

---

28. See de Lubac, *Medieval Exegesis,* vol. 2, 129. He cites Robert of Melun: "*Tropologia* means speech that turns [*sermo conversivus*] because it designates a deed of such a sort that it is necessary for us to be converted to it with respect to the establishment of moral edification."

29. On this theme, see de Lubac, *Medieval Exegesis,* vol. 2, 142-43; for the Augustinian references see vol. 2, 364, note 95.

30. See John Cassian, *Conferences* 14.8 (Luibheid, 160).

therefore, allowed it to be read *for us;* it stood as an existential invitation in the present to change — and not so much our behavior as our interior attitudes, the intentions of our hearts.[31]

Abelard may have been the leading voice in promoting this new emphasis on intentionality in ethics in the mid-twelfth century, but it was the Cistercian exegetical tradition, and above all its preaching, that practiced the extension of this sense of the biblical text with special fervor during this period. In this tradition of monastic reading, preaching was meant to interiorize a text's meaning rather than exploring the biblical vision of salvation history through the literal sense. As a direct consequence of this, allegorical readings preoccupied monastic exegetes throughout the twelfth century. One example of this was the tradition of interpreting the four arms of the cross allegorically as signifying the cosmic dimensions of the salvation wrought by Christ — in the East and in the West, for the North and for the South, as well as up and down, right and left.[32] Bernard of Clairvaux extended this reading to interpret them as the four "virtues of the soul," which he elaborated following a well-worn tradition as continence, patience, prudence, and humility.[33] But his exegetical reading of such a passage did not seek to explain a text. Rather, he sought to apply it to the inner motions and experiences of the soul, such as sadness and anxiety, remorse and contrition, release and forgiveness, and above all he followed Augustine's insistence that every interpretation of Scripture was to encourage the love of God and neighbor.

Bernard's exegesis might well strike casual readers as pure allegory, but he would have been surprised by such an assessment. For while he prized the "spiritual senses" found in biblical texts, and recognized that

31. Abelard is often cited as a key figure in the development, during the twelfth century, of a theory of intentionality as central for ethics; see, for example, Jean Porter, "Responsibility, Passion, and Sin: A Reassessment of Abelard's Ethics," *The Journal of Religious Ethics* 28 (2000): 367-94.

32. The great representative of this tradition was Rabanus Maurus with his stunning treatise on the Praises of the Holy Cross, which combines visual media (drawings) and poetry in an intricate theological presentation. See the critical edition *Hrabanus Maurus: In honorem sanctae crucis,* ed. Michel Perrin, Corpus Christianorum Continuatio Mediaevalis 100 and 100A (Turnhout: Brepols, 1997).

33. De Lubac, *Medieval Exegesis,* vol. 2, 374, note 135, cites a sermon of Bernard "de quatuor cornibus cruces" on the Feast of St. Andrew the Apostle, where these four are mentioned. Bernard also discusses them at some length as the true meaning of the "ointments" mentioned in Song of Songs 1:3; see Sermon 22.10 in *On the Song of Songs,* vol. 2, trans. Kilian Walsh, Cistercian Fathers Series 7 (Kalamazoo, MI: Cistercian Publications, 1976), 23.

these "lifted" the reader or hearer into the "mysteries" of God, he insisted as a preacher that there was always a corresponding movement toward the "inner sense" of the text — and this depended not on vision but on hearing what he simply calls the "voice" of the text, which is his way of gesturing toward its moral sense. Commenting on Psalm 34:3 (Vulgate), "I am the salvation of my people," he reminds his monastic audience that when spiritual health is experienced, one cannot keep silent about its benefits; "the inner sense finds outward expression."[34] In other words, the monks' experience of the "sweetness" of the spiritual life inevitably led them back — a "downward" return, following the ascent of contemplation — to service, to moral actions on behalf of others.

De Lubac called the kind of interpretation found in Bernard's writings "mystical tropology,"[35] and one can easily see why. He claims that it followed the precedent of Gregory the Great who, as we saw, did not give his students the desired practical recipes for their behavior, but rather promoted the intimate turn of the text of Job away from the facts of the story and from doctrinal speculation to the hearer — and thus to the intimate dialogue between the soul and God. As mystical tropology, the moral sense was held to be superior to allegory, since the latter can easily deteriorate into doctrinal formalism. In the Pauline triad of faith, hope, and love, in other words, tropology came to correspond to love, and love is the greatest among these virtues — not in the form of outward deeds, but rather of inner attitude and affection.

The understanding of the moral sense as an actualization of the biblical text — that is, its meaning for me as a reader — may explain a strange phenomenon some time later. We have previously discussed how the young Luther polemicized against the fourfold sense, already as early as 1516, but in his first course on the Psalms, the *Dictata* of 1513-15, he still used it — even though it is clear that the literal sense (and for the Psalms this included the *sensus de Christo*) was for him the "principal" one. Among the spiritual senses, however, Luther repeatedly named tropology as primary: "As we have frequently said, tropology is the primary sense *(sensus primarius)* of Scripture. When it is grasped, allegory, anagogy, and the application to special circumstances follow easily."[36] If, as scholars today assume, the

---

34. Sermon 15.8 (*On the Song of Songs,* vol. 2, 112).

35. De Lubac, *Medieval Exegesis,* vol. 2, chapter 9, "Mystical Tropology," 127-77.

36. *Scholae: Psalmus LXXVI,* D. Martin Luthers Werke, Weimarer Ausgabe 3, 531:33-35. See also Karl Holl, *Gesammelte Aufsätze zur Kirchengeschichte,* vol. 1: *Luther* (Tübingen: J. C. B. Mohr, 1921), 546-48.

contours of Luther's mature theology are adumbrated here, the surprising elevation of the moral sense may give us a precious hint as to why this is so: for Luther, tropology did not refer to isolated moral directives, but rather pointed to the nature of the gospel itself — and this underscores the unified nature of the Scriptures. It had to do with an "understanding of Scripture" *(intelligentia scripturarum),* and this required the transformation of the reader. It could not simply be a sense somehow provided by the reader, however learned or clever he or she might be.

It seems clear from the quotation that, at least when judged within the framework of the quadriga, Luther regarded the step from the *sensus de Christo* to the *sensus de anima* as crucial. When Christ is the meaning of the text, it is Christ *for me:*

> This is the rule for tropology: Wherever in the Psalms Christ laments and prays in bodily affliction in the literal sense, with the same words every believing soul which has been begotten, brought up in Christ and acknowledges its sinfulness laments and prays. To this day, Christ is being spat upon and killed in ourselves.[37]

Gerhard Ebeling has described this "tropological actualization," as he calls it, as an early expression of Luther's "existential hermeneutics."[38] What is said of Christ in the Bible comes to acquire its full truth when it affects our existence:

> The person who wants to understand the Apostle and other Scriptures wisely must understand all those terms tropologically: truth, wisdom, power, salvation and, righteousness, that is, as realities by which God makes us strong, saved, righteous, wise, and so on.[39]

The unrepeatable history of Christ is being given to us today, here and now, in faith. "The righteousness of God . . . is tropologically faith in Christ."[40] Ulrich Mauser even goes so far as to suggest that the primacy of tropology constitutes Luther's deliberate reversal of the traditional order of the senses: what can and must be said of Christ in the text literally and allegorically is

---

37. *Scholae: Psalmus XXX, v. 10,* D. Martin Luthers Werke, Weimarer Ausgabe 3, 167:20-25.
38. Gerhard Ebeling, "Die Anfänge von Luthers Hermeneutik," in *Zeitschrift für Theologie und Kirche* 48 (1951): 226-30.
39. *Scholae: Psalmus LXX, v. 19,* D. Martin Luthers Werke, Weimarer Ausgabe 3, 458:8-10.
40. *Scholae: Psalmus LXXI,* D. Martin Luthers Werke, Weimarer Ausgabe 3, 463:1 and 466:26.

determined by what faith knows — a faith, that is, that has experienced the justification of the sinner.[41] Such faith must rule doctrine, not the other way around!

Faith is thus a comprehensive notion for Luther. Since it includes the full awareness of the human predicament, which goes deeper than the outward imperfections of our everyday works and behavior, it must appropriate the entire Christ, not isolated features or specific moral precepts. This faith comes "from hearing" *(fides ex auditu),* as Luther never tires of repeating, citing this text from Romans 10:17 in its Vulgate rendering. But what is it that faith "hears"? Luther's insistent answer is that it means hearing the Word — which is to say, hearing the truth, and this means both the troubling truth about ourselves and humanity and, at the same time, the good news about the Triune God and his saving work. In this sense, this "Word of God" *(verbum Dei),* this truth, is not simply a verbal claim. It points to a person, one who is witnessed and mediated through the Word of Scripture — and through not only our preaching and hearing of this Word, but also and necessarily through our living of it. Of course, for Luther this meant that the act of "hearing" this Word presumed an encounter with the Bible; Scripture was the means God had established for our encountering this "person." And for Luther, this "circle" points to the principle of interpretation, establishing the horizon into which the text must be lifted — certainly through the efforts of the interpreter, but primarily and effectively by the one who stands at the end of every exegetical and existential journey, just as he stood at its beginning.

At the outset of this chapter, we spoke of the miracle of the human ear, which in its most important part is fully developed by about four and a half months after conception. But what, we might wonder, does the fetus want to listen to? What does it need to hear so early? One answer might be that it needs to hear the heartbeat of the mother, the very sound of life — which is also pulsing as one throughout its own developing body. It needs assurance of this, and finds it through this most intimate conveyance of sound, by which its body and that of its mother are bound as one: "I hear, therefore I am." But as hearing is the first sense experience in our lives, so it will be the last. As the bracket around life, hearing by nature stands at a threshold, and this finally points to the threshold of silence, if we consider the scene from our perspective: hearing characterizes the total short span of our active ex-

---

41. Ulrich Mauser, *Der junge Luther und die Häresie* (Gütersloh: Gütersloher Verlagshaus Gerd Mohn, 1968), esp. 59-61.

istence during which we have the chance to, and cannot help but, listen and respond. For hearing is a journey from the silence where life originates to the silence of death — and, beyond this, into an ultimate silence which hides the Word and the Truth beyond our experience, even beyond our existence, the silence that is our final home.

A Japanese story tells of a ninth-century sage who went on an extended trip abroad, visiting many countries. When he returned, the emperor sent for him and inquired eagerly what the traveler had seen and heard. For a long time, the sage kept silent. Then he took a little bamboo flute from his pocket and blew one long, single tone, after which he took a deep bow and departed. The emperor was disappointed. But he kept that one tone in his heart amidst the interminable noises of a busy life, and tradition has it that in his old age he, too, finally found illumination.

CHAPTER FIVE

Anagogia: Tasting Reality

In this chapter, we turn finally to the last of the quadriga, the four traditional senses of Scripture symbolized by the imaginative — and imaginary — chariot of Aminadab in Song of Songs 6:12. On the basis of the first three, which Christian interpreters understood as a hierarchy proceeding from the bottom up, as it were — namely, the literal, allegorical, and tropological — the final sense, *anagōgē,* represents the high point. It stands as the crowning achievement in the necessary process of interpretation, a task, as we have suggested, that the predicament involved in facing such biblical texts requires of us.

Surprisingly, however, this was not always the perception. There seemed to be much insecurity among exegetes and theoreticians over the place and use of this particular sense. Indeed, anagogy is missing from many medieval lists of these scriptural senses, including, oddly enough, the one we find in Hugh of St. Victor's writings, as we shall see. Other medieval exegetes had difficulties distinguishing it from allegory and "mystical tropology," senses explored in the previous two chapters; perhaps for this reason, most modern writers on medieval hermeneutics often just mention it in passing, with little in the way of substantial discussion.

Why the diminution or outright omission of anagogy in medieval treatments of the fourfold sense? At first the reason seems obvious enough: after extracting doctrinal and ethical meaning from the letter of a biblical passage, what else was one to look for? Was there anything more to find? Yet such an argument is entirely too facile and finally will not suffice, if only because it does not accord with the vital role that anagogy plays in this interpretive schema. There must be something beyond the first three — that is, the foundational literal sense and the first two spiritual senses of allegory and tropology. Aminadab's chariot, after all, is a quadriga, a vehicle drawn by four horses. The extra sense, moreover, is a *third* spiritual sense, as we have seen, though its exact assignment within this triad seemed to present persistent problems for medieval interpreters. It is to these that we now turn our attention.

To describe the difference between literal sense and spiritual meaning, theorists from the early and medieval church often used comparative metaphors drawn from the world of plants and foods: bark and marrow; shell and nut; chaff and kernel; honeycomb and honey. To proceed from the one to the other requires effort, skill, and an investment of time. All these pairs — and it should be noted that they are all found in the Bible — have one feature in common: the experience of reaching the second of this pairing, which is the overarching goal of the effort, promises to reward the interpreter with "sweetness" — one tastes the sweet marrow, the sweet nut, the sweet kernel, sweet honey, and so forth. If we take into account that honey was the main sweetener in pre-modern cuisine, we begin to grasp how important this metaphor was for illustrating the delight to be discovered in biblical interpretation.

The Bible itself offers many instances of this. Consider the intricate logic of Samson's riddle: "Out of the eater came something to eat; out of the strong came something sweet" (Judg. 14:14). This allusion points to the hero's experience of finding a honeycomb in the carcass of a lion he had killed. Another passage, this one from the Book of Deuteronomy, mentions "honey from the rock" (32:13), and the wisdom literature includes the admonition to "eat honey, my son, for it is good; the drippings of the honeycomb are sweet to your taste" (Prov. 24:13), an urging that establishes the connection between honey and sweetness, but also goodness and the sense of taste. In the latter passage, ethics and aesthetics are yoked in the experience of taste. Commenting on this text, Rabanus Maurus, abbot of Fulda in the ninth century, explains:

> Honey which is ready for consumption suggests the moral surface of the letter. The honeycomb, in which the honey is squeezed out from the wax, indicates figuratively an allegorical expression. When the veil of the letter is drawn back, the sweetness of the spiritual sense is perceived somehow through the investment of labor and time.[1]

---

1. *In Proverbia Solomonis* 2.24, Patrologia Latina 111, ed. J.-P. Migne, 757D-758A.

Elsewhere he voices the more general claim that "divine Scripture is a honeycomb filled with the honey of spiritual wisdom," an affirmation that wisdom as the highest goal of knowledge is something to be tasted and not merely known.[2] But what is clear in this fascinating passage is that interpretation, as a form of tasting, takes time and work. It does not simply "happen" for us — as any cook who labors to prepare a delicious meal knows well enough!

Let us return once more to Aristotle's hierarchy of the five bodily senses, a theme he explored in some detail in his treatise *On the Soul*. We have already noted that he discusses taste as a particular form of touch, determining that it is among the two least significant senses in the hierarchy of value.[3] The reason for this, according to the philosopher, is obvious: the human face itself positions the mouth as the organ of taste in the lowest position. Beyond this physiological observation, Aristotle goes on to make some valid observations: even more than the other senses, taste as he interprets it always works in pairs — for example, sweet/bitter and sour/salty — and in order to be activated, taste needs the presence of moisture. We know today that he was right in this, since our taste buds function by perceiving chemical substances only in solution; a dry mouth enjoys little experience of flavor.

What emerged as more important in the Christian tradition than it had been in this Aristotelian analysis was the biblical material itself. Surprisingly, except for the implied connection of sweet, bitter, and sour with the sense of taste, the word "taste" itself does not occur with any frequency in the Bible. There are the references to the heavenly manna which "tasted like wafers made with honey" (Exod. 16:31), and of course taste is implied in the poignant image of the Promised Land as one "flowing with milk and honey" (e.g., Exod. 33:3). We find taste expressed in the expression "to taste death," evoked by death's metaphorical bitterness, which occurs in one of Jesus' sayings (Mark 9:1) and in the Fourth Gospel is quoted by Jesus' interlocutors (8:52). But in the case of such scant references, the exception proves the rule: taste is generally a neglected sense in Scripture.

When we turn to the early Christian literature, of course, we find a much more abundant usage of taste. For the expression that speaks of "tasting death," the commentaries suggest the general meaning of "experiencing," but it seems that the metaphor actually serves as an *intensification*

---

2. *De universo* 22.1, Patrologia Latina 111, ed. J.-P. Migne, 594C.

3. See above, chapter 1, n. 21; Aristotle, *De Anima* 2.

of experience. This is certainly the case when a prophet or seer is ordered to eat a scroll on which the Word of God is written, an image that occurs in Ezekiel's prophecy (2–3) and again in the Book of Revelation (10:8-11). Ezekiel reports that in his mouth the scroll was "as sweet as honey," while the author of the Revelation to John says the same about the taste in his mouth but adds, "When I had eaten it, my stomach was made bitter." The metaphorical act together with its sensory result serve to underscore the thorough assimilation — or intensification — of the divine word by the recipients: the word has become their own in a deeply personal way. Indeed, we now know, given our scientific knowledge of digestion as a transformative process, that the act of ingesting takes the nutrition of what is tasted into the very substance of the body itself. In these ways one might even say that the experience of tasting far surpasses that of hearing in its intensity.

The most important biblical verse suggesting a metaphorical use of the sense of taste is found in the Psalms: "O taste and see that the Lord is good" (34:8). From early times on, this verse found a prominent place in the Eucharistic liturgy. The two echoes of it in the New Testament — 1 Peter 2:3 and Hebrews 6:4-5 — may well reflect this context already. In a famous passage of his *Address on Religious Instruction,* Gregory of Nyssa argued that in the Eucharist, bread and wine as the immortal body and blood of Christ become physically part of our body, being tasted and consumed as nourishing food.[4] In faith, this is the full reality of the presence of the Lord necessary for the salvation of the whole person, both soul *and body.* In this sacrament, we are quite literally "in-corporated" into Christ, and Christ into our bodies. Such a taste leads to a kind of mutual embodiment, as it were.

This verse from the Psalms, however, was not only used in the context of Eucharistic eating and tasting. It also provided the biblical warrant for the language of "tasting God" as the expression of an intimate spiritual experience of God's presence, an intensification which could be described if at all only in metaphorical language. This interpretation was greatly increased in the West by a slight change in the medieval Latin rendering of the verse: "O taste and see that the Lord is *sweet" (quia dulcis est Dominus),* instead of "good." This change is part of an intriguing phenomenon by which the Latin Bible greatly enlarged the use of "sweetness" language, employing words like *dulcis* ("sweet") or *dulcedo* ("sweetness")

---

4. *Address on Religious Instruction 37,* in *Christology of the Later Fathers,* ed. Edward Hardy, Library of Christian Classics (Philadelphia: Westminster Press, 1954), 318-20.

to translate the Hebrew root *tôb* ("good") as well as its Greek equivalent *chrēstos* ("good" or "helpful").[5] For Latin readers, the trees found in the second creation story of Genesis (2:9 and 3:6) were not "good" for food, but "sweet," and Jesus was pronouncing his yoke to be not "easy" but "sweet" (Matt. 11:30). Through this change, not only God's "good" law or God's "helpful" Word was declared to be "sweet," but even the divine persons could be called "sweet" and thus in some way also the object of "tasting" — an intimate spiritual experience analogous to tasting pleasant food. All this seems to take its cue from Psalm 34:8, with the terminology of tasting and sweetness emerging to play a considerable role in the way Western theologians described the mystical experience of God's presence — in Eucharistic reception, of course, but also in the interior union of the soul with the divine. For this to occur, the entire body and not merely the tongue or mouth came to be identified as the organ of the tasting experience, or the "reception," if we might speak in this way.

In his day, Augustine moved beyond the common notion that the experience of sweetness in prayer as well as in other forms of serving God represented a spiritual consolation. But he pressed this point further, speaking of God's own presence as the highest form of sweetness — "*vera tu et summa suavitas.*"[6] The notion of sweetness came to function particularly in the monastic exegesis of the medieval Cistercians via the yearning for a remembered taste; in this sense, the memory of this sweetness serves as an intensification of experience, precisely because such a remembering can stimulate the desire for God in a time of a felt absence.[7] As Bernard of Clairvaux once put it, "blessed are those who know by the taste of this happy experience, how sweetly, how wonderfully the Lord deigns to grant revelation in prayer and the meditation of Scripture."[8] We will return to this topic.

Drawing on biblical food imagery, Gregory of Nyssa distinguished

5. See Jean Châtillon, "Dulcedo," in *Dictionnaire de Spiritualité, Ascétique et Mystique,* vol. 3 (Paris: Beauchesne, 1967), 1781-83.

6. See *Confessions* 9.1.1, Corpus Christianorum Latinorum 27 (Turnhout: Brepols, 1981), 133, line 16.

7. For further discussion of this theme of "sweetness" in the early Cistercian literature, see Henri de Lubac, *Medieval Exegesis: The Four Senses of Scripture,* vol. 2, trans. E. M. Macierowski (Grand Rapids: Eerdmans, 2000), 173-75, where the English translation renders "suavité" as "smoothness."

8. *Sermo de duobus discipulis euntibus in Emmaus* 20, Patrologia Latina 184, ed. J.-P. Migne, 976C.

stages of spiritual progress, all of them labeled "sweet": thus, "beginners" taste the sweetness of milk, those who are "advanced" in their faith receive the taste of bread and honey, and the "perfect" ones come to taste the inebriating wine of ecstasy, which one experiences as a "spiritual inebriation."[9] The reference here to Ephesians 5:18 — "Do not be drunk with wine, but with the Spirit" — became a classic text for this experience. Gregory took his cue from Origen, who was the first to build the metaphor of "tasting sweetness" into the very structure of what we have described as a biblical hermeneutics of ascent, one based in a doctrine of spiritual progress.[10] For Origen, all sweet foods of the Bible functioned as figures of spiritual realities, arousing and enticing the inquisitive soul which hungers for just such a taste. In his Seventh Homily on Exodus, he interpreted the manna which the Israelites received in the wilderness as the Logos, Christ, the Bread from Heaven, lifting the text from its somatic or bodily/literal level to the spiritual, and he interprets the word of God as a manna that produces a sweetness corresponding to each person's desires.[11] Only the latter discloses to us, according to Origen, the true spiritual meaning of what began with a physical experience. He could call this procedure *allēgoria*, but preferred the term *anagōgē* to describe it, drawing on an Aristotelian word-creation used by Neoplatonic sources to denote the movement between higher worlds, the "aeons." Origen made it a technical term of biblical hermeneutics, one that graphically described the upward or ascending dynamics of interpretation. He described this dynamic experience in various ways, as "bringing up," "lifting up," or "leading upward"; at this early point, the terminology was not yet fixed. Indeed, Gregory of Nyssa could still speak of the "anagogical interpretation" as "tropology or allegory or some other name. We shall not quarrel about the name."[12]

A decisive step toward clarification was taken by the enigmatic author of the early sixth century, Pseudo-Dionysius. This theologian, whose important treatises circulated under the name of the Athenian convert of the apostle Paul (see Acts 17:34), seems to have nurtured this pseudonym in

---

9. Gregory of Nyssa, *Homilies on the Song of Songs*, trans. Richard A. Norris (Atlanta: Society of Biblical Literature, 2012), 279-85.

10. See Châtillon, "Dulcedo," 1783-84.

11. Origen, *Homilies on Genesis and Exodus* 7.5-8, ed. Ronald Heine, Fathers of the Church 71 (Washington, DC: Catholic University Press, 1982), 307-15.

12. Gregory of Nyssa, *Homilies on the Song of Songs,* 3-5. On Gregory's indifference to the terminology of anagogy see Hans Boersma, *Embodiment and Virtue in Gregory of Nyssa: An Anagogical Approach* (New York: Oxford University Press, 2013), 66-70.

order to keep alive the fictive presumption of an early date of his writings as a means of claiming their authority.[13] He did not use the term "anagogy" in Origen's technical sense, however; nor did he endorse Origen's super-plenary inspiration of the words of Scripture. The human authors of the Bible, according to Pseudo-Dionysius, were to be understood as instruments of a comprehensive divine pedagogy through which God the creator wants to effect the restoration of his created and fallen world.[14] This Eastern theologian, who probably lived no earlier than the late fifth century, was not much concerned with plain passages; his focus persistently falls on those he called "symbolic." Through their obvious inadequacy and even absurdity in expressing spiritual truth, such texts exposed the logic of the entire process in which anagogy finds its precise role.[15]

To understand this, Pseudo-Dionysius conceived of God's revelation as descending into the manifold verbal affirmations of the Bible, which gives rise to what he calls *kataphatic* or "positive" theology — or what we commonly think of as "God-talk." The countermovement, anagogy or uplifting, reminds us that the initiative in theology always belongs to God and not to the interpreter; it suggests a return through the symbols of the biblical language via an ever-increasing negation of their adequacy, until the point that they reach up to the realm of noetic or intelligible truth. It is here, at this apex of the ascent, where God dwells, beyond all language and images and concepts, in utter silence, darkness, and simplicity. What is important to note here is that this double movement reflects the fundamental nature of reality, structured as it is in the dynamic model of Platonic cosmological speculation by a movement of *exitus,* or "procession," and *reditus,* or "return."[16] The interpreter of the Bible thus finds this dynamic motion not only in creation, but discovers how it is everywhere present in biblical texts, which represent an instance of a larger and all-encompassing cycle — one initiated and sustained by God and only entered into, as it were, by the scriptural reader. This second motion of return as an uplifting is an accom-

---

13. For my understanding of Pseudo-Dionysius, I am indebted to the work of Paul Rorem; see his *Biblical and Liturgical Symbols within the Pseudo-Dionysian Synthesis* (Toronto: Pontifical Institute of Medieval Studies, 1984); *Pseudo-Dionysius: A Commentary on the Texts and an Introduction to Their Influence* (New York: Oxford University Press, 1993); and his contributions to the volume *Pseudo-Dionysius: The Complete Works,* Classics of Western Spirituality (Mahwah, NJ: Paulist Press, 1994).

14. Rorem, *Biblical and Liturgical Symbols,* 54.

15. See Rorem, *Biblical and Liturgical Symbols,* 51.

16. Rorem, *Biblical and Liturgical Symbols,* 58-65.

modation to our nature, and finds expression in what Pseudo-Dionysius refers to as the *apophatic* or negative theology.[17]

The *rules* of interpretation thus require the exegete to trace these dynamics — that is, of procession and return — to the originating *principle* of the ineffable deity, identical with the infinite One of the Neoplatonic tradition. That is, the fundamental "motor" of the entire movement — the initiating and sustaining energy of this cycle — is Divine Love, and here it is useful to remember that Pseudo-Dionysius does not differentiate between *eros* and *agape*. This movement lies at the root of God's primal ecstasy in the very act of creation, an experience of God "going out" of God's own self as a mode of being that exemplary humans can experience by participation as well: Moses, Paul, and Pseudo-Dionysius's mysterious teacher Hierotheos were such models of participatory ecstasy. But what is crucial is that it also places the interpreter in the role of participant in a dynamic energy that flows through all that is — including, of course, the biblical text in its larger patterns as in its only apparently isolated details.

Pseudo-Dionysius's biblical vision of descent and anagogy, pointing to a pattern shaping the "universe" above, the realm of the angels, as well as the "universe" below, the realm of the church's life, has been immensely influential on the theology and practices of Eastern Orthodoxy. And, though the Dionysian corpus of writings had remained unknown in the West until the early Middle Ages, their discovery and translation into Latin by Western theologians established them as a foundational text in the rise of Scholasticism, thereby helping to shape this new form of theological argumentation. These schoolmen looked to the Apostle Paul as one of the original authorities of Christian theology — and such *auctores,* as "creators" or "authors," established for them the basis for *auctoritas,* or "authority." They regarded this "Dionysius" clearly as an authority. He had a supposed relationship with the Apostle, their patron and colleague. But they also found the writings of Pseudo-Dionysius immensely useful in clarifying a pattern within which the interpreter's work could be understood, one grounded by his notion that "it would be unreasonable and foolish to look at words rather than at the power of the meanings."[18]

Early Latin authors often used the term "mystical" for any higher sense of the Bible, focusing on the mysterious, concealing aspect of the anagogi-

---

17. Rorem, *Pseudo-Dionysius: A Commentary,* 194-205.

18. *The Divine Names* 4, Patrologia Graeca 3, ed. J.-P. Migne, 708B-C; see Rorem, *Biblical and Liturgical Symbols,* 26.

cal interpretation in the Origenistic tradition. The veil lying over all reality — and thus, too, over the Scriptures — has to be lifted for the sake of those who need to be and desire to be taught. As Gregory the Great described the situation, Scripture does not yield its savory juice if it is not pressed by hard work.[19] For him, scriptural references to honey did not suggest the spiritual senses as such but rather pointed to the sweetness which results from spiritual understanding.[20] However, when Gregory divided the higher senses into three for teaching purposes, "anagogy" became the technical term for the last one, suggested by Paul's image of the *anō Ierousalēm,* the "Jerusalem above," in that foundational passage of Galatians 4:21-26.[21] With eschatology being assigned a place, the group of senses was now complete: faith and love were joined by hope to cover the full range of the interpretive possibilities, and these were seen to relate to the temporal referents of past, present, and future.

There was, however, a problem here with the Origenistic term, at least in the way that John Cassian had already kept it in its Greek form as *anagōgē.* Origen used it as a designation for the move from the level of the letter to that of the spirit, a spatial concept without any regard to a possible temporal dimension. For John Cassian, however, eschatology as the discourse about last or final things implied both an upward and a forward movement: "In anagogy, the message is transferred to things invisible and future."[22] It points to what lies beyond us, not only in the "reach" of our bodies in space but in the longing we experience as shaped by time. One might even say that anagogy, within the trajectory of this patristic tradition, came to represent not only an upward-lifting dynamic but a forward-reaching one as well; in this sense, the motion of such a spiritual interpretation came to be experienced as a temporalizing of spatial categories.

19. "So many truths were written there simply, to nourish children, but some in obscure sayings that they may occupy the strong, since things understood with effort are the more welcome." *Saint Gregory the Great: Homilies on the Book of the Prophet Ezekiel,* trans. Theodosia Gray (Etna, CA: Center for Traditionalist Orthodox Studies, 1990), 2.5.4. For a more extensive discussion of Gregory's exegetical principles, see G. R. Evans, *The Thought of Gregory the Great* (Cambridge: Cambridge University Press, 1986), 87-95; on the present topic, 94-95.

20. See Châtillon, "Dulcedo," 1789.

21. See above, p. 52.

22. "[Anagoge] per quam ad invisibilia et futura sermo transfert." John Cassian, *Collatio* 14.8.2, Corpus Christianorum Latinorum Online 406, line 12; compare John Cassian, *Conferences* 14.8, trans. Colm Luibheid (New York: Paulist Press, 1985), 161. Boersma finds the same double dimension in Gregory of Nyssa; see his *Embodiment and Virtue,* 2.

Sixteenth-century humanists ridiculed the Latinized form of the fourth sense as it appeared in our jingle: *Quo tendas anagogia.* In a sarcastic vein, Melanchthon suggested that the Greek word should be read differently — not as *ana-gōgia* (leading upward), but as *an-agōgia,* deriving from *an-agōgos,* "rude" or "uneducated," and meaning "insolence" or "boorishness."[23] We should today translate the term in such a way that it suggests more than simply an upward direction ("the upward path to pursue"), since the Latin leaves room for both upward and forward motion: the word suggests "where one should be headed." Yet the understanding of anagogy as an upward eschatology was totally dominant in the Middle Ages, as the standard definitions make clear: "anagogy is the sense about the things above"; "anagogical figures drench us with the things divine"; "anagogy is when we should understand one thing as another which is the object of our desire, the eternal happiness of the blessed above."[24]

Hugh of St. Victor, indomitable educator that he was, had much to say in his "summa" *On the Sacraments,* borrowing most of what he discusses here from the final three books of Augustine's *City of God* to describe life as a movement of what we have described as "forward eschatology." That is, he situates our life in relation to what is ultimately before us — namely, the end of the world and its fulfillment in history. But in Hugh's exegetical handbook, the *Didascalicon,* he consistently mentions three scriptural senses only: history, allegory, and tropology.[25] Anagogy is altogether missing from his discussion, a strange omission to say the least. Apparently, at least one of Hugh's later readers found this to be so odd that he "corrected" what he perceived as an unfortunate shortcoming in the text. In an unpublished treatise on the fourfold sense penned in 1486, one that reproduces much of Hugh's text word for word, Johannes Trithemius, monk and subsequently abbot of a small Benedictine monastery at Sponheim in the Rhineland, inserted anagogy as the fourth of these senses in every passage where Hugh discussed them — showing himself more loyal to the model of the quadriga than to the master's own intent.[26] The author's explanation for his addition

23. Melanchthon, *Elementa Rhetorices,* ed. Karl Gottlieb Bretschneider, Philippi Melanthonis Opera 13 (Halle, 1846), 467-68.

24. De Lubac, *Medieval Exegesis,* vol. 2, 180-81.

25. See Hugh of St. Victor, *Didascalicon* 6.2-6; for English translation see *The Didascalicon of Hugh of St. Victor: A Medieval Guide to the Arts,* trans. Jerome Taylor (New York: Columbia University Press, 1961), 135-46.

26. I have discussed this text in my article "Johannes Trithemius on the Fourfold Sense of Scripture: The *Tractatus de Inuestigatione Sacrae Scripturae* (1486)," in *Biblical Interpre-*

was quite simple: within the building metaphor, as Hugh had developed it, anagogy suggested "putting on the roof." But this is finally an embarrassing witness to this later schoolmaster's mentality, which sees eschatology simply as the final subject in a neatly organized scholastic curriculum. And, as his argument proceeds, he overlooks entirely what Hugh himself says about the omission at the end of the *Didascalicon:*

> And now those things which pertain to reading have been explained as lucidly and briefly as we know how. But as for the remaining part of learning, namely meditation, I omit saying anything about it in the present work because so great a matter requires a special treatise.[27]

Note that the term Hugh himself uses here is "meditation"; Hugh did think that anagogy as "the upward path to pursue" was "teachable" in some limited way. But he distinguished between two aspects: the objective or propositional one which "declares" and "discusses," and the subjective one which is defined not by an object but by a mode of apprehension, an experiential mode that "contemplates" and hopes "to behold." The person discoursing about eternal things is not automatically transported into the mystery of the age to come; speculating about last things is not the same as being caught up in an ecstasy. This latter mode was the kind of anagogy that really interested Hugh. He had read Pseudo-Dionysius, of course, but he worked in a monastic context, and it was this context that led him to place the real anagogy as beyond what one might learn from others. This seems to reflect his view of prayer as not confined simply to the public expression of monastic prayer as the *opus Dei* or "work of God," but also including its more "private" form — namely, the ruminative process by which monks read Scripture by themselves.[28]

It was the university teachers of the later Middle Ages, however, who kept the temporal element in view. As one of them put it, "The fourth [sense] is the anagogic when we want to signify through the things designated in Scripture still further something that pertains to the state of the

tation in the Era of the Reformation: Essays Presented to David C. Steinmetz in Honor of His Sixtieth Birthday, ed. Richard A. Muller and John L. Thompson (Grand Rapids: Eerdmans, 1996), 23-60.

27. *Didascalicon* 6.13 (Taylor, 151).

28. See Ivan Illich, *In the Vineyard of the Text: A Commentary to Hugh's* Didascalicon (Chicago: University of Chicago Press, 1993), esp. 51-65 on "monastic reading."

life to come."[29] In order to be teachable, anagogy had to be reduced to instruction about *futura,* the events that take us forward toward the end time, whenever that may be, or to logical speculation about the upward things that are "above." This movement thus leads toward what is above us, but also what lies ahead of or before us. It had to do with the "not yet" in the experience of the "eternal happiness of the blessed," as Bonaventure put it, those "things" which for us pilgrims in this life are still ahead of us as objects of desire and hope.[30] Understood in this particular way, anagogy acquired a meaning unknown in the earlier tradition — namely, as a goal that draws us in time, and encourages our desire for what awaits us.

In the last chapter we spoke of tropology as an interiorization and personalization of the text's meaning through this form of moral engagement with it, and observed the prominence of this emphasis in Cistercian circles. Contemporary with Hugh, this emerging circle of monastic teachers witnessed a notable inflation of "sweetness" language. The images of honey, honeycomb, wax, and bees became regular metaphors to describe what it meant to extract the sweetness of the various spiritual senses from the Bible's "literal sense." Bernard of Clairvaux, the greatest of the Cistercian exegetes, was even known as *doctor mellifluus,* the "honey-dripping doctor," because of the eloquence — or "sweetness" — of his writings. In this milieu, anagogy held a special place: "There is quite a sweet drink in history already; a sweeter still in allegory; the sweetest in morality; but it is by far incomparably sweet in anagogy, that is, in contemplation."[31] In this sense, Bernard could speak of the *suavitas spiritus* as a taste of "sweetness" that we experience in our hearts.[32] Moral engagement had a wonderful taste, according to Bernard.

Of course, "contemplation" had been part of the vocabulary of Western Christian mysticism for a long time. As the Latin equivalent of the Neoplatonic *theoria,* it referred to the experience of God in the human soul as the result of an anagogical process. Gregory the Great offered a magnificent biblical image for it. In his *Homilies* on the vision of Ezekiel 1, he interpreted the faces and wings of the "four living creatures" as symbols of the two goals of biblical interpretation: "The face pertains to the clear conceptual

29. Alphonsus Tostatus (fifteenth century), as cited in de Lubac, *Medieval Exegesis,* vol. 2, 181.

30. Bonaventure, *Breviloquium,* Prologue 4.1, trans. Erwin Esser Nemmers (St. Louis: Herder, 1947), 12.

31. Alexander of Canterbury, as cited in de Lubac, *Medieval Exegesis,* vol. 2, 177.

32. See de Lubac, *Medieval Exegesis,* vol. 2, 175.

notions of faith; the wings to contemplation."[33] The "flying" of the creatures lifts up the understanding of the text beyond a merely "noetic" faith. For Gregory, the freedom of this flight was the privileged experience of monks and nuns, those who embraced the "contemplative life." This *Sitz im Leben* of contemplation in monastic exegesis rather than in the biblical exegesis of the schools remained a basic assumption throughout the Middle Ages. Thus, Hugh of St. Victor connected the tropological sense with the active life, the anagogical with the contemplative. As such, he was careful to distinguish the "height" of contemplation, which brings us the full experience of *dulcedo,* from the hard work of meditation:

> Meditation is an assiduous and shrewd drawing back of the thought, either laboring to explicate something complicated or seeking to penetrate a mystery. Contemplation is a sharp and free observation of the mind, expanding everywhere to behold things.[34]

Contemplation as the higher of the two has a universal dimension, directing its activity everywhere; we must note, however, that the activity here is a gazing or looking, one that is expansive in enabling us not simply to "look at" things but rather to "see through" them.

For Pseudo-Dionysius and Eastern theology generally, in contrast, contemplation was the final return in the process of knowing and unknowing, not the process itself but rather its result. It was an experience of communion with and assimilation to the deity "as far as is permitted" in the divine realm of the so-called "intelligibles." But the Western tradition had a quite different bent. When it spoke about the end of this ecstatic journey, it normally marked the limits of the achievable union by including the dimension of a forward eschatology. Augustine had made this point quite clear: "complete" or "full" anagogy, the final end and fulfillment of contemplation, is reserved for the life we will come to know fully only *in patria.* That is, when we are finally "home" after death, there will be no need for reading and interpreting any longer; then we will "contemplate" the Word of God itself.

Despite the enthusiasm for Pseudo-Dionysius and his concepts of silence, unknowing, and darkness, Western theologians rarely embraced the

---

33. *Homilies on the Book of the Prophet Ezekiel* 3.1 (Gray, 31-32).

34. *In Salomonis Ecclesiasten,* Patrologia Latina 175, ed. J.-P. Migne, 116-17. See Ann Astell, *The Song of Songs in the Middle Ages* (Ithaca: Cornell University Press, 1995), 78.

authentic Dionysian mysticism, as Paul Rorem has reminded us.[35] They regularly "enriched" and thereby adulterated his thought by adding two Augustinian themes, the very ones that were conspicuously absent in the Dionysian treatise on *Mystical Theology*, namely, love and Christ. Bonaventure states the correction with great clarity: after negation comes love, and love's path is the love of the Crucified.[36] But these "enrichments" had already moved to the center of the anagogical interpretation as we find it expressed in the writings of Bernard of Clairvaux. "Love" *(caritas)* for Bernard belongs to the realm of the "affections," to the heart and not to notions of the mind — or what today we would refer to as feelings or emotions rather than ideas or thoughts. Any ascent as an experience of God's presence happens in the ultimacy of this realm of the *affectus,* and love as an affective experience has Christ as its object. But there is even more to be said here: such an experience has Christ as its subject, its goal, and its motor as well. The biblical material on which Bernard practiced what we might well call his "hermeneutics of affection" was wide-ranging, with extant sermons that cover the lectionary texts of the church year in its entirety. His central text, however, was generally the Song of Songs, a book he exalted as the "highest" of all the many songs found in Scripture.[37] Over the course of the last twenty-five years of his life, he explored this biblical treasure in eighty-six sermons, and at that only reached the opening verses of the third chapter.[38]

We do well to remember the controversy over the Song of Songs in the early second century CE, which questioned whether this book of Scripture should be included in the emerging canon. In its literal sense this ancient text, referred to as *Canticum canticorum* or the "Canticle of Canticles" in the Latin Bible, is plain love-poetry; as such it is very beautiful, very human, very sensuous, but not "theological" — at least in its literal sense. God is never mentioned in the entire text. The poem certainly has its place in the history of Jewish literature, but hardly in the history of Jewish religion. Or does it? It was the persuasive argument of no less a theological authority

35. See especially Rorem, *Pseudo-Dionysius: A Commentary,* 237-40.

36. See Rorem, *Pseudo-Dionysius: A Commentary,* 220.

37. See Bernard of Clairvaux, Sermon 1.6-8, in *On the Song of Songs,* vol. 1, trans. Kilian Walsh, Cistercian Fathers Series 4 (Kalamazoo, MI: Cistercian Publications, 1971), 4-5.

38. The standard English translation of these sermons, by Kilian Walsh and Irene M. Edmonds, has been published as volumes 4, 7, 31, and 40 in the Cistercian Fathers (CF) series under the title *On the Song of Songs.* Volume 1 (CF 4) contains sermons 1-20; volume 2 (CF 7), sermons 21-46; volume 3 (CF 31), sermons 47-66; and volume 4 (CF 40), sermons 67-86. Our citations are taken from this translation.

than Rabbi Akiba, the great *darshan* of the early second century, arguing in its favor, that assured its canonicity within the Jewish canon.[39] But others were not so favorable toward its inclusion, basing their assessment on the "plain" text before them. Theodore of Mopsuestia, for example, a theologian of the Antiochene tradition, saw the problem: he identified the poem as a "table song" for a banquet or a wedding feast, suggesting that Solomon had written it to defend his dark-skinned Egyptian bride — mentioned in 1 Kings 3:1 — against murmurs at the court. As a result of this sensible piece of genre analysis, Theodore could find no reason for its canonical standing.[40] Much later, a humanist scholar writing in the sixteenth century, the Reformed theologian and preacher Sebastian Castellio, echoed this position. He denounced the book as carnal and unworthy of being kept in the canon. The reactions in both cases are noteworthy: Theodore's opinion was condemned at the Fifth Ecumenical Council in 553, and Castellio was censured by Calvin, who, as the minutes of the official meeting reported, "approved the book as holy."[41]

How in the world could this happen? How could the Jewish community and the Christian churches keep this thoroughly secular and explicitly erotic book in their theologically normative canon, and reject the arguments of its clear-sighted critics? The answer, of course, lies in a universal assumption about the language of the Song: what the book says, it was held, is metaphor from beginning to end, intended by the author — whether divine or human — to mean something different from what it seems to say. As we earlier noted, they borrowed Quintilian's definition of allegory from his classical handbook on rhetoric as *metaphora continuata,* or "sustained metaphor."[42] By such a definition, whether in the church's or synagogue's understanding, the Song of Songs was simply a case of rhetorical allegory. And

---

39. See Judith Kates, "Entering the Holy of Holies: Rabbinic Midrash and the Language of Intimacy," in *Scrolls of Love: Ruth and the Song of Songs,* ed. Peter Hawkins and Lesleigh Cushing (New York: Fordham University Press, 2006), 201-13. A useful orientation to the Jewish interpretation of the Song of Songs is presented in Peter Kuhn, "Hoheslied II. Auslegungsgeschichte im Judentum," *Theologische Realenzyklopädie,* vol. 15 (1986), 503-8.

40. See Nestor C. Kavvadas, "Theodor von Mopsuestia zur Kanonizität des Hohenliedes," in *Studia Patristica,* vol. 52, ed. Allen Brent and Markus Vinzent (Louvain: Peeters, 2012), 275-83.

41. The Geneva Council's report is printed in *Calvini Opera Omnia,* vol. 21: *Thesaurus epistolicus Calvinianus* (Braunschweig, 1879), 329. For more detail see Heinz Liebing, *Humanismus, Reformation, Konfession: Beiträge zur Kirchengeschichte* (Marburg: Elwert, 1986), 60-61.

42. See above, p. 47.

if, as Thomas Aquinas argued, metaphor was part of the literal sense, then the literal sense of the Song of Songs included the meaning of the allegory intended by its author — and for Thomas, the *auctor* of Scripture was God.

But the fathers of the early church took the presence of the Song of Songs in the canon as proof positive of the need for interpretive allegory in biblical interpretation. Origen, who explained the high pitch of erotic fervor by classifying the Song in its literal sense as an *epithalamium,* a wedding song composed by Solomon to be recited by his Egyptian bride on their wedding day, suggested already the two standard meanings of the anagogy: the bridegroom stands for God or for Christ, the bride for the Church or for the human soul.[43] The Marian interpretation which flourished from the twelfth century on — that is, the bride as standing for Mary — simply extended the ecclesiological and individual allegory by presenting Mary as the perfect exemplar, either of the Church or of humankind.[44]

One of the most intriguing medieval commentaries on the Song is that of Honorius of Autun (ca. 1150).[45] It is one of the very few that expound the Song of Songs systematically according to all four senses. Honorius's literal sense assumes Solomon and Pharaoh's daughter as the main dialogue partners. But he was careful to distinguish literal from what we have come to think of as "historical." "Whether this was so in reality, does not matter, since a mystical reality must be understood here."[46] In fact, Honorius introduces three other brides as additional speakers: a Babylonian princess, the Sunamite, and "Mandragora" (a misunderstanding of the mandrake herb mentioned in 7:13), all in order to support his reading of the Song as teaching a complex scheme of salvation history. Going carefully through the text, Honorius retells the entire content of the Bible as the love story of a woman betrothed to the Prince of Heaven: she is Sarah, Rebecca, Rachel, the daughter of Zion, and *ecclesia* ("Church"); and her consorts are Abraham, Isaac, Jacob, Solomon, and Christ, respectively. With this power to signify the whole sweep of God's history with humanity as a movement that

---

43. A standard translation of Origen's commentary is *Origen: The Song of Songs; Commentary and Homilies,* trans. R. P. Lawson, Ancient Christian Writers 26 (Westminster, MD: Newman Press, 1957). On his interpretation, see E. Ann Matter, *The Voice of My Beloved: The Song of Songs in Western Medieval Christianity* (Philadelphia: University of Pennsylvania Press, 1990), 20-48.

44. Astell, *The Song of Songs,* 42-72.

45. The *Expositio* is printed in Patrologia Latina 172, ed. J.-P. Migne, 347-496. For a discussion of the work, see Matter, *The Voice of My Beloved,* 58-85.

46. *Expositio,* 364A. See also the remarks by Astell, *The Song of Songs,* 31-33.

culminates in the eschatological Wedding Feast, the language of the Song of Songs becomes, literally, anagogy, as Anne Astell has correctly observed, a preview of heaven. It is the "new song" which the Elders of the heavenly Jerusalem are singing, an allusion to the Revelation to John (see Rev. 5:9).

Most medieval commentaries on the Song of Song — and more than one hundred are extant — were produced by monastic authors. And, given the dominance of this mystical reading during that period, this fact should not surprise us. In a recent book on these commentaries, Denys Turner explores the question as to why the erotically explicit language of the Song was so highly valued in the cloister, of all places, seeing it as the supremely appropriate expression of the affective union of the soul with God in contemplation.[47] His answer to this apparent puzzle points to the confluence of two streams in the monastic literature of this period: the Greek tradition of *eros* — to be translated as "yearning" — which goes back to Plato's *Symposium* and reached the Middle Ages via Origen and Pseudo-Dionysius, on the one hand; and, on the other, a monastic theology of history nourished by an eschatological hermeneutics of the Bible.[48] This seems to be a useful argument, but two major difficulties emerge as one ponders the question more closely. The first concerns the role Turner assigns to Pseudo-Dionysius, for as we earlier noted *eros* as yearning does not play a key role in the Dionysian system of procession and return where scriptural anagogy has its place. Turner himself does not claim direct Dionysian influence on this monastic tradition, but speaks of what he describes as a "high-level ideological osmosis."[49] If he were right, it would be hard to explain why Pseudo-Dionysius had a much greater impact on the secular masters in the schools, including that of St. Victor, than on monastic theologians such as St. Bernard. The argument is unconvincing.

The second difficulty has to do with Turner's central thesis: namely, the specific adequacy of erotic language for the experience of the monastic contemplative life. He may be right about the strong parallel between the structure of eroticism and the eschatological tension between "already" and "not yet," the dialectic of presence and absence, and the yearning for fulfillment and union so characteristic of monastic spirituality. He may even be correct about the polarity of freedom and necessity, oneness and differenti-

---

47. See Denys Turner, *Eros and Allegory: Medieval Exegesis of the Song of Songs*, Cistercian Studies Series 156 (Kalamazoo, MI: Cistercian Publications, 1995).

48. Turner, *Eros and Allegory*, 42.

49. Turner, *Eros and Allegory*, 139.

ation, which marks the experience of sexual union, a tension that paradoxically does not allow for the extinction of individual identity, being a close parallel to the contemplative experience at its peak. But Turner, like most of us, still seems to be a victim of the modern obsession with sex: few of us are able to shed the notion that spiritual union with God must have its highest mirror-image in the ecstasy of carnal union here on earth. Turner does note the paradox: in the monastic exegesis of the Song of Songs, erotic love had to be totally detached from its carnal reality — even in marriage. And the more the love story of the Song was evacuated of its narrative reality, the more it became available as an allegory of the road of monastic spirituality. But the epitome of the paradox for Turner is still about sex: "The reality of *eros*," he insists, "is found in the inversion of its own significance, in celibacy."[50]

It would seem that the logic of monastic contemplation as the final spiritual sense of the Song of Songs developed along lines far richer and deeper than this narrow scope can allow. Bernard does exploit the metaphorical potential of the language of physical love to the full, invoking the image of spousal union time and again. But he himself says, "I am not so much interested in expounding words as in imbuing hearts."[51] He does not just speak about love, as an idea; he is in love with Christ, who is the true sense of the Song of Songs as well as the central "content" of the whole Bible. "If I feel that my eyes are opened to understand the Scriptures . . . , I have no doubt that the Spouse is here."[52] For Bernard, this is a reality experienced neither physically nor solely in the mind; it is rather an affective experience, a total involvement of the heart — and this meant a kind of intensification of experience for a person in his or her totality, as we earlier suggested. For this reason, Bernard approached reading the Song of Songs as a hunt for the prized game animal: the lure of the game leads us as hunters down many paths, now hiding, now granting a glimpse of its beauty and glory. But it is always leading us further, beyond what we know, to new experiences of yearning and delight. Bernard recognizes the importance of touch in this pursuit, but sees how the coursing of the hunt depended on the dogs' sense of smell to guide the hunters in their search for their prey.[53] Smell is the

50. Turner, *Eros and Allegory*, 155.

51. "Nec studium tam esse mihi, ut exponam verba quam et imbuam corda." *In Cant. Sermo* 16.1, Patrologia Latina 183, ed. J.-P. Migne, 849A; cited in de Lubac, *Medieval Exegesis*, vol. 2, 424, note 24.

52. Sermon 69.6 (*On the Song of Songs*, vol. 2, 33).

53. See Mark S. Burrows, "Of Hunters, Hounds, and Allegorical Readers: The Body of

guide to the entire hunt, after all, which leads to the eventual tasting of what was pursued in the search!

Following a tradition found already in Origen, Bernard also assumed a set of inner senses corresponding to the physical ones and feeding directly into the affective life. It is interesting to note that he here plays down the sense of touch, which is so closely linked to the sexual experience. Touch is invoked in the interpretation of the kiss of the opening verse of the Song of Songs Canticle (1:2), but when Bernard interprets the risen Christ's warning to Mary Magdalene, "Do not touch me" (John 20:17), he paraphrases it to mean, "Depend no longer on this fallible sense. Lean on the Word; rely on faith."[54] In contrast, the sense referenced by him most frequently in his sermons is sight. But in the description of the anagogical ascent the most powerful sense invoked is taste: "Blessed are they who know by the taste of this happy experience how wonderfully the Lord deigns to grant revelation in prayer and the meditation of Scripture."[55] When he speaks of the three rooms to which the king introduces the soul — namely, the "garden," "wine-cellar," and "bedroom"[56] — Bernard suggests that it is in the wine-cellar of the moral sense that the fruit collected in the garden of history begins to be sweet, but it is reserved for the one who enters the bedroom to taste the mystery of contemplation, completing the apostle Paul's description: "What eye has not *seen* and ear has not *heard* nor the human heart *conceived*" (1 Cor. 2:9).[57] This kind of experience happens, as he goes on to suggest, in the "mystical and deep heart" where alone faith "is borne, as if wrapped in a covering and kept under seal."[58] It is an inner sense, one hidden from the immediate surfaces of experience.

Taste is the image Bernard accords to the final and highest sense of biblical interpretation, or anagogy: "*Taste* and see that the Lord is sweet." Bernard comments on the word order as found in Psalm 34:8, and interprets this as clear biblical proof privileging the sense of taste as higher than sight in the experience of union. In his Sermon 71 on the Song, he turns to com-

---

the Text and the Text of the Body in Bernard of Clairvaux's *Sermons on the Song of Songs*," *Studies in Spirituality* 14 (2004): 114-37.

54. Sermon 28.9 (*On the Song of Songs*, vol. 2, 95).

55. *Sermo de duobus discipulis euntibus in Emmaus* 20, Patrologia Latina 184, ed. J.-P. Migne, 976C; cited by de Lubac, *Medieval Exegesis*, vol. 2, 397, note 188.

56. See especially Sermon 23, where Bernard describes the "three rooms of the King," as he puts it; he returns to explore the second of these — the "wine-cellar" — in Sermon 49.

57. De Lubac, *Medieval Exegesis*, vol. 2, 162.

58. Sermon 28.9 (*On the Song of Songs*, vol. 2, 96).

ment on the text "He feeds among the lilies" (Song of Songs 2:16), pointing to how this image conveys an amazing description of tasting, suggesting that the strange and startling image of the Bridegroom "feeding on" us and even "eating" us — just as we "eat" him. For Bernard, such an extended metaphor of mutual eating offers the ultimate expression of love's mutuality:

> I myself am his food. Does he not eat ashes as though they were bread? [Ps. 102:9] For I, as a sinner — it is I who am the ashes to be eaten by him. I am chewed as I am reproved by him; I am swallowed as I am taught; I am digested as I am changed; I am assimilated as I am transformed; I am made one as I am conformed. . . . He eats me that he may have me in himself, and he in turn is eaten by me that he may be in me, and the bond between us will be strong and the union complete, for I shall be in him, and he will likewise be in me.[59]

The image of mutual tasting says more, and conveys the depth and completeness of this union more graphically, than any of the other senses could do — whether seeing, hearing, or touching.[60] For taste is superior to all the other senses in terms of its immediacy and the intensity of perception it enables. One can imagine Bernard's monastic audience hearing in such a passage echoes to the monastic trope that described the monk's meditative engagement with Scripture as a "mastication" or "rumination."[61] Here, of course, the tables are turned: it is Christ as the "Bridegroom" who chews, swallows, digests, and transforms us into his body so that we come to be in him just as he is in us.

What is striking in this passage, furthermore, is Bernard's realization that this process of ingesting and digesting leads to an assimilating that happens by a transforming of one into the other to the point of a final conforming. But it all begins with the divine Bridegroom claiming us as his "bread": "I am his food" — and here the word he chooses, *cibus,* also suggests the "fodder" eaten by animals, an allusion that strengthens his reference to the bridegroom's chewing of the ashes as if it were bread. This experience of a

---

59. Sermon 71.5 (*On the Song of Songs,* vol. 4, 52).

60. For a detailed discussion of this question and its context, see Ulrich Köpf, *Religiöse Erfahrung in der Theologie Bernhards von Clairvaux* (Tübingen: J. C. B. Mohr [Paul Siebeck], 1980), 156-61.

61. On this theme, see Jean Leclercq, *The Love of Learning and the Desire for God: A Study of Monastic Culture,* trans. Catharine Misrahi (New York: Fordham University Press, 1961), esp. 73-75.

mutual tasting establishes an example that Bernard considers to be even stronger than the sexual allusions found in this narrative.

In various passages in these sermons, Bernard describes this deepest spiritual experience, this "tasting of the sweetness of the Lord" that beckons us as the end of the road of scriptural interpretation, as "mystical."[62] But it is also clear that we experience something of this "taste" already in this life. In one remarkable passage where he describes monastic reading as a "chewing" of the text "with the teeth of one's understanding," he points out that the "honey" is in the honeycomb — to be tasted — just as true devotion lies within the "letter."[63] Yet he rarely speaks of anagogy explicitly, preferring to describe his exegesis as "tropological" — here obviously in the second understanding we discussed in the preceding chapter on this sense, one that suggests a personalization, interiorization, and intensification of experience. Such metaphors of taste surely accomplish just this.

With the talk about union as suggested in Sermon 71, however, Bernard marked some clear limits. First, this union is not among equal partners; it is not a union of essences; in fact, he devotes the entire second part of this sermon to establishing the difference between the union tasted by the soul and the oneness enjoyed by Father, Son, and Spirit in the Trinity. Second, as an experience of oneness of will and love, this is a rare, brief, and fleeting experience, one that can never be final but always kindles fresh desires.[64] And, third, while Bernard does not hide his bias for the contemplative life in the cloister and an unwavering devotion to the anagogy of affective love, he knows that even for the monk active love in practice usually and necessarily takes precedence: "Those whose faith is strong have no need of a contemplative experience."[65] In fact, in his treatise *On Loving God,* when he discusses the four "degrees" (*gradūs*) — or what we might now come to think of as "intensifications" — of love, the third of these which speaks of our love of God for God's sake is a state when love is purified and

---

62. Sermon 52.2; Bernard elaborates on this experience later in the same sermon, describing this kind of "ecstasy" *(excessus)* — which alone should be referred to as "contemplation" — as a state of "going out of [oneself]," "transcending the self" such that one "gazes without the use of bodily likenesses." He goes on to elaborate on this experience of "ecstasy of spirit" in a remarkable passage, describing this experience as a kind of "sleep . . . in the arms of [the] bridegroom"; Sermon 52.4-6.

63. Sermon 7.5 (*On the Song of Songs*, vol. 1, 40).

64. See Köpf, *Religiöse Erfahrung*, 170-71.

65. Sermon 46.2 (*On the Song of Songs*, vol. 2, 167). See also Sermon 50.4-6 (*On the Song of Songs*, vol. 3, 32-35).

thus free to love the neighbor. To be led beyond this to the "fourth" and highest *gradus,* he insists, is a rare and special gift, an experience of "grace upon grace." This accords with his concession elsewhere in these sermons that he himself only knew about this "ecstasy" through others, and he is quick to add in this discussion of the fourth degree that "brotherly love [immediately] calls us back."[66]

For Bernard each of these dimensions of love actually serves as an intensification, leading us through the flesh and toward a deepening experience of our spiritual natures. As he summarizes this in the treatise:

> Since we are carnal and born of concupiscence of the flesh, our cupidity or love must begin with the flesh, and when this is set in order, our love advances by fixed degrees, led on by grace, until it is consummated in the spirit, for "Not what is spiritual comes first, but what is animal, then what is spiritual." It is necessary that we bear first the likeness of an earthly being, then that of a heavenly being.[67]

This is a telling passage, conveying as it does Bernard's insinuation that only those in a position to devote themselves to the "ordering" of love that monks could come to experience through the disciplined life of prayer were in a position to experience the presence of this truer image, the *imago caelestis.* He would not have presumed that only monks had this image; it was given to all. But the experience of this was the privilege of monastic contemplation by means of an intensification of human experience, and led from the earthly image we know through carnal love to the heavenly image that reflects our true spiritual nature. Returning to the metaphor of eating and taste, we see the same dynamic in his use of a passage from Sirach, "The one who eats still hungers for more" (24:21[29]): the longing for Christ is like a "hidden manna" — a reference to Revelation 2:17 — and those who begin to taste it are never satisfied in this life. Desire and not duty is what drives them on.[68]

Bernard's emphasis here on mystical anagogy, which he roots in the work of monastic prayer, is a theme Meister Eckhart comes to pursue two centuries later. Eckhart accomplishes this not by referring to the Song of

---

66. Bernard, *On Loving God* 10.27, ed. Emero Stiegman, Cistercian Fathers Series 13B (Kalamazoo, MI: Cistercian Publications, 1995), 29-30.

67. *On Loving God* 15.39 (Stiegman, 40).

68. See Sermon 15.3, *De quaerenda sapientia,* Patrologia Latina 183, ed. J.-P. Migne, 578A.

Songs but rather by turning to the familiar Gospel story of Mary and Martha (Luke 10:38-42) and offering a famous reversal of the way it had generally been expounded during the earlier Middle Ages. In this version, Jesus speaks approvingly when he says, "Martha, Martha, you are full of care and concern," and he might have explained the compliment, as Eckhart suggests, in this way: "Mary still is stuck in her loving affections, her longing for the sweet consolations of her soul. You have moved on. You are in the holy business of virtuous living. You have found the truth: only one thing is needful, namely God, and therefore you are free. Mary is not there yet. But take heart, she *has* chosen the best part. She is on track. This current mood will leave her and in due time she will be as blessed as you are."[69] In this startling reversal of a well-worn tradition that privileged the contemplative over the active life, Eckhart emphasizes the height of Martha's devotion through her service. Contemplation should finally lead to action, turning us back, as Bernard had also suggested, to the needs of others.

We have already seen that the Protestant Reformers of the sixteenth century rejected the quadriga as a scholastic word-game, one which they considered useless for the task of authentic biblical interpretation. But what is surprising is the realization that Bernard was not an advocate of this specific scheme either. His references to the traditional spiritual sub-senses are imprecise, inconsistent, and often downright confusing. What he was vitally interested in, however, was the anagogic dynamics of the interpretive process. Scripture for him was a table where we are being constantly fed, from sweetness to sweetness; as such, the parameter or horizon of our interpretation is not a method but an experience — in this case, the intimate delight in the Bridegroom's presence. Bernard sometimes called the result "wisdom," or *sapientia,* a word he suggested to be derivative from the Latin root *sapere,* meaning "to savor." As he puts it in a particularly vivid passage,

> For where there is love, there is no toil, but a taste. Perhaps *sapientia,* that is wisdom, is derived from *sapor,* that is, taste, because, when it is added to virtue, like some seasoning, it adds taste to something which by itself

69. Sermon 86, "Intravit Jesus in quoddam castellum," in *Meister Eckhart: Teacher and Preacher,* ed. Bernard McGinn, Classics of Western Spirituality (Mahwah, NJ: Paulist Press, 1986), 338-45. For a discussion of this text, see Dennis Tamburello, OFM, *Ordinary Mysticism* (Mahwah, NJ: Paulist Press, 1996), 86ff. Tamburello also points to a sermon on Sirach 24:21(29) where Eckhart says, "God as infinite truth and goodness and infinite existence is the meat of everything that is true, and that is good. And he is hungered for. They feed on him because they exist, are true, and are good. They hunger because he is infinite" (McGinn, 174).

is tasteless and even bitter. I think it would be permissible to define wisdom as a taste for goodness.[70]

In this passage, virtue stands as the pathway to beauty, with aesthetic enjoyment becoming the motor to move us forward and keep us going in our moral striving. Ethics, as Bernard here and elsewhere suggests, is not of itself sufficient to motivate us to a life of virtue and sustain us in that effort. Incidentally, the poetic eloquence of Bernard's Latin in this passage intensifies the hearer's experience of delight. The work of interpretation becomes a delightful way of "tasting" the words themselves, here by means of an ingenious poetic "game" of rhyming: *"ubi autem* amor *est,* labor *non est sed* sapor."* The wordplay here is lost in translation, which would be rendered literally "and yet where love is, [it is] not a work but a taste." It is as if Bernard, realizing how delightful language can be in the ear, also honors its taste on the monk's tongue, as it were. It was surely a line worth chewing on to extract all the *devotio* found in the words — like the honey trapped in the wax of the honeycomb. One can imagine his early auditors remembering this little rhyming jingle when much of his prosody might have faded away: *amor — non labor — sed sapor.* "Love — not work — but taste."

It has long been noted that Bernard held a special place in the estimation of the Reformers. Recent studies have confirmed this impression and clarified the details. Luther's "political" interpretation of the Song of Songs — he suggested it was Solomon's poetic praise of God for the blessings of his reign — demonstrates that he had no use for Bernard's anagogical exegesis.[71] In fact, he actually berates the "inappropriate and monstrous" commentaries of what he calls the "tropologists," and while Bernard is not mentioned, he certainly cannot be excused from this indictment.[72] Of course, we do find in Luther something like a bridal mysticism, but elsewhere and not in connection with the Song of Songs.[73] It was nourished in his writings by texts like Psalm 45, or the parable of the great wedding feast in Mat-

---

70. Sermon 85.8 (*On the Song of Songs,* vol. 4, 204).

71. Luther himself wrote a short exposition of the Song of Songs in 1539: "Lectures on the Song of Solomon," in *Ecclesiastes, Song of Solomon, and the Last Words of David,* trans. Ian Siggins, Luther's Works 15 (St. Louis: Concordia Publishing House, 1972), 191-264. On his interpretation see Endel Kallas, "Martin Luther as Expositor of the Song of Songs," *Lutheran Quarterly* 2 (1988): 323-41.

72. *Luther's Works,* vol. 15, 194-95.

73. Reinhard Schwarz, "Mystischer Glaube — die Brautmystik Martin Luthers," *Zeitwende* 52 (1981): 193-227.

thew 22, and above all in the Letter to the Ephesians (especially 5:28-32). Here, the bride comes to represent the church, the entire community of those who hear the Word, not the "soul" as an individual figure. And Luther's emphasis is not on love and union, as had been the case in this earlier tradition of monastic anagogy, but rather on promise and trust suggested by the bridegroom's dowry and the community of goods — in short, the "happy exchange" in which Christ gives all the riches of his grace in return for the bride's poverty and unworthiness. Despite the inequality of the mutual gifts, however, it is an exchange where one heartbeat takes over.

We also find statements in which Luther criticizes Bernard's exegesis, sometimes quite savagely: Bernard, he says, too often avoids the literal sense of a text, and is *mirabilis artifex,* an "amazing expert *in katachresibus,*" the art of using terms improperly, and Luther goes on to criticize the spiritual interpretation of his monastic reading as often leading away from the right understanding because it assumes that God's Word is dark and not perspicuous or clear.[74] Nonetheless, Luther had a lifelong admiration for the French abbot. For him, Bernard was a singular witness to the true faith during the dark ages of papalism; Luther knew his writings and quoted from them nearly five hundred times.[75] And, among this deluge of citations, two passages from Bernard's works reappear with a particular persistence, neither having anything to do with the abbot's anagogy but rather with themes central to Luther's own theology. The first is the beginning of a sermon for the Feast of the Annunciation, a text Luther quotes verbatim in his lectures on Romans in 1516 (see his comments on Rom. 8:16). In that passage, Bernard addresses the fact that all things needful for us — forgiveness of sins, good works, and eternal life — are unmerited gifts of God's sheer grace, given to us so that our faith might grasp the gift as real through the witness of the Holy Spirit in our hearts: Your sins are forgiven.[76]

---

74. Theo Bell, *Divus Bernhardus: Bernhard von Clairvaux in Martin Luthers Schriften* (Mainz: Verlag Philipp von Zabern, 1993), 325-27.

75. Bell, *Divus Bernhardus,* 361-62. As Bell points out, fully one-third of these references are to Bernard's phrase "Perdite vixi" in Sermon 20.1 (*On the Song of Songs,* vol. 1).

76. "We ought to believe, in the first place, that we cannot obtain the pardon of our sins otherwise than through the mercy of God; secondly, that we are powerless to do any good work whatever except by his grace; thirdly, that by no works of ours can we merit eternal life, unless it is His good pleasure to bestow upon us this also as a free gift." "First Sermon for the Feast of the Annunciation," in *St. Bernard's Sermons for the Seasons and Principal Festivals of the Year,* trans. A Priest of Mount Melleray, vol. 3 (Westminster, MD: The Carroll Press, 1950), 134. See also Bell, *Divus Bernhardus,* 91-99.

According to Melanchthon, Luther repeatedly told the story of an older monk who comforted the young brother during his early struggles in the monastery by reminding him of the phrase, "forgiveness of sins," in the third article of the Creed, and pointing him to this passage in Bernard.[77] The second text is a prayer from Bernard's Sermon 20 on the Song of Songs: "Take from this miserable life, I beg you, the years that remain. And instead of those which I lost while I lived them — for I lived them wickedly *(perdite vixi)*, you, O God, will not refuse a humble and contrite heart."[78] Luther remembered these words — wrongly — on his own deathbed; they assured him that the great saint understood the need for lifelong penitence and had finally given up his monasticism for the simple trust in his Savior. Both these texts show that Luther heard in Bernard a witness to the central truth of the gospel; he saw this saint not as a mystic, but as a preacher and a theologian.[79]

Calvin's attitude was similar in some ways, but also significantly different. We mentioned earlier that Calvin had defended the Song of Songs as a "holy" book against Castellio's dismissive rejection of it. A passage in the *Institutes of the Christian Religion* suggests that Calvin understood the bride of the Song as the faithful soul, in contrast to Beza's commentary of 1586 — the first written by a Reformed author — which pursued an ecclesiological interpretation. In this regard, Calvin generally seems to avoid criticizing Bernard, and while his earliest two references were negative — one saying that Bernard "wrote rather obscurely" — all further references in the *Institutes* were positive.[80] Like Luther, Calvin remained an admirer of the abbot all his life. He praised Bernard's style and skills, and used him in his polemic in order to demonstrate the continuity of Reformed theology with the best of the medieval Catholic tradition. But it is striking that Calvin nowhere quotes Bernard's mystical treatises, and the exegetical procedure in Bernard's commentary on the Song of Songs remains largely unmentioned in his works.[81]

---

77. Melanchthon, *Epistolarum Liber X*, no. 3478, Corpus Reformatorum 6 (Halle, 1839), 159. See Bell, *Divus Bernhardus*, 33.

78. Sermon 20.1 (*On the Song of Songs*, vol. 1, 147). See Bell, *Divus Bernardus*, 290-92, 363, 373.

79. Bell, *Divus Bernhardus*, 366-68.

80. See Anthony N. S. Lane, *Calvin and Bernard of Clairvaux*, Studies in Reformed Theology and History 1 (Princeton, NJ: Princeton Theological Seminary, 1996), 28-31.

81. Lane, *Calvin and Bernard*, 31. Lane notes that Calvin *does* "quote from [Bernard's] *Sermones in Cantica*, but his interest is primarily polemical (in his attack on free will and

That said, Calvin himself proved unafraid of mystical terminology, using the very term "mystical union" *(unio mystica)* — which Bernard did not use — twice in the *Institutes*. In the most remarkable of these, a passage found in his discussion of the nature of the "sanctified" life of the Christian — "in Christ," as he was wont to write — we come upon this description:

> That joining together of Head and members, that indwelling of Christ in our hearts — in short, that mystical union — are accorded by us the highest degree of importance, so that Christ, having been made ours, makes us sharers with him in the gifts with which he has been endowed. We do not, therefore, contemplate him outside of ourselves from afar in order that his righteousness may be imputed to us, but because we put on Christ and are engrafted into his body — in short because he deigns to make us one with him.[82]

Interpreters are often suspiciously quick to assert that Calvin cannot be speaking of mystical union in the "normal" sense of a fusion of essences that would have entailed an obliteration of individual identities. This point is well taken; such an argument would have been nowhere in his mind. The passage cited above occurs in the context of a polemic against Andreas Osiander, whom Calvin accuses of the "monstrous" notion of essential righteousness, as if God "pours himself into us as a gross mixture."[83]

As the careful language in this quotation demonstrates, however, Calvin was vitally interested in the biblical and soteriological concept of the believer's intimate union with Christ. Indeed, he chose explicitly experiential language like that of "engrafting" to describe this union as an overcoming of "distance" or "separation" — and correct a weak notion of justification as an "imputed" righteousness, against more extreme voices in the Reformed camp. His language offers another example of what we have called the intensification of the believer's experience of God — for

---

merit) and secondarily literary (in his appreciation of Bernard's apt sayings). He shows no interest in the specifically mystical teaching of Bernard" (34). The latter claim no longer seems accurate; see below.

82. Calvin, *Institutes of the Christian Religion* 3.11.10, trans. Ford Lewis Battles, Library of Christian Classics 21 (Philadelphia: Westminster Press, 1960), 737.

83. See François Wendel, *Calvin: The Origins and Development of His Religious Thought,* trans. Philip Mairet (New York: Harper, 1963), 235-38. See also Gunter Zimmermann, "Calvins Auseinandersetzung mit Osianders Rechtfertigungslehre," *Kerygma und Dogma* 35 (1990): 236-56.

here, as Calvin is careful to say, we must speak of a "sharing," and even an "indwelling." As he goes on to say, "With a wonderful communion, day by day, [Christ] grows more and more into one body with us until he becomes completely one with us" — and, in the edition of 1545 adds, "in one and the same substance."[84] In another passage, this one from his commentary on Ephesians, he goes even further: "As Eve was formed of the substance of Adam so that she was like unto a part of him . . . so we communicate in [Christ's] substance and by that communication are assembled into one and the same body."[85] And, finally, in the most daring of ways he claims — at least, assuming that this text is reliable: "By communion with Christ we are inserted into his body, that we become his members, that we have life in common with him and even as he is one with regard to the father, we become one with regard to him."[86]

Not even Bernard used language quite like this. Bernard also never spoke of a fusion of essences or of the obliteration of identities. Apparently, he was not a "normal" mystic. But what does Calvin's bold reference to "mystical union" really mean? Calvin asserts in ever new phrases that it is close, complete, and total: "The spiritual union that we have with Christ belongs not only to the soul, but also to the body, so much so that we are flesh of his flesh and bone of his bone."[87] "[Christ] so labors by the virtue of the Holy Spirit that we are united with him more closely than are the limbs to the body."[88]

In probing this theme, David Willis has argued that "Calvin's doctrine of the union with Christ is perhaps the single most important teaching which animates the whole of his thought and personal life."[89] If this assessment is correct, Edward Dowey's persistent reminder that we look closely at the structure of the *Institutes* for clues to Calvin's intentions may have pointed to what I take to be the possible basis for it: namely, Book 3 offers

---

84. *Institutes* 3.2.24 (Battles, 570).

85. This text is an explication of Eph. 5:29. *Calvini Opera*, Corpus Reformatorum 51 (Halle, 1895), 225.

86. "Homilia 11 in I Lib. Samuelis," *Calvini Opera*, Corpus Reformatorum 52 (Halle, 1885), 353. "Quemadmodum unum est in patre, ita nos unum in ipso fiamus."

87. Commentary on 1 Cor. 6:15, *Calvini Opera*, Corpus Reformatorum 49 (Halle, 1892), 398.

88. Sermon 9 on the Passion, *Calvini Opera*, Corpus Reformatorum 46 (Halle, 1891), 953.

89. David E. Willis-Watkins, "The Unio Mystica and the Assurance of Faith According to Calvin," in *Calvin: Erbe und Auftrag; Festschrift für Wilhelm Heinrich Neuser zum 65. Geburtstag*, ed. Willem van't Spijker (Leuven: Peeters Press, 1991), 78.

Calvin's explication of the Holy Spirit's activity in applying Christ's work to humans, a discussion introduced not by a discussion of "justification" but rather by the Reformer's teaching about union with Christ.[90] In other words, Calvin's pastoral interests seem to be framing his theological concerns here, insisting as he does that in order to reap the benefit of Christ's gifts we must be united as closely as possible with him — and this happens in faith through the Holy Spirit.[91] From there, the discussion proceeds to explore the realities of our life "in Christ," entailing a consideration of illumination, regeneration, justification, and election, all of which leads to the final culminating treatment of the resurrection of the body.[92]

It may not be inadmissible to call the sweep of this structure in Book 3 of the *Institutes* an example of the practice of biblical anagogy. After all, Calvin wrote this treatise, as he reminds us in his "Prefatory Address to . . . Francis," as the necessary introduction to the interpretation of Scripture, which remained the work to which he devoted most of his energy and effort. One notices in this summary the strong presence of the scriptural teaching of both forward and upward eschatology, with the accent on the reality of our union with Christ now — that is, the experience of the saving presence of God in our life experience, a gift that comes to us through faith through the Spirit. God has laid the foundation for the process: "It is God's plan (as I often reiterate) to lift us to himself by appropriate means."[93] In Calvin's formulation, this "means" points to the relationship of Israel's circumcision and the Church's baptism as an "anagogic" one.[94] All this suggests that we might rightly begin to think of Calvin, in line with the rich tradition we have been discussing up to this point, as an "anagogical theologian." But does it follow that this leaves us with a *Calvinus mysticus,* Calvin as a mystic in a manner not unlike Bernard of Clairvaux?

Anthony Lane, to whom we owe a thorough study of Calvin's use of Bernard, refuses to draw conclusions about any deeper affinity between the two in this matter.[95] Yet the Franciscan historian David Tamburello, in a

---

90. Edward A. Dowey Jr., *Knowledge of God in Calvin's Theology,* 3rd ed. (Grand Rapids: Eerdmans, 1994).

91. Dowey notes how knowing Christ, for Calvin, did not suggest a speculative knowledge, but rather pointed to an enjoyment of the living presence of Christ within us. See Dowey, *Knowledge of God,* 198-201.

92. See Dowey, *Knowledge of God,* 204.

93. *Institutes* 4.17.15 (Battles, 1372).

94. *Institutes* 4.16.3-4 (Battles, 1326-27).

95. Lane, *Calvin and Bernard.*

more recent study of Bernard and Calvin, is less hesitant.[96] Applying the typical ecumenical methodology *en vogue* today, he moves through comparison, compatibility, and convergence to a thesis: if Bernard was a mystic, he suggests, so was Calvin — though not, of course, of the usual kind of which we spoke earlier. Rather, he represents what Tamburello calls an "ordinary mysticism" of a practical, affective kind, one that the author proposes in another volume as something every Christian should consider in his or her own personal life.[97] Yet while the substance of this last point seems defensible, it seems doubtful to describe it by means of this particular label. For the word "mysticism" means too many things to too many people, even if nuanced by a qualifying adjective like "ordinary." Calvin does, however, in speaking of our union with Christ, align himself with Bernard — not least because of the Reformer's recognition of the high esteem his predecessor held for the sense of taste and its organ: "Faith," he says, "is the mouth by which we eat Christ."[98] What a wonderful statement! Would a Reformed theologian say this today? One can certainly hope so, for by so doing they would be aligning themselves with Calvin, certainly the most venerable authority among the esteemed *doctores ecclesiae,* or "doctors of the church," found in this tradition.

---

96. Dennis Tamburello, OFM, *Union with Christ: John Calvin and the Mysticism of St. Bernard* (Louisville: Westminster/John Knox Press, 1994).

97. Tamburello, *Ordinary Mysticism.*

98. *Commentary on the Gospel of John* 6.56, in *Calvin's Commentaries,* vol. 17 (Grand Rapids: Baker Book House, 1989), 267-68.

CHAPTER SIX

Sense or Nonsense? The Power of Biblical Language

Our discussion of the history of interpretation began by examining the predicament the interpreter faces with the text from the Song of Songs 6:12, a verse that makes no sense as it stands. A literal translation of the garbled words would read, "I did not know — my soul — he/she set me — chariots of my princely people." In this form, it is nonsense. But it is also part of Scripture, and therefore invites us to make an effort. We *have* to interpret such a text. We have seen how medieval exegetes, spurred on by the challenge such a passage presented, pursued various exegetical strategies. They looked to the attempted translations made earlier from the Hebrew into Greek and Latin, in the Septuagint and in the Vulgate respectively, and discovered that these translators had rendered this impossible verse as a reference to the *quadriga Aminadab*. And, with this, "Aminadab's chariot" offered itself as a compelling "brand" for the fourfold sense of Scripture.

Such an assignment of the image also placed it in the company of a host of further cross-connections: to other biblical chariots such as the *merkavah* of Ezekiel's vision with its four living creatures and four wheels, but also other biblical "fours" — the four rivers of Paradise, the four-legged table of Moses' tabernacle, the four-wheeled trolleys in Solomon's temple (1 Kings 7:27-37) — a whole web of related significations and meanings, its threads crisscrossing the Bible.[1] If nothing else, this "second life" of the problematic verse demonstrates that the predicament of having to interpret

1. See the wide-ranging discussion of this topic in Anna C. Esmeijer, *Divina Quaternitas: A Preliminary Study in the Method and Application of Visual Exegesis* (Assen: Van Gorcum, 1978), esp. 30-58.

requires that the interpreter use a great deal of imagination and demonstrate a ready willingness to go out on a limb. For medieval exegetes, as we have seen, there was no predicament; they did not feel that it was some extraneous burden to solve such problems. Difficulty is what they delighted in, sending them as it did into the complexity found in the Scriptures, in the wider literature of ancient and contemporary sources, and in their own experience of themselves and their world. The challenge of a verse like this one from the Song of Songs presented not simply a problem, but an opportunity for discovery as well. It invited them to dive into the inexhaustible ocean of biblical meaning, a journey, as Augustine noted, that mirrored their experience of themselves as well.

They faced the same question, of course, that we do: "How is one to do this?" Or, in the context of this study, "How did *they* do it?" which seems like a question about method. As we have suggested, however, it would be a mistake to write a history of biblical interpretation as an account of method. Method in biblical interpretation deals with the rules of handling language, and that means language in general as well as the specific languages of the biblical texts: its Hebrew and its Greek garb, its grammar and syntax, its conventions, and its peculiar mode of speaking. These rules, almost without exception, are not just applicable to the Bible, but were shared in the wider literary cultures of the day. As we noted earlier, classical education was geared toward mastering authoritative texts. In the school of the *grammatikos,* young people learned how to establish, copy, recite, and analyze the Greek and Latin classics according to vocabulary, forms, syntax, rhetorical structure, background, and content.

These rules were rational, codified, and thus understandable and teachable. Early Christians used them, too; in fact, they kept the system of classical schooling itself as the preferred propaedeutic for their Bible-centered education. Of course, interpreters faced a real problem with Hebrew, for which no teachable code existed. Until the sixteenth century when the first Hebrew grammar books were published in the West, the language had to be learned in a social context where it was read and spoken. This is the reason, as noted in an earlier chapter, why Jerome did not "know" Hebrew: he could read the Hebrew script, knew words, and inquired about their meaning and etymology. But he could not and therefore did not know how everything fit together since he never lived in a linguistic community that could have taught him such things. Indeed, it seems clear today that some of the Latin Hebraists of the twelfth century knew far more than he. Yet these obstacles to Hebrew learning had no great effect, since interpreters during late antiquity and throughout the Middle Ages elevated the importance of the Septuagint — the Greek translation of the Old Testament — because of their awed acceptance of the stories about its inspiration. In fact, this conviction was held so deeply in Christian circles that it even cast shadows over Jerome's efforts to redo the standard Latin version.

Throughout the Christian centuries the Greek and Latin forms of the Bible were taught on the basis of the same methods and rules that prevailed in classical times. When Origen began teaching, he taught as a *grammatikos,* offering public lectures on the Bible on the side. Augustine had taught classical rhetoric and included plenty of "rules" material in his textbook *On Christian Doctrine* to help with the specific difficulties of biblical language, adding a discussion of biblical rhetoric in Book 4 based on the model Cicero had provided. The sixteenth-century humanists, furthermore, worked at bringing about a revival of classical learning. Melanchthon, the "teacher of Germany," had his academic location in the arts faculty at Wittenberg, not in the faculty of theology. He taught Hebrew and Greek, classical authors and subjects, and wrote schoolbooks in many fields, including a Latin primer and a Greek grammar. The draft curriculum for theologians at the University of Basel was formulated in 1536 by Andreas Bodenstein von Karlstadt, Luther's former colleague at Wittenberg, who had found refuge in Basel. The sole subject of study in that faculty was the reading and interpretation of the Bible, aided by a full day each week of disputation exercises. Questions to be pursued included "What?" which examined a text's literal sense and argument of a passage; "How?" which explored its rhetorical structure and conventions; "To what end?" which considered its scope and goal; "Collation," which analyzed parallel texts; and, finally, "Conciliation," which sought to harmonize apparent contradictions.[2] These steps clearly reflect the methods of textual analysis in use by the classical *grammatikoi* and rhetoricians. Methods and rules of interpretation had not changed much.

Karlstadt added to this sequence a final topic, "Accommodation." As he explained its purpose, "professors shall apply their proven doctrine and the Scriptural witness to the contemporary world, support good habits, but also break Satan's edifice which he has constructed through false teaching or injustice."[3] Yet this was no longer a matter of "method." It was rather

---

2. See Rudolf Thommen, *Geschichte der Universität Basel, 1532-1632* (Basel: C. Dettloffs Buchhandlung, 1889), 18-20. The draft is printed in Appendix IV, 319-21.

3. Thommen, *Geschichte,* 320.

an instance of what we are calling "principles," that is, the parameter or "horizon" of understanding into which the interpretation finally seeks to lift the text. Classical scholarship, as we have seen, called this final step the *meros kritikon,* or "criticism," a strategy of interpretation to be taught by the philosopher. Methods or rules are thus to be distinguished from principles.

In our historical exploration thus far, we have suggested how such principles were far more important for the progress of biblical interpretation than methods. They reflect theological intentions, and while they all share a common core they vary widely among persons and across periods. Indeed, one might well write an entire history of theology using these principles of biblical interpretation as a guide.[4] Yet today one senses in many quarters a discomfort with the theological pluralism this requires us to face when approaching this history. In our exegesis, too, we too often prefer clear rules, those which can be taught and learned such that we can come to a rational assessment of the results. We dislike what we consider to be the "wild allegorization" of premodern interpretation, the supposedly uncontrolled and irrational *eisegesis* involved in the "spiritual" reading of the Bible. This is why modern attempts to write a history of biblical interpretation normally have focused on a history of methods, since these seemed to suggest a more rational and thus scientific way forward.

Our leading example of this was Frederick Farrar's *History of Interpretation,* published as the Bampton Lectures of 1885. Farrar shared in the excitement over the light of scientific progress, which in his time had finally reached the dark corners even of biblical scholarship. For him, only one valid method mattered, and that was a soberly pursued historical criticism which would treat the Bible like all other literature and thus "discover what the writers really meant and said" in the "immediate and primary sense of the sacred writings."[5] Judged from this perspective, all former methods — and particularly what he called "the dreary fiction of the fourfold senses"[6] —

4. This would be a somewhat more focused enterprise than Gerhard Ebeling's comprehensive vision of "Church History as the History of Biblical Interpretation," which he sketched in his Tübingen inaugural lecture in 1947; see *The Word of God and Tradition: Historical Studies Interpreting the Divisions of Christianity,* trans. S. H. Hooke (Philadelphia: Fortress Press, 1968). I have discussed the implications of Ebeling's thesis in my own 1977 inaugural lecture at Princeton Theological Seminary. See "Church History and the Bible," in *Biblical Hermeneutics in Historical Perspective: Studies in Honor of Karlfried Froehlich on His Sixtieth Birthday,* ed. Mark S. Burrows and Paul Rorem (Grand Rapids: Eerdmans, 1991), 1-15.

5. Farrar, *History of Interpretation* (1886; Grand Rapids: Baker Book House, 1961), i, 29.

6. Farrar, *History of Interpretation,* 327.

appeared to be misguided, erroneous, and even perilous. In fact, the entire history of biblical interpretation, in Farrar's judgment, was little more than a systematization of the "art of *mis*interpretation," "augmented at each stage by the superaddition of fresh theories no less mistaken."[7] Unfortunately, Farrar did not notice that he was consistently confusing methods and principles. And if "criticism," the old *meros kritikon,* established the principles rather than the methods of interpretation, then what Farrar called his "method" was really a "principle." And, in this sense, it was driven by an ideology which wanted to move the biblical text into the parameter of a purely human history, like Kant's horizon of "religion within the boundaries of pure reason." Instead of a dynamics of ascent, this principle advocated a dynamics of descent, the descent into the limited world of human motivations, projections, and values — those values, for Farrar, that were most properly Protestant and the only ones appropriate in modern times.

The consequences of this fatally reduced perspective appear with an almost embarrassing clarity in Farrar's evaluation of the Antiochene exegetes of the fourth and fifth centuries. "They were the Reformers, the Protestants, the Puritans of the Ancient Church," he suggested, an island of reasonableness in a morass of perversion.[8] As he went on to say, "Their system of biblical interpretation approached more nearly than any other to that which is now adopted by the Reformed churches throughout the world" and "[t]he superiority of the Antiochene over the Alexandrian method may be readily seen by comparing the sober, moral, practical manner in which Chrysostom treats [this subject]."[9] For Farrar, however, there could be no appreciation of Antiochene spirituality and no mention of the Antiochene *theoria,* which seem to be evoking such interest today.

Let us return here to David Steinmetz's provocative thesis against this reductionism, cited already in the opening chapter: "The medieval theory of levels of meaning in the biblical text, with all its admitted defects, flourished because it is true, while the modern theory of a single meaning, with all its demonstrable virtues, is false."[10] Steinmetz's primary argument is that the biblical evidence itself forces upon the Church where the Scriptures are read something like a distinction between "letter" and "spirit," and thus suggests a dynamics of ascent: here we find metaphor and figure, a relation

---

7. Farrar, *History of Interpretation,* 9, 19.
8. Farrar, *History of Interpretation,* 216.
9. Farrar, *History of Interpretation,* 210, 212.
10. See above, p. 11, note 20.

between Israel and the Church, and the need to find some meaning in apparently unedifying materials. In terms of the history of exegesis, Steinmetz makes the case for recognizing multiple principles at work, even in the use of the fourfold sense; after all, interpreters were never interested solely in the biblical text, but rather in the text as enriched by its own later history. At stake is the question of a text's later "context," the "second life" it experienced in synagogue and church, an illustration of the ongoing testimony Hans-Georg Gadamer called its *"wirkungsgeschichtliches Bewußtsein,"* or its "historically effected consciousness."[11]

The great advantage of the fourfold sense was its flexibility in serving the dynamics of ascent. With its help, medieval exegetes could take seriously and pursue more than one agenda at the same time, accommodating different accents and emphases. For them, as Gregory the Great said, "[Scripture is] like a certain river, if I may describe it like this, one that is smooth and deep, in which the lamb walks and the elephant swims."[12] Or, consider the interpretation given by a fourteenth-century Dominican to the story of David slaying Goliath:

> Intended historically [this] is understood of the killing of Goliath by his own sword by the boy David. Allegorically, it signifies Christ conquering the devil with the same cross which the latter had prepared for him. Tropologically, it denotes the war of the just against the devil tempting the flesh; for when the flesh is curbed and kept in check, the [devil's] head is cut off, when his first attacks are rendered defeated and fruitless. And anagogically, the victory of Christ on the day of judgment is implied, when death the final enemy is finally destroyed.[13]

Henri de Lubac, unrivaled master of the medieval material and ardent defender of the fourfold sense, included this citation in the second volume of his indispensable four-volume study. He found in the traditional system an amazing coherence and complex interplay of factors which reminded him of the "wheel within the wheel" of Ezekiel's vision.[14] *Allegoria* is the truth of

11. See Gadamer, *Truth and Method,* trans. Joel Weinsheimer and Donald Marshall (London: Continuum, 1989), 172-382; esp. 298ff.

12. *The Letters of Gregory the Great,* trans. John R. C. Martyn, Medieval Sources in Translation 40 (Toronto: Pontifical Institute of Medieval Studies, 2004), 384.

13. J. M. de Turre, OP, as cited in Henri de Lubac, *Medieval Exegesis: The Four Senses of Scripture,* vol. 2 (Grand Rapids: Eerdmans, 2000), 197-98.

14. de Lubac, *Medieval Exegesis,* vol. 2, 204-06.

historia, but in order to fill this role fully, it needs unfolding in two directions: namely, inward as well as outward. There is a clear temporal sequence at work here: history precedes mystery, figure precedes truth, deeds done come before deeds to be done, and spiritual life now before life eternal. A logical sequence is also operative: the object of allegory "recapitulates" the object of history in the person of Christ, who signifies himself in the dimensions of community, self, and final destination.

De Lubac lifts up one point in particular: the fourfold sense exhibits what he describes with a vivid image as an "incurable character of incompleteness."[15] There is always motion between the senses, ever new depth in each. Like manna, this interpretation adapts itself to the reader's insight and capacity. As Gregory the Great had put it, "Holy Scriptures grow with the one who reads them."[16] And Rabanus Maurus: "To the extent that a person advances on high, to that extent the sacred speeches speak of higher things."[17] In other words, this approach affirms that the world of the Bible was not created once for all; rather, the Spirit creates it afresh each day by opening the Scriptures to the reader's understanding. By such a means, *"translatus est Christus ad Ecclesiam"*: "Christ is brought over into the church."[18] As the etymology of the verb suggests, this movement implies a "bringing over" of meaning from "there" to "here," an emphasis on the consistency between the two Testaments and the coherence these effect as both an intensification and an expansion of meaning *within the interpreter.* For de Lubac, this meant that allegory, hardly the "wax nose" method Luther berated, brought forward what he considered the "truth" of *historia.*

We may not share de Lubac's enthusiasm as it found expression some fifty years ago, nor should this study be construed as a revival of the fourfold sense as an exegetical tool for today. Even in his day, de Lubac admitted that the dynamics of this tradition were easily lost on those who just read the handbooks. We have suggested that the very organization of this scheme for teaching purposes was problematic, for one can teach methods, but not the ascent. Under the principle of a dynamic "uplifting," however, the method of the fourfold sense displayed an amazing flexibility, as we have seen, above all in its resistance to becoming a rigid or closed system. We noticed this resistance time and again at the transition from one sense

---

15. de Lubac, *Medieval Exegesis,* vol. 2, 204.

16. *Homiliarum in Ezechielem prophetam,* lib. 1, hom. 7.8, Patrologia Latina 76, ed. J.-P. Migne, 843D: "Divina eloquia cum legente crescunt" (on Ezek. 1:19).

17. de Lubac, *Medieval Exegesis,* vol. 2, 419, note 73.

18. de Lubac, *Medieval Exegesis,* vol. 2, 418, note 46.

to another: these boundaries were fluid, the distinctions not clear-cut, and the dividing lines at best fuzzy.

Indeed, the literal and allegorical senses seem to be opposites by nature, a point reinforced by their derivation from the Pauline antithesis of letter and spirit. But the situation could be different within the framework of the fourfold sense. Hugh of St. Victor stated that two things are sought in Scripture: first, the knowledge of truth, and second, the form of virtue. The first is found through history and allegory together, the second through the moral sense. We spoke in the third chapter about Hugh's expansion of the scope of allegory. Following the Augustinian notion of God's two books, Hugh developed a Christocentric vision of the whole cosmos — from the book of nature and the book of history — as the content of his allegorization.[19] For him, this did not in the least degrade the literal sense. On the contrary, Hugh reserved his sharpest rebuke for those who said, "[w]e do not care for the letter; we teach allegory. *If the letter is taken away, however, what is Scripture?*"[20] Christian instruction, or what we today might call "formation," needs both — or rather, such *doctrina* or teaching is both. Hugh called his own doctrinal *summa, De sacramentis christianae fidei*, the "second part of sacred rhetoric," the first being the full assimilation by the student of the biblical text and history in its literal form.

Another development strengthened this close bond between the literal and allegorical senses of the Bible. Recall that Origen and the patristic tradition had included all metaphorical language in the "spiritual" sense in order to demonstrate the need for a hermeneutics of ascent. In a similar fashion, and a more precise grasp of the role of *littera* and *historia* in the interpretive enterprise, Thomas Aquinas later taught that metaphor is part of the convention of human language and must therefore be reckoned as part of the literal sense — which he equated with the author's intention.

19. Augustine already paired the "two books" with the senses of hearing and seeing: "Liber tibi sit pagina divina, ut haec audias; liber tibi sit orbis terrarum, ut haec videas." See *Enarrationes in Psalmos* 45.7, Patrologia Latina 36, ed. J.-P. Migne, 518D.

20. *De scripturis et scriptoribus sacris*, c. 1: "Non curamus de littera sed allegoriam docemus . . . Si enim littera tollitur, Scriptura quid est?" Patrologia Latina 175, ed. J.-P. Migne, 13A-B; see Hartmut Freytag, "Quae sunt per allegoriam dicta: Das theologische Verständnis der Allegorie in der frühchristlichen und mittelalterlichen Exegese von Gal. 4,21-31," in *Verbum et Signum. Festschrift für Friedrich Ohly*, vol. 1, *Beiträge zur mediävistischen Bedeutungsforschung* (München: W. Fink, 1975), 237, note 50. See also Freytag, *Die Theorie der allegorischen Schriftdeutung und die Allegorie in deutschen Texten besonders des 11. und 12. Jahrhunderts* (Bern: Franke, 1982).

This decision allowed for a considerable expansion of literal interpretation, including in its scope the domain of allegory when this was "intended" by the author — or "rhetorical" allegory. Luther stands in line with this development. While he rejected the quadriga emphatically and argued for what he considered to be the obvious, natural, and literal or grammatical sense of the Bible, he insisted early and late that this one sense had to carry the entire load of the dynamics of ascent. He never relinquished this conviction, or questioned its practice. One part of his solution involved the way he redefined what "literal" meant. Thus, in the second Psalms commentary of 1519, he cautioned: "A large part of the understanding is located in figurative language, especially in the Holy Scriptures which have their own idiomatic expressions; ignorance of these produces thick fog, sometimes in bright daylight!"[21] Luther's contention that his Christological interpretation of the Psalms was "literal" suggests this very expansion, aligning his approach with a critical development we have noted in Aquinas's thought.

An even more striking case of this is found in his 1539 commentary on the Song of Songs. Luther accepted the tradition that Solomon was the text's author, but in the preface he revealed that a courtly epic, the *Theuerdank* authored by the Emperor Maximilian, had suggested to him the key to the metaphorical language of the Song: secular rulers sometimes use the fiction of amorous poetry to express their view of important matters concerning their realm and rule. Thus, in the person of the bride, Solomon honors God with his loving praises, meaning by this that "he commends his own government to us and composes a kind of encomium in praise of the peace and present state of his kingdom, giving thanks to God for that highest blessing, external peace."[22] Luther's idea did not catch on, though he was convinced he had discovered the true literal sense of this biblical poem.

As we have seen, the three spiritual senses as these were developed by medieval interpreters subdivided what the earlier tradition had simply called the "spiritual" or "mystical" sense. It cannot come as a surprise that the boundaries between them were also fuzzy and fluid. Allegory and tropology were originally interchangeable, and when the distinction was made, tropology could precede allegory — at least until Gregory fixed the sequence by means of clear logic: "We do not reach faith via the virtues; we advance to the virtues through faith."[23] In the rational climate of the me-

---

21. On Psalm 3:4; D. Martin Luthers Werke, Weimarer Ausgabe 5, 84: 29-31.
22. See Luther's Works 15, 195.
23. "Non enim per virtutes venitur ad fidem, sed per fidem pertingitur ad virtutes." Greg-

dieval schools, biblical allegory was restricted more and more to doctrinal meaning. As systematic academic "theology," it lost its appeal for a new generation of pastors who used it primarily as a tool for their tropology — a means, that is, to get at what they considered to be the all-important moralizing of biblical texts.

Even today, this is still the situation that prevails among us. We avoid any use of allegory in exegesis, but we are entirely comfortable with employing it in sermons as a means of ethical exhortation. That is, Christian theology in its contemporary approach to *doctrina,* or in its "teaching" function, tends to avoid expressing ultimate propositional truth, but rather aims at shaping and encouraging the Christian life. As Ellen Charry explores this question, she suggests that such "doctrine" focuses on the formation of character, and this occurs as a process of personal transformation.[24] She points to how this builds a needed bridge between systematic and pastoral theology. On the basis of the present study, however, we would go further to suggest that this is also an attempt to restore the dynamic of ascent between the allegorical and the tropological senses of Scripture. Given the "departmentalized" situation of academic theology, both these senses have the tendency to swallow the other, in the thirteenth century as much as in our own.

We also noted earlier in this study an additional blurring of the lines between allegory and tropology in the Middle Ages. As the attribute of "sweetness" wandered from allegory to tropology in the climate of the newly dominant monastic spirituality of the twelfth century, exemplified by Bernard of Clairvaux, the interiorizing tendency of "mystical tropology" led to an experience of the power of the text in the affective realm of contemplation. Drawing on a number of sermons by Godfrey, abbot of Admont in Styria, whom he pictures as a twelfth-century spiritual brother to Bernard of Clairvaux, de Lubac describes how this happens: The person who experiences the mysterious visit of God at the height of contemplation "rests, as did the Apostle John at the supper, upon the chest of Jesus, which is no other than Sacred Scripture. There, in this Heart, life gushes forth; there resides the power of the mysteries; there the life-giving secrets that escape those who are merely doctors are concealed. . . . At such a degree of

---

ory the Great, *Homiliarum in Ezechielem prophetam,* lib. 2, hom. 7.9, Patrologia Latina 76, ed. J.-P. Migne, 1018A.

24. See Ellen Charry, "The Moral Function of Doctrine," *Theology Today* 49 (1992): 31-45. See also Charry's full-length treatment of this theme: *By the Renewing of Your Minds: The Pastoral Function of Christian Doctrine* (New York: Oxford University Press, 1999).

interiority, allegory is no longer distinct from tropology; mystery and morality are united in a single mystic vision full of sweetness."[25]

Bernard also showed that no real boundaries existed between "mystical tropology" and anagogy, though his Cistercian confrere Gilbert of Hoyland, who tried to complete the unfinished series of Bernard's sermons on the Song of Songs, could draw a sharp dividing line: "I may perhaps seem foolhardy in trying to explain mysteries not experienced, even concerning the little bed of the bride [3:1], for perhaps she built it too delicately and too secretly beyond the reach of our conjectures. Therefore, let us descend from the mysteries to the morals."[26] But he hardly meant it. Like Bernard, he was very much committed to the openness of the exegetical process beyond morality and to the superiority of contemplation as his master had established it.

The point of all the fuzziness of boundaries and transitions between the senses, of course, is that the scheme was not meant to be tight, but rather serve as a teachable method. At bottom, it simply reflected the underlying assumption of interpretation as a fluid and dynamic movement — and not just forward but upward, from letter to spirit, from milk to solid food, from water into wine. Mauritius of St. Victor spelled this out in a memorable image:

> Christ is the grain from which the flour of Scripture is milled, the bread of heaven . . . The two millstones between which the grinding takes place are the letter and the spirit. The letter is the stone below which does not move, coarse, vile, and lowly as it is. The spirit is the stone above; its motion, enabled by the water of natural intelligence, releases the multiple senses, allegory, tropology, and anagogy. . . .[27]

Following patristic precedent, the new generation of preaching masters, like Master Mauritius, saw the freedom of the spirit as a special characteristic of tropology: "History is done and does not have the capacity to expand, but tropology is free."[28] Yet they did not see or apply this freedom

---

25. de Lubac, *Medieval Exegesis,* vol. 2, 175.

26. Gilbert of Hoyland, Sermon 2.8, in *Sermons on the Song of Songs,* trans. Lawrence Braceland, Cistercian Fathers Series 14 (Kalamazoo, MI: Cistercian Publications, 1978), 62-63.

27. See his *Sermo 6 De sancto Augustino,* 97-106, Corpus Christianorum Continuatio Mediaevalis 30, ed. Jean Châtillon (Turnhout: Brepols, 1975), 228-29.

28. "Historia stricta est et evagandi non habet facultatem. Tropologia libera est." Jerome, *Commentary on Habakkuk* 1.7-11, Patrologia Latina 25, ed. J.-P. Migne, 1281D. De Lubac,

as license to do whatever they wanted; it only functioned properly when the inferior stone — the "literal sense" — was firmly in place. The spiritual interpretation must always be based on the properties of the words used and the things signified.

Let us recall here how Origen, with all his anagogical ingenuity, took interest in every word and phrase, every variant and grammatical detail, and how Bernard's imagination seemed unlimited in his determination not to neglect a single iota of the text — for even the smallest crumbs must be gathered, chewed, digested, remembered. Yet despite a difference in style, Calvin's approach to interpreting Scripture as an "anagogical theologian" continued this focus, not by emphasizing the analytical method of such an exegetical approach but rather by pointing to the importance of the experience of "union" with Christ in faith as a gift of the Holy Spirit.[29] This faith, as Calvin understood it, was inextricably tied to Scripture, which for this very reason must be taken seriously as a whole — and, following this tradition, this meant in every detail and in the rhetoric of every phrase. And for all these authors, as we have seen, the sweetness of anagogy always begins with the "touch" of the literal sense, which remains the foundation that undergirds the "building" of this interpretive approach.

The Bible translator William Tyndale included in one of his polemical tracts a section devoted to exploring the "Fourfold Sense of Scripture."[30] He begins with the merciless destruction of the quadriga, arguing that allegory serves only the pope's cause by making tradition the key to all biblical meaning. Following from this, he insists, tropology and anagogy are but "Roman inventions" and unnecessary as specific forms of allegory — namely, allegory of manners and allegory of hope. Allegory itself — and he intends here what we have earlier discussed as rhetorical allegory — is "strange speaking or borrowed speech . . . as when we say of a wanton child: this sheep has maggots in his tail; he must be anointed with birch salve, which speech I borrow of the shepherds." There is one sense of the Bible only, Tyndale insists, and that is the literal; but, like all human language, this sense makes constant use of allegories, of proverbs and similitudes, that is, of metaphorical language — and this alone is the sense we ought to hold

---

Medieval Exegesis: The Four Senses of Scripture, vol. 1 (Grand Rapids: Eerdmans, 1999), 16, alludes to this phrase but identifies the source incorrectly (280, notes 11 and 12).

29. See also William Bouwsma, *John Calvin: A Sixteenth-Century Portrait* (New York: Oxford University Press, 1988), 318.

30. See his *The Obedience of a Christian Man,* 1528, ed. David Daniell (London: Penguin, 2000), 156-80.

onto: "God is a Spirit, and all his words are spiritual. His literal sense is spiritual, and all his words are spiritual . . . if thou have eyes of God to see the right meaning of the text and whereunto the Scripture pertaineth and the final end and cause thereof."[31]

Tyndale is pointing here to what we would today call the hermeneutical "circle" of biblical interpretation. But he also clearly reckons with a "final end and cause" of the Bible; in the last analysis, the Bible is not an end in itself, the object of a dispassionate approach, but rather a means to an end. If the end or goal and thus the principle of its interpretation is the common theme underlying its various expressions — that is, as life in the Spirit, life in the presence of God, union with God or Christ — then one question becomes inevitable: is the Bible really necessary for this? Could we not reach this goal by some other road? And thus, at the deepest level: why bother with the Bible at all? Of course, this question is not new. At the very beginning of his Matthew Commentary, Chrysostom wrote,

> It would indeed be right for us not to require the aid of the written word but to exhibit a life so pure that the grace of the Spirit would stand there instead of books for the instruction of our souls, and as the books are written with ink, so our hearts would be written on by the Spirit. But since we have forsaken this grace, let us at least embark on the second best course.[32]

And, in the West, as we earlier observed, Augustine embraced a strikingly similar view: "Thus, a person supported by faith, hope, and charity, with an unshaken hold upon them, does not need the Scriptures except for the instruction of others."[33] Of course, he is here thinking of the desert saints, who, as he put it, "live by these three virtues in solitude without books." But even Martin Luther, with all his love for Scripture, was under no illusion about the Bible's secondary character: "That one had to write books is already a great deterioration and a limitation of the spirit dictated by necessity — it is not the way of the New Testament."[34]

Yes, the Bible is not absolutely needed. It is not totally indispensable.

---

31. Tyndale, *Obedience,* 162.

32. *First Homily on the Gospel of Saint Matthew,* in Nicene and Post-Nicene Fathers (First Series) 10 (Grand Rapids: Eerdmans, 1986), 1.

33. Augustine, *De doctrina christiana* 1.39.43; see *On Christian Doctrine,* trans. D. W. Robertson Jr. (Indianapolis: Bobbs-Merrill, 1958), 32.

34. *Weihnachtspostille 1522,* D. Martin Luthers Werke, Weimarer Ausgabe 10.1.627, 1-3.

There *are* other ways to the goal. Today this argument is sometimes heard to a more ominous tune. For many good people, the Bible has become an embarrassment. Rather than being helpful for the spiritual journey, they feel that it gets in the way of its own supposed message and goal. They wonder what we are to make of the patriarchal language of the Bible, which many find offensive to the ear and out of touch with current cultural sensitivities. They worry, too, about its content. Modern scholarship has exposed the extent of bias and prejudice that it harbors: thus, some have contended that the Bible is anti-Semitic, anti-democratic, anti-women, and anti-gays and lesbians. By our standards, it is often plainly wrong — not only in matters of fact, but in questions of faith and ethics as well. It condones war and violence, child abuse, exploitation of the environment. There are serious people among us — not only outside the churches but inside as well — who find it too much of a burden to carry on with the Bible. They are ready to abandon the places where the authority of the Bible still holds sway — and leave the church.[35]

Indeed, the authority of the Bible has been under a cloud for a long time, ever since the Enlightenment, and has shared in the general trend of the erosion of authority in modern society.[36] The Latin noun *auctoritas*, "authority," is derived from the designation of a person, an *auctor*, or "author." In legal parlance, it referred to the moral influence an ancestor had on later generations. Thus, it is a relational term. The Catholic theologian Avery Cardinal Dulles defines authority as "that which (or the person whom) one has reason to trust."[37] With the mention of "reason" we find ourselves in the world shaped by the Enlightenment. The important point, however, is that authority has to do with trust and therefore with power. When trust is extended, power is bestowed. Something or someone is allowed to impact, to influence, or even govern my life. This is why authority is eyed with so much suspicion in an age of human self-determination and autonomy. And

---

35. These concerns are persuasively presented by Terence E. Fretheim in a volume containing the texts and discussions of the Hein-Fry Lectures for 1995; see Terence E. Fretheim and Karlfried Froehlich, *The Bible as Word of God in a Postmodern Age* (Minneapolis: Fortress Press, 1998). My own portion of the lectures, 3-77 and 127-32, develops in more detail the thoughts expressed on the following pages here.

36. See Jeffrey Stout, *The Flight from Authority: Religion, Morality, and the Quest for Autonomy* (Notre Dame, IN: University of Notre Dame Press, 1981).

37. Avery Dulles, "The Authority of Scripture: A Catholic Perspective," in *Scripture in the Jewish and Christian Traditions: Authority, Interpretation, Relevance*, ed. Frederick E. Greenspahn (Nashville: Abingdon Press, 1982), 14.

yet authority is indispensable for human existence. If authority means trust, we live by it. From earliest childhood on, we must trust those who are close to us simply in order to survive, to develop, to live. There is certainly something like natural parental authority.

Well, if not the Bible, then what? What other authority can be invoked as the guide on the road to an authentic life? For the Christian, an authentic life is one lived out in the Spirit of God and of Christ. Our culture as a whole has turned to *experience*. Experience as the result of scientific experimentation guarantees for us the objectivity of our view of the world; it defends the facts, so the argument goes, against conceit and illusion. Personal experience, on the other hand, guarantees the subjectivity of individual freedom, *my* right to choices and self-determination against imposed demands and external compulsion. Even in the orbit of traditional Christian theology, the emphasis on experience looks promising. We have encountered it in this study time and again, especially in our discussion of the anagogical sense. The Cistercian tradition insisted on supplementing the immediate meaning derived from reading the Bible by "touching and fingering it, so to speak, with the hand of experience," or, as Bernard put it, by learning how to read *in libro experientiae,* "in the book of experience."[38] Christianity itself began with the experience of the life, death, and resurrection of Jesus of Nazareth, first of all among those who knew him and later among those who heard or read about him. Scriptures — and in the earliest generation of disciples this meant the Hebrew Scriptures and their interpretation — were only the means to make sense of this experience.

It is no secret that in recent feminist theology and other expressions of liberation theology experience plays a crucial role as an authorizing power. Representatives of a radical wing have given up on both the Bible and the church, many taking their cue from Mary Daly and others who have advocated organizing sympathizers into marginal communities with their own life of faith and new priests and ministers to guide them. But even among those who are willing to work from within the Women-Church Convergence or other networks or associations of feminist women, authority is shifting away from "officers" and rather to experience, women's experience. Letty Russell speaks of a new "partnership" of theological sources shared by Scripture, tradition, historical criticism, and experience, but it is the fourth

---

38. "Hodie legimus in libro experientiae," *Bernard of Clairvaux: On the Song of Songs* 3.1, trans. Kilian Walsh and Irene M. Edmonds, Cistercian Fathers Series 4 (Kalamazoo, MI: Cistercian Publications, 1971), 16.

element of this "quadrilateral" — experience as the experience of oppressed women — that she gives priority.[39] The same holds for Elisabeth Schüssler-Fiorenza, whose scholarly work concentrates on biblical and early Christian sources; she also contends that the locus of revelation and grace is neither the Bible nor the tradition of the patriarchal church, but rather "the experience of women . . . struggling for liberation from patriarchy."[40] Rosemary Ruether has been concerned with the need for liturgical expressions of faith within women-church and for a new canon. She sees her *Womenguides,* with its collection of women's lore from many sources, as "a handbook from which a new canon might emerge."[41] As she goes on to say, "human experience is both the starting point and the ending point of the circle of interpretation," including the interpretation of the "prophetic-messianic tradition of the Bible," which establishes the understanding of the faith. Faith obviously must involve experience as an authorizing power. In the present situation, women's experience must have a right to assert itself powerfully in women's faith. So why should experience not be enough as the basis of an authentic faith?

The answer, frankly, must be that experience alone is not enough. There is a fundamental difficulty with the raw material of experience. Like all else in Russell's *quadrivium,* experience — whether women's experience or any other — suffers unavoidably from ambiguity. It always encompasses multiple possibilities. Experience can lead in many directions. And, importantly, the deeper it reaches the more ambiguous it becomes. Experience needs to be defined, given perimeters, and this form-giving event occurs in language. "Out of the abundance of the heart, the mouth speaks" (Matt. 12:34). In the light of this simple truth it should not surprise us to realize that all experiential theologians are rather loquacious — they have much to

39. See her essay "Authority and the Challenge of Feminist Interpretation," in *The Feminist Interpretation of the Bible,* ed. Letty M. Russell (Philadelphia: Westminster Press, 1985), 136-46. The "quadrilateral" is a variation of what Methodist ecumenist Albert Outler proposed as the fourfold source of authority for the Christian life: viz., Scripture, tradition, reason, and experience; Russell explored these themes in her 1986 Warfield Lectures at Princeton Theological Seminary, subsequently published as *Household of Freedom: Authority in Feminist Theology* (Philadelphia: Westminster Press, 1987).

40. Elisabeth Schüssler-Fiorenza, "The Will to Choose or Reject: Continuing Our Critical Work," in *The Feminist Interpretation of the Bible,* ed. Russell, 128.

41. Rosemary R. Ruether, "Feminist Interpretation: A Method of Correlation," in *The Feminist Interpretation of the Bible,* ed. Russell, 111. See also her *Womenguides: Readings Toward a Feminist Theology* (Boston: Beacon Press, 1985), and *Women-Church: Theology and Practice of Feminist Liturgical Communities* (San Francisco: Harper & Row, 1985).

say. Among this group, the mystics are among the most productive writers of the Christian tradition. Augustine "spoke" his experiences into being in his effusive *Confessions*. And, since he had the training of a rhetorician, he did so by choosing his language carefully — and he shaped this treatise by using the language of prayer, the "speech" of intimate conversation with the God to whose providence he attributed every one of his several "conversions."

Paul's personal account of his conversion on the road to Damascus sheds light once more on this dynamic. It is buried in a dependent clause in a larger argument so that it is easily overlooked. "But when the one who had set me apart from my mother's womb and had called me through his grace, *was pleased to reveal his Son in me* . . ." (Gal. 1:15-16). Paul's self-understanding as a Christian, his life's commitment, and his sense of mission are all expressed in these few words describing an experience. What exactly did he experience? We do not learn what Paul felt, what he saw or heard. The later accounts in Acts, chapters 9, 22, and 26, supply some details: a vision of light and a voice from heaven. The Apostle himself is less dramatic: "God revealed his Son in me." The phrase implies that he knew the person he was talking about. He knew him as the enemy of God, the false messiah who had met his just deserts and whose followers had to be destroyed. Now he began to know him differently, as the Son of God — a different definition of the same person. There is still much debate among exegetes about the background of the term "Son of God." But "God's Son" is radically different from "enemy." Paul's experience of a radical change of perception finds expression in a simple but precise linguistic turn. This is the point: Experience needs definition, and therefore it is aimed at language. It is human language that gives experience the form through which it acquires its reality. Language is our access to reality.

"Real" faith needs language, and this language, whatever its specific shape, has a clear priority in the sequence of existence. Language is already there prior to experience. Paul borrows the language of his contemporary religious environment when he calls Jesus "Son of God." Faith needs language in order to be, and it needs experience to move from the mere sound of words to their truth. Christian faith needs its specific language: we know that there is something like a Christian "mother tongue" for our faith, terms and phrases we learn from our mothers and fathers in the faith. But we need to remember that all its forms go back to the matrix from which they grew: this mother soil is Scripture.

In the Church, we want to say that it is God who speaks in Scripture, and that the Bible is not "just literature" like any other book. But God *speaks*. Even an inspired Bible does not solve the problems we as readers have in making sense of its content. On the contrary, this task opens up the real problem — which is language itself. God *speaks*. When we say this we mean that God uses language, a human phenomenon, and thereby puts the deity at the mercy of our language's limitations. We said earlier that experience is ambiguous and therefore aims at language, but language is not unambiguous either. It can reveal and it can hide; it can speak the truth and pronounce a lie; it can heal and it can hurt. As a human phenomenon, language is always imperfect, groping, and vulnerable; it can be misunderstood, misused, and manipulated. It participates in the openness of all human speech which must be filled with specific meaning through specific human experience. As a record of past experience with God, the Bible will never replace the need for personal faith experience today. But the Bible — its stories, its prayers, visions, admonitions, and words — can help us in our personal experience find our own language. It can interpret *us*.

Understood in this way, we come to know biblical language not as coming directly from heaven as a block of truth from which anyone is free to quarry bits and pieces for his or her own agenda. It comes to us rather as an invitation to our faith — nothing more than this, but surely also nothing less. The language of the Bible in its many expressions is as tentative, fragile, and experimental as any human speech to which we listen every day. It is sitting there, gently extending an invitation to our experience and to our faith, as if it is beckoning us, "Come in! Settle down! Make yourself at home!" One of the convenient things about invitations is that they can be turned down — which we do when we find that they interfere with what we think are more important preoccupations. But in exploring this metaphor, one thing is clear: if we accept *this* invitation, we are in for a long party, not just for some brief happening — in fact, a life-long exercise. The exchange between experienced faith and the Bible can become a rhythmic movement, a breathing-in and a breathing-out. It happens within the same house, and when faith goes out to meet the challenges of the day, it can come home from its necessary excursions, and return to the language of the Bible.

In a thoughtful and provocative article published in 1994, Gerhard Ebeling shows how deeply this precise rhythm is embedded in Luther's theology.[42] For Luther, the power of the Word of God in Scripture manifests

---

42. See Gerhard Ebeling, "Hermeneutik zwischen der Macht des Gotteswortes und

itself in a paradoxical movement characterized by several hermeneutical shifts or reversals. The first has to do with the reader's laborious and initially frustrating wrestling with a difficult text, a struggle that sometimes ends on the opposite note — namely, in the joyful and liberating experience of being overpowered and enlivened by the text. "Note that the power of Scripture is of this kind: Scripture is not being conformed to the one who studies Scripture but transforms into itself and its powers the one who loves it."[43] The second reversal occurs within the Scriptures themselves when they speak to us as the Word of God. It is a reversal in the function of this Word being pondered and experienced. God's Word shifts from being law to being gospel, from killing to making alive, in a single motion; and only through the old self dying can the new self be raised. As Luther suggests, the task of rightly dividing the law and the gospel "makes" the theologian. But this is not a matter of distributing law and gospel by texts, such that today's lesson is law but next Sunday's will be gospel. Nor is it a matter of figuring out the proper dosage of each required for counseling or pastoral work. Sensitivity certainly is needed in all branches of pastoral care, but it is not enough if it is sensitivity to the human situation into which the Word is spoken; it must be in equal measure sensitivity to the awesome power of the Word itself, which not only sounds forth but performs. The third reversal occurs in the turn from the written to the oral word, from Scripture to proclamation, the "living voice of the gospel." Ebeling points out that for Luther "there is an essential affinity between Scripture and the Law": the written page means distance, and breathes permanence, a stern "once-for-all-ness." The gospel, on the other hand, is not in its essence a written phenomenon; it is "good news, to be published not with the pen, but with the mouth," to be poured into public hearing with a living voice.

But who is willing and able to hear this news, through and beyond these three "reversals," and thus to receive it as "good news"? We seem to be living in an age of unprecedented devaluation of the word, written as well as oral. The reason for this, however, seems to have less to do with a distrust of words as a consequence of their inflation and cheapening in the many voices that seem to be constantly assailing us. We have learned to use, manipulate, and "read" words, and have figured out ways to decide when they are serious or safe, alarming or affirming. We are aware of their

---

seiner Entmachtung in der Moderne," in *Theologie in den Gegensätzen des Lebens,* Wort und Glaube 4 (Tübingen: Mohr Siebeck, 1994), 209-25.

43. *First Psalms Commentary 1513-16,* on Psalm 68; Luther's Works 10, 332.

limitations and their usefulness. Methods of interpretation have brought home to us the ambiguity of all words, but we have grown accustomed to living with a pluralism of approaches, voices, and critiques. Rather, the devaluation of the word stems from the distrust of the *auctores,* the *authors* of words, the human minds behind them: as the old saying has it, *omnis homo mendax* — "all humans are liars." To be sure, this attack on the reliability of human *auctoritas* or "authority" is a biblical pronouncement, one made by the Psalmist (116:11). It is also, however, a general truth that seems to impose itself more powerfully today than at any previous point in time. We have lost faith in humanity.

How does this mood change affect our Bible? In a way, the "Good Book" is caught in the middle. Insofar as the Bible is literature, a collection of books by human authors, the loss of faith in humanity must affect it; if we treat the Bible just as part of our human world, we have every reason to begin with a "hermeneutics of suspicion" — it will be amply vindicated. One can easily understand the reaction of women and other readers who find the book hopelessly patriarchal, set it aside with disappointment, and concentrate on building their spiritual home elsewhere. The church of Christ is certainly not the "church of man." But it is not exclusively Women-Church or the church of any other "special-experience" group either, as important as the particularity of experience as well as particular concerns and gifts are. The church is being gathered out of a wealth of diverse human experiences as an inclusive, pluralistic group of people, men and women of all races and nations — in short, as the kind of gathering which it is worth striving for. It is a church that embodies or at least lives toward the Pauline image of being "in Christ," in which "there is no longer Jew nor Greek, slave nor free, male nor female, for all . . . are one in Christ" (Gal. 3:28).

Such a church is a church that, while realizing the limitations of the language of the Bible, can reckon with an *auctor* of Scripture who does not have to be mistrusted like another human, but can be supremely trusted. Or can he, really? A growing number of contemporaries in our world seem prepared to give up on God as well. God-talk for many does not make sense anymore. For them, God is no longer an authority because He or She cannot be trusted. There are loudly announced events these days promoting atheism as a faith option, and the first atheist "churches" have made their appearance in recent years. All the trappings are there: a worship space, a congregation, a liturgy, a sermon, fellowship. What is conspicuously absent are prayers — and the Bible. Mainline Christian churches may have to live with such nonsense copies of their own outward shell on the next street corner just as they are living with the temples and worship houses of other religions and faith communities. But these new "churches" will not have to be the final station on the way to finding sense and spiritual meaning for troubled lives. Faith experience is strong in Christian churches which are moving from isolation, exclusivity, and authoritarian privilege to new forms of community, inclusivity, and openness precisely with the experience of a helpful presence of the Bible — helpful in addressing the task of creating language for experience. They are on the way into an open future, and even those who are tempted to leave can formulate ways in which the Bible, vulnerable and ambiguous as it is, may be granted authority. Letty Russell writes, "For me, the Bible is 'Scripture,' or sacred writing, because it functions as 'script' or prompting for life. Its authority in my life stems from its story of God's invitation to participation in the restoration of wholeness, peace, and justice in the world. Responding to this invitation has made it my own story, or script, through the power of the Spirit at work in communities of struggle and faith."[44]

For the Christian church of the future, the Bible and its language will remain the house in which the "breathing-in" will be done, the concentration on the center of faith which is Jesus Christ, but it will also be the house in which the "breathing-out" has its beginning, the "living voice" we come to know in and as witness and proclamation. Both happen in the same house. Once again, as Ebeling puts it, "From the Word, faith emerges, and from faith the Word comes forth again in ever new acts of interpreting and directing the Gospel — but in such a way that any such language-event always returns to its [biblical] origin so that it might come forth from it purified and ready to enter again the ever-changing course of time."

This rhythm of "in" and "out," listening and speaking, creating and re-creating Christian life, has been a constant reality over the centuries, unleashing an incredible amount of creative thought and action. These "ever new acts of interpreting and directing the Gospel" have been capable of triggering dramatic as well as less dramatic transformations in the course of individual lives, in the life of the church, and even in society. On the basis of biblical texts, often no more than individual verses, rightly or wrongly, huge thought structures have been erected, some with dire and repulsive consequences, others with the potential of great benefit for gener-

---

44. Letty Russell, "Authority and the Challenge of Feminist Interpretation," in *The Feminist Interpretation of the Bible,* ed. Russell, 138.

ations.[45] Today more and more of these constructions are being scrutinized in terms of their origins and the dynamics of their development, often with surprising results.[46] In the field of biblical studies, the history of biblical interpretation is moving to the center of attention.

Probably the most astonishing case of a single text growing tall through the centuries is the case of John 1:14: "The Word became flesh." It spells out a specific theological interpretation of the birth of Jesus, the story of which is told in Matthew 1 and Luke 2 and alluded to by Paul in a side remark in Galatians 4:4. This four-word interpretation formed the basis for the concept of incarnation. The word "incarnation" itself is a neologism, a new Latin word creation parallel to the Greek Christian term *ensarkōsis*, meaning "enfleshment." It does not yet occur in the New Testament and rarely in the early centuries. Yet, eventually it became the key to major tenets of the Christian faith — the doctrinal formulations of Christology, soteriology, and even the theology of images[47] — they all depend on it, and "incarnation" is still used as a household word in today's language expressing the Christian faith.[48]

As the previous chapters have demonstrated, the practitioners of the exegetical quadriga in early and medieval times regarded it as their special privilege as well as a deeply satisfying spiritual undertaking to draw ever new meanings from the pages of the Bible. For them, the fourfold sense was a means to organize the immense flow of ideas which occurred to creative minds when they heard and read the biblical texts. They were, of course, "pre-critical" readers by our standards, but their interpretive proposals

45. One might think, e.g., of Exodus 22:18 ("Thou shalt not suffer a witch to live"); Luke 14:23 ("compel them to come in"); 1 Timothy 2:12 ("I suffer not a woman to teach"); Romans 13:1 ("Let every soul be subject unto the higher powers").

46. In my own doctoral dissertation I traced the history of Matthew 16:18-19 ("You are Peter, and upon this rock I will build my church") in the Middle Ages. I found that the papalist interpretation of the rock as Peter and his successors constituted only a small stream of the tradition. The majority of exegetes interpreted the "rock" as Christ on the basis of 1 Corinthians 10:4. See the essay "Saint Peter, Papal Primacy, and the Exegetical Tradition," in my *Biblical Interpretation from the Church Fathers to the Reformation* (Farnham: Ashgate, 2010), 3-44.

47. On this last point, see my essay "The Libri Carolini and the Lessons of the Iconoclastic Controversy," in *The One Mediator, the Saints, and Mary*, ed. H. George Anderson, J. Francis Stafford, and Joseph A. Burgess, Lutherans and Catholics in Dialogue 8 (Minneapolis: Augsburg Fortress, 1992), 193-208 and 374-76.

48. On the problems with this concept see John Hick, ed., *The Myth of God Incarnate* (London: SCM Press, 1977). In the preface to the 1993 edition, Hick reports on the subsequent theological journeys of the individual contributors.

were no less sophisticated than those of present-day scholars. Living intensely in the world of the Bible and its language every day, monks, nuns, and academic teachers displayed an astonishing versatility, imagination, and ingenuity in their attempts to find cross-connections, similitudes, allusions which would grow out of their close scrutiny of the text and lead back to it as part of the anagogical rhythm.

We began our journey by considering the conundrum facing interpreters of that impossible verse, Song of Songs 6:12 and of the introduction in the Greek and Latin Bible of "Aminadab's chariot." Compared with the frustrations of modern commentators, it is exhilarating to see what kind of imaginative insights occurred to those pre-critical minds when they read in their Vulgate, "I did not know. My soul disturbed me on account of the quadriga of Aminadab."

Honorius of Autun in the early twelfth century took his initial cue from the following verse, 6:13, which mentions a name in the context of the Marian interpretation of the Song to which he subscribed: "Return, return, O Sunamite!" Honorius saw this "Sunamite" as the representative of the Jewish Christian church, the church from the Synagogue, and understood the verse as "the words of the penitent church when it had to be converted from being just Jewish":

> She is grieving at having erred so long with regard to the Virgin and her offspring, and with these words makes amends for her error. "I did not know," glorious Virgin, that you were full of grace and that the fountain of grace flowed from you. "My soul was troubled," that is, the zeal of the Lord which I had for my soul's sake, it taught me to do what I did, and this happened "on account of the chariot of Aminadab," that is, on account of the gospel of Christ, so that, repulsed by me, yea impelled by me, they might roll through the zones of the earth. "O Sunamite," long held captive by the devil, "return" to Christ's mysteries through faith, "return" through hope, return through love of God and neighbor, return through doing so that those who have already long been in Christ may look at you imitating your words and deeds![49]

What a wealth of new context! What a rich story spun from the thin yarn of the few biblical words! What careful attention to the images of the exe-

---

49. Honorius of Autun, *Sigillum B. Mariae Virginis*, Patrologia Latina 172, ed. J.-P. Migne, 512C.

getical tradition, and what a strenuous attempt to draw a lesson from the unyielding material! The reader has a hard time catching up with the unexpected turns in almost every sentence.

About the same time, Rupert of Deutz commented on Aminadab's chariot in a section on 2 Samuel 6:1-16, boldly identifying Aminadab with the Abinadab of Gibeah. He titled the section "What the new cart is, what the house of Abinadab is, and what the disdain of Saul's daughter Michal is as she is looking out of the window":

> It is written: "And they set the Ark of the Lord on a new cart and brought it out of the house of Abinadab." The new cart on which this Ark of the Covenant of the Lord is carried is the new gospel of Christ by which his Resurrection is proclaimed in the whole world according to the prediction. For the four wheels are the four gospel writers. But the house of Abinadab (the word means "the voluntary one of my people"), this house, I said, of Abinadab, that is, of Christ who gave himself voluntarily for the people, once was the synagogue, but now his house is the church who accepted the faith in Christ's Resurrection while the former looks on with envy. And now she [the synagogue] mocks our dancing and jumping David, not restraining its blasphemous mouth, just as here Saul's daughter Michal looking from her window at David jumping and dancing before the Lord despised him in her heart. The time is still in the future that she will say: "I did not know. My soul was troubled on account of the chariot of Abinadab." "I did not know," she says, "my soul is troubled" by the unexpected change of things, and I did not understand the chariot of the gospels which carried the Ark of the Lord from the house of Abinadab. But when the fulness of the Gentiles will have come in, then that Michal will no longer look through her window and despise the glorious king David but will herself follow and accept the Ark of the Lord, the faith of Christ's Resurrection. Now, however, in the interim she is watching so to speak through the window for, unwilling to participate in such great joy, she devises in secret her plots [thinking about] in what way and whence she can direct her blasphemies.[50]

We will certainly have to object strongly to the vicious denunciation of the living Jewish community and the unmitigated Christian triumphalism that

---

50. Rupert of Deutz, *De Trinitate. In libros Regum*, lib. II, c. 27, Patrologia Latina 167, ed. J.-P. Migne, 1127A-B.

come to expression in these very "medieval" lines. Yet it is astonishing to observe what a rich potential of interconnected biblical stories, images, and explanatory combinations is spread before our eyes. All interpretive stops are pulled: philological knowledge, textual comparison, psychological sensitivity, contemporary polemics, eschatological awareness — everything is here. Honorius and Rupert were masters of broadening their readers' outlook on a fragment of a text which makes little sense, because they believed even this verse had a message in the framework of the task of encouraging the spiritual ascent. Like all medieval exegetes, they had to be masters of anagogical ingenuity.

Not only theologians delighted in the challenge of such texts. Medieval artists joined them with enthusiasm, employing to the full the interpretive potential of their tools — artistic media, form, color. One of the best-known visual representations of Aminadab's chariot is found on a twelfth-century stained glass window panel at the abbey church of Saint-Denis in Paris. We do not know the artist who executed the work, but its real *auctor*, Abbot Suger, who commissioned the windows, described it in his report on the church's decoration by quoting the inscription which he ordered to be included:[51]

> In the same window, above the Ark of the Covenant:
> "On the Ark of the Covenant is established the altar with the
> Cross of Christ.
> Here Life wishes to die under a greater covenant."

Exegetes as well as artists and patrons were well aware that their interpretive efforts were part of the "breathing out," the attempt to help readers and viewers in the task of participating in the anagogical dynamics, the upward journey which was the ardent desire of every soul reading the Bible or entering a church. Suger himself describes the particular window in which the Aminadab panel is located as "urging us onward from the material to the immaterial."

---

51. "In eadem vitrea, super arcam foederis: / Foederis ex arca Christi cruce sistitur ara; / Foedere majori vult ibi vita mori." Suger of Saint-Denis, *De Administratione* 34; see *Abbot Suger On the Abbey Church of St.-Denis and Its Art Treasures,* ed. and trans. Erwin Panofsky (Princeton, NJ: Princeton University Press, 1979), 74. About the Aminadab panel see the brief discussion in *The Royal Abbey of Saint-Denis in the Time of Abbot Suger (1122-1151),* ed. Sumner McKnight Crosby et al. (New York: Metropolitan Museum, 1981), 86. More recently, see Jacqueline Frank, "The *Quadrige Aminadab* Medallion in the 'Anagogical' Window at the Royal Abbey of Saint-Denis," *Gazette des Beaux-Arts* 141 (1999): 219-34.

Saint-Denis, Abbey Church: "Quadrige Aminadab" panel (line drawing)
In Karl Künstle, *Ikonographie der christlichen Kunst,* vol. 1
(Freiburg: Herder, 1928), 61, fig. 14

The panel itself is round, symbolic of the perfect world of God's cosmos. It features a uniform blue background which displays the color of "air," one of the four elements. The subject of the scene is indicated by a title at the bottom; it reads: *"quadrige Aminadab,"* and with this wording Suger establishes a clear link to Song of Songs 6:12. In the center one sees the golden Ark, styled as an open cart with filigreed side panels and a bottom on which the two tablets of the Law and Aaron's rod are placed. The cart is a rectangular box with the four corners being strongly emphasized. In fact, there are many more "fours" in the picture: the four wheels of Ezekiel's vision are quite prominently placed at the corners of the cart — each has eight (= 2 × 4) spokes. The four winged creatures appear in the quadrants. They symbolize the four evangelists; three of them hold a book, the "angel" of John a scroll, and the cross in the center as well as the corpus display the extension in four directions. The half-figures of the creatures emerge from stylized clouds. These clouds are reminiscent of representations of the waves of the four rivers of paradise which frequently stand for the four senses of the one Scripture, just as the one stream in Eden divided into four branches (Gen. 2:10). From the bottom of the cart rises the cross with the crucified Christ held by a nimbed God-Father whose features, following earlier tradition, are those of Christ. The cross itself is a living, "greening" cross covered with vines and leaf scrolls, representing the Tree of Life (Gen. 2:9). In front of the God-figure behind the cross down to the back panel of the cart a yellow cloth or veil hangs from the cross bar. The scene is sometimes classified as an early example of the "throne-of-grace" motif which became prominent in later centuries.[52] But Suger's own inscription suggests a more precise interpretation: Giving the scene the name of the *Quadrigae Aminadab* Suger alludes to the fourfold sense of the Scriptures. Scripture comprises the Old and the New Testament as the revelation of two progressive covenants, the "greater" of which is established by Christ's sacrifice on the Cross. But this second covenant must be understood as being based on the earlier one established by the Law of Moses, which is carried in the Ark of the Covenant. The cart seems to be in motion but it is unclear whether upward or forward. The wheels are rolling just as the evangelists in the quadrants seem poised to carry the gospels to the four corners of the world.

Again, a number of quite disparate biblical strains are imaginatively

---

52. Representations of this type show the Trinity of God the Father presenting a crucified Christ with the dove of the Holy Spirit between his beard and the head of Christ. See Fides Buchheim, *Der Gnadenstuhl — Darstellung der Dreifaltigkeit* (Würzburg: Echter-Verlag, 1984).

combined into one picture here: the quadriga of Song of Songs 6:12; the Ark of the Covenant and its journeys (1 Sam. 7; 2 Sam. 6), Ezekiel's throne wagon with the creatures and the wheels (Ezek. 1, 10), the rivers of paradise (Gen. 2:10), the cross and the veil. The connections and associations between the various items are imprecise, somewhat fuzzy, but allusive and intuitively coherent. Suger knows that Aminadab is not identical with Abinadab, the Ark of the Covenant is not itself a chariot or Ezekiel's throne wagon; the creatures are not necessarily the four evangelists; and the interpretation of the veil confronts the viewer with several options: it could be the veil in front of the Ark (Exod. 40:3), the temple curtain (Matt. 27:51), or even the veil over Moses' face to which Paul refers (2 Cor. 3:13-18). Together, however, all these individual elements form a comprehensive icon of God's ongoing history of salvation which forms the content of the message of the Bible. The same God is the author and giver of both saving covenants (and written "Testaments"!), the Old and the New. He provided the Law for ancient Israel and the sacrifice of the Son for the salvation of the entire world. Clearly the sacrificed Christ constitutes the center of the icon, the "altar" of the church's offering as Suger says. The eyes of all four creatures or evangelists are fixed on the Crucified, giving the roundel its shape of a wheel turning around its hub.

One intriguing detail must not go unnoticed. Undoubtedly God looks out from the picture. God looks straight at you and me. God seeks eye contact with the beholder. Once more the horizon of this icon summarizing the biblical message expands into a new dimension: The viewer, the reader is being integrated into the picture. He or she becomes part of the dynamics which so clearly describe the motion of the spiritual ascent. As an image of the biblical God these eyes extend the invitation: "Come in! Make yourself at home in this humble dwelling of scriptural language and allow it to become the language of your faith experience. You may feel you have to re-mold, re-shape, transform it, but then it could also turn on you and use its power to transform *you,* because this power is not its own but the power of God." "My power is made perfect in weakness" — these are words of God spoken to Paul as the Apostle himself reports (2 Cor. 12:9).

We cannot help it. As human beings left with an embarrassingly imperfect Bible in the garb of human language, "sensing the Scriptures" remains a never-ending task for Christians. It needs time and effort, and it is not always successful. But it is worth spending our time on. *Our* time — the most precious personal gift we humans have received for living the one life we have on this earth.

Bibliography

Alan of Lille. *Anticlaudianus, or The Good and Perfect Man*. Translated by James J. Sheridan. Toronto: Pontifical Institute of Medieval Studies, 1973.

Alexander Minorita. *Expositio in Apocalypsim*. Edited by Alois Wachtel. Monumenta Germaniae Historica: Quellen zur Geistesgeschichte des Mittelalters 1. Weimar: Böhlau, 1955.

Anderson, H. George, J. Francis Stafford, and Joseph A. Burgess, eds. *The One Mediator, the Saints, and Mary*. Lutherans and Catholics in Dialogue 8. Minneapolis: Augsburg Fortress, 1992.

Archambault, Paul J., ed. *A Monk's Confession: The Memoirs of Guibert of Nogent*. University Park: Pennsylvania State University Press, 1996.

Aristotle. *De anima*. Edited by William David Ross. Oxford: Clarendon Press, 1961.

———. *Metaphysics*. The Student's Oxford Aristotle 4. Translated by W. D. Ross. New York: Oxford University Press, 1942.

———. *Parva Naturalia*. Edited by William David Ross. Oxford: Clarendon Press, 1955.

Astell, Ann W. *The Song of Songs in the Middle Ages*. Ithaca, NY: Cornell University Press, 1995.

Augustine. *Confessiones*. Corpus Christianorum Latinorum 27. Turnhout: Brepols, 1981.

———. *Confessions*. Translated by Henry Chadwick. New York: Oxford University Press, 1992.

———. *Expositions on the Book of Psalms*. Nicene and Post-Nicene Fathers (First Series) 8. Edited by Philip Schaff. Grand Rapids: Eerdmans, 1980.

———. *On Christian Doctrine*. Translated by D. W. Robertson Jr. Indianapolis: Bobbs-Merrill, 1958.

———. *On Genesis: A Refutation of the Manichees, Unfinished Literal Commentary on*

Genesis, The Literal Meaning of Genesis. Translated by Edmund Hill. New York: New City Press, 2002.

――――. *Questionum in Heptateuchum Libri Septem.* Corpus Christianorum Latinorum 33. Turnhout: Brepols, 1958.

――――. *Sermons on Selected Lessons of the New Testament.* Nicene and Post-Nicene Fathers (First Series) 6. Edited by Philip Schaff. Grand Rapids: Eerdmans, 1986.

――――. *Tractates on the Gospel of John.* Nicene and Post-Nicene Fathers (First Series) 7. Edited by Philip Schaff. Grand Rapids: Eerdmans, 1986.

Bataillon, L.-J. "Early Scholastic and Mendicant Preaching as Exegesis of Scripture." In *Ad Litteram: Authoritative Texts and Their Medieval Readers.* Edited by Mark D. Jordan and Kent Emery, 165-99. South Bend, IN: Notre Dame University Press, 1992.

Bell, Theo. *Divus Bernhardus: Bernhard von Clairvaux in Martin Luthers Schriften.* Mainz: Verlag Philipp von Zabern, 1993.

Berendt, Joachim Ernst. "Ich höre, also bin ich." In *Über das Hören: Einem Phänomen auf der Spur.* Edited by Thomas Vogel, 69-90. Tübingen: Attempto Verlag, 1998.

Bernard of Clairvaux. *On Loving God.* Edited by Emero Stiegman. Cistercian Fathers Series 13B. Kalamazoo, MI: Cistercian Publications, 1995.

――――. *On the Song of Songs.* Translated by Kilian Walsh and Irene Edmonds. 4 volumes. Cistercian Fathers Series 4, 7, 31, 40. Kalamazoo, MI: Cistercian Publications, 1971-.

――――. *St. Bernard's Sermons for the Seasons and Principal Festivals of the Year.* Translated by A Priest of Mount Melleray. Westminster, MD: The Carroll Press, 1950.

Bernard, Robert. "The Rhetoric of God in the Figurative Exegesis of Augustine." In *Biblical Hermeneutics in Historical Perspective: Studies in Honor of Karlfried Froehlich on His Sixtieth Birthday.* Edited by Mark S. Burrows and Paul Rorem, 88-99. Grand Rapids: Eerdmans, 1991.

Berndt, Rainer, SJ. "Das 12. Jahrhundert. Überlegungen zum Verhältnis von Exegese und Theologie in *De Sacramentis Christianae Fidei* Hugos von St. Viktor." In *Neue Richtungen in der hoch- und spätmittelalterlichen Bibelexegese.* Schriften des Historischen Kollegs, Kolloquien 32. Edited by Robert Lerner, 66-78. Munich: Oldenbourg, 1996.

Bizer, Ernst. *Fides ex Auditu: Eine Untersuchung über die Entdeckung der Gerechtigkeit Gottes durch Martin Luther.* Third edition. Neukirchen: Neukirchener Verlag, 1966.

Boersma, Hans. *Embodiment and Virtue in Gregory of Nyssa: An Anagogical Approach.* New York: Oxford University Press, 2013.

Bonaventure. *Breviloquium.* Translated by Erwin Esser Nemmers. St. Louis: Herder, 1946.

Bibliography

Borst, Arno. *Der Turmbau von Babel: Geschichte der Meinungen über Ursprung und Vielfalt der Sprachen und Völker.* Stuttgart: Anton Hiersemann, 1959.

Bostock, Gerald. "Allegory and the Interpretation of the Bible in Allegory." *Journal of Literature and Theology* 1 (1987): 39-53.

Bouwsma, William J. *John Calvin: A Sixteenth-Century Portrait.* New York: Oxford University Press, 1988.

Buchheim, Fides. *Der Gnadenstuhl — Darstellung der Dreifaltigkeit.* Würzburg: Echter-Verlag, 1984.

Burrows, Mark S. "Of Hunters, Hounds, and Allegorical Readers: The Body of the Text and the Text of the Body in Bernard of Clairvaux's Sermons on the Song of Songs." *Studies in Spirituality* 14 (2004): 114-37.

Burrows, Mark S., and Paul Rorem, eds. *Biblical Hermeneutics in Historical Perspective: Studies in Honor of Karlfried Froehlich on His Sixtieth Birthday.* Grand Rapids: Eerdmans, 1991.

Calvin, John. *Thesaurus epistolicus Calvinianus.* Calvini Opera Omnia 21. Corpus Reformatorum. Braunschweig, 1879.

———. *Commentary on the Gospel of John.* Calvin's Commentaries 17. Grand Rapids: Baker Book House, 1989.

———. *Institutes of the Christian Religion.* Translated by Ford Lewis Battles. Library of Christian Classics 20, 21. Philadelphia: Westminster Press, 1960.

Campenhausen, Hans von. *The Formation of the Christian Bible.* Translated by J. A. Baker. Mifflintown, PA: Sigler Press, 1997.

Cassian, John. *Conferences.* Translated by Colm Luibheid. Classics of Western Spirituality. New York: Paulist Press, 1985.

Charry, Ellen. *By the Renewing of Your Minds: The Pastoral Function of Christian Doctrine.* New York: Oxford University Press, 1999.

———. "The Moral Function of Doctrine." *Theology Today* 49 (1992): 31-45.

Châtillon, Jean. "Dulcedo." In *Dictionnaire de Spiritualité, Ascétique et Mystique: Doctrine et Histoire.* Edited by Marcel Viller, F. Cavallera, and J. de Guibert, vol. 3, 1781-83. Paris: Beauchesne, 1967.

Chrysostom. *Homilies on the Gospel of St. Matthew.* Nicene and Post-Nicene Fathers (First Series) 10. Edited by Philip Schaff. Grand Rapids: Eerdmans, 1986.

Clark, Mark John. *A Study of Peter Comestor's Method in the Historia Genesis.* Ph.D. Dissertation, Columbia University, 2002.

Clement of Alexandria. *Eclogae propheticae.* In *Clemens Alexandrinus: Excerpta und Eclogae propheticae.* Die griechischen christlichen Schriftsteller der ersten drei Jahrhunderte 17. Edited by Otto Stählin. Leipzig: Hinrich, 1909.

Colish, Marcia L. *The Mirror of Language: A Study in the Medieval Theory of Language.* Lincoln: University of Nebraska Press, 1968.

Crosby, Sumner McKnight, Jane Hayward, Charles T. Little, and William D. Wixom. *The Royal Abbey of Saint-Denis in the Time of Abbot Suger (1122-1151).* New York: Metropolitan Museum, 1981.

Dilthey, Wilhelm. "The Understanding of Other Persons and Their Manifestations of Life." In *Selected Works.* Volume 3: *The Formation of the Historical World in the Human Sciences.* Translated by Rudolf A. Makkreel and Frithjof Rodi. Princeton: Princeton University Press, 2010.

Dowey, Edward A., Jr. *The Knowledge of God in Calvin's Theology.* Third edition. Grand Rapids: Eerdmans, 1994.

Drewermann, Eugen. *Tiefenpsychologie und Exegese.* Volume 1: *Die Wahrheit der Formen: Traum, Mythos, Märchen, Sage und Legende.* Olten: Walter-Verlag, 1984.

———. *Was ich denke.* Munich: Goldmann Verlag, 1994.

Dulles, Avery, SJ. "The Authority of Scripture: A Catholic Perspective." In *Scripture in the Jewish and Christian Traditions: Authority, Interpretation, Relevance,* edited by Frederick E. Greenspahn, 14-40. Nashville: Abingdon Press, 1982.

Ebeling, Gerhard. "Die Anfänge von Luthers Hermeneutik." *Zeitschrift für Theologie und Kirche* 48 (1951): 172-230.

———. "Hermeneutik zwischen der Macht des Gotteswortes und seiner Entmachtung in der Moderne." In *Theologie in den Gegensätzen des Lebens,* 209-25. Wort und Glaube, 4. Tübingen: Mohr Siebeck, 1994.

———. "Schrift und Erfahrung als Quelle theologischer Aussagen." *Zeitschrift für Theologie und Kirche* 75 (1978): 99-116.

———. *The Word of God and Tradition: Historical Studies Interpreting the Divisions of Christianity.* Translated by S. H. Hooke. Philadelphia: Fortress Press, 1968.

Eckhart, Meister. *Meister Eckhart: Teacher and Preacher.* Edited by Bernard McGinn. Classics of Western Spirituality. Mahwah, NJ: Paulist Press, 1986.

Ehrman, Bart. "The Text of Mark in the Hands of the Orthodox." In *Biblical Hermeneutics in Historical Perspective: Studies in Honor of Karlfried Froehlich on His Sixtieth Birthday.* Edited by Mark S. Burrows and Paul Rorem, 19-31. Grand Rapids: Eerdmans, 1991.

Esmeijer, Anna C. *Divina Quaternitas: A Preliminary Study in the Method and Application of Visual Exegesis.* Assen: Van Gorcum, 1978.

Evans, Gillian Rosemary. *The Thought of Gregory the Great.* Cambridge Studies in Medieval Life and Thought (Fourth Series) 2. Cambridge: Cambridge University Press, 1986.

Farrar, Frederick W. *History of Interpretation.* 1886. Grand Rapids: Baker Book House, 1961.

Fleming, John. "Christopher Columbus as a Scriptural Exegete." In *Biblical Hermeneutics in Historical Perspective: Studies in Honor of Karlfried Froehlich on His*

Sixtieth Birthday. Edited by Mark S. Burrows and Paul Rorem, 173-83. Grand Rapids: Eerdmans, 1991.

Frank, Jacqueline. "The *Quadrige Aminadab* Medallion in the 'Anagogical' Window at the Royal Abbey of Saint-Denis." *Gazette des Beaux-Arts* 141 (1999): 219-34.

Freeland, Cynthia. "Aristotle on the Sense of Touch." In *Essays on Aristotle's De Anima*. Edited by Martha C. Nussbaum and Amélie Oksenberg Rorty, 227-48. Oxford: Clarendon Press, 1999.

Fretheim, Terence E., and Karlfried Froehlich. *The Bible as Word of God in a Postmodern Age*. Minneapolis: Fortress Press, 1998.

Freytag, Hartmut. *Die Theorie der allegorischen Schriftdeutung und die Allegorie in deutschen Texten besonders des 11. und 12. Jahrhunderts*. Bibliotheca Germanica 24. Bern: Francke, 1982.

―――. "*Quae sunt per allegoriam dicta:* Das theologische Verständnis der Allegorie in der frühchristlichen und mittelalterlichen Exegese von Gal. 4,21-31." In *Verbum et Signum: Festschrift für Friedrich Ohly*. Volume 1: *Beiträge zur mediävistischen Bedeutungsforschung*. Edited by Hans Fromm, Wolfgang Harms, and Uwe Ruberg, 230-45. Munich: W. Fink, 1975.

Fritsch, Charles T. "Principles of Biblical Typology." *Bibliotheca Sacra* 104 (1947): 214-22.

Froehlich, Karlfried. "'Always to Keep the Literal Sense in Holy Scripture Means to Kill One's Soul': The State of Biblical Hermeneutics in the Beginning of the 15th Century." In *Literary Uses of Typology from the Late Middle Ages to the Present*. Edited by Earl Miner, 20-48. Princeton: Princeton University Press, 1977.

―――. "Bibelkommentare — Zur Krise einer Gattung." *Zeitschrift für Theologie und Kirche* 84, no. 4 (November 1987): 465-92.

―――. *Biblical Interpretation from the Church Fathers to the Reformation*. Variorum Collected Studies Series 951. Farnham: Ashgate, 2010.

―――. "Church History and the Bible." In *Biblical Hermeneutics in Historical Perspective: Studies in Honor of Karlfried Froehlich on His Sixtieth Birthday*. Edited by Mark S. Burrows and Paul Rorem, 1-15. Grand Rapids: Eerdmans, 1991.

―――. "The Glossa Ordinaria and Medieval Preaching." In *Biblical Interpretation from the Church Fathers to the Reformation*, 1-21. Variorum Collected Studies Series 951. Farnham: Ashgate, 2010.

―――. "Interpretation of the Old Testament in the High Middle Ages." In *Hebrew Bible/Old Testament: The History of Its Interpretation*. Volume 1: *From the Beginnings to the Middle Ages (Until 1300)*, Part 2: *The Middle Ages*. Edited by Magne Sæbo, 496-558. Göttingen: Vandenhoeck & Ruprecht, 2000.

―――. "Johannes Trithemius on the Fourfold Sense of Scripture: The *Tractatus de Inuestigatione Sacrae Scripturae* (1486)." In *Biblical Interpretation in the Era of the Reformation: Essays Presented to David C. Steinmetz in Honor of His Sixtieth Birthday.* Edited by Richard A. Muller and John L. Thompson, 23-60. Grand Rapids: Eerdmans, 1996.

———. "The Libri Carolini and the Lessons of the Iconoclastic Controversy." In *The One Mediator, the Saints, and Mary.* Edited by H. George Anderson, J. Francis Stafford, and Joseph A. Burgess, 193-208. Lutherans and Catholics in Dialogue 8. Minneapolis: Augsburg Fortress, 1992.

———. "Saint Peter, Papal Primacy, and the Exegetical Tradition." In *Biblical Interpretation from the Church Fathers to the Reformation,* 3-44. Variorum Collected Studies Series 951. Farnham: Ashgate, 2010.

Froehlich, Karlfried, trans. and ed. *Biblical Interpretion in the Early Church.* Sources of Early Christian Thought. Philadelphia: Fortress Press, 1984.

Gadamer, Hans-Georg. *Truth and Method.* Second edition. Translated by Joel Weinsheimer and Donald Marshall. London: Continuum, 1989.

———. "Über das Hören." In *Hermeneutische Entwürfe: Vorträge und Aufsätze.* Edited by Hans Förster, 49-57. Tübingen: J. C. B. Mohr [Paul Siebeck], 2000.

Gese, Hartmut. "Erwägungen zur Einheit der biblischen Theologie." *Zeitschrift für Theologie und Kirche* 67, no. 4 (1970): 416-36.

Gilbert of Hoyland. *Sermons on the Song of Songs.* Translated by Lawrence Braceland. Cistercian Fathers Series 14. Kalamazoo, MI: Cistercian Publications, 1978.

Gilbert, Avery N. *What the Nose Knows: The Science of Scent in Everyday Life.* New York: Crown Publishers, 2008.

Grant, Gerard G. "The Elevation of the Host: A Reaction to Twelfth Century Heresy." *Theological Studies* 1, no. 3 (1940): 228-50.

Graves, Michael. *Jerome's Hebrew Philology: A Study Based on His Commentary on Jeremiah.* Supplements to Vigiliae Christianae 90. Leiden: Brill, 2007.

Gregory the Great. *Homilies on the Book of the Prophet Ezekiel.* Translated by Theodosia Gray. Etna, CA: Center for Traditionalist Orthodox Studies, 1990.

———. *The Letters of Gregory the Great.* Translated by John R. C. Martyn. Medieval Sources in Translation 40. Toronto: Pontifical Institute of Medieval Studies, 2004.

Gregory of Nyssa. *Address on Religious Instruction.* In *Christology of the Later Fathers.* Edited by Edward Hardy, 318-20. Library of Christian Classics. Philadelphia: Westminster Press, 1954.

———. *Homilies on the Song of Songs.* Translated by Richard A. Norris. Writings from the Greco-Roman World 13. Atlanta: Society of Biblical Literature, 2012.

Grimm, Jacob. *Rede auf Wilhelm Grimm: Rede über das Alter.* Im Auftrag der Brüder Grimm-Gesellschaft Kassel herausgegeben. Kassel: Bärenreiter-Verlag, 1963.

Gross-Diaz, Teresa. "What Is a Good Soldier to Do? Scholarship and Revelation in the Postills on the Psalms." In *Nicholas of Lyra: The Senses of Scripture.* Edited by

Philip D. W. Krey and Lesley Smith, 111-28. Studies in the History of Christian Thought 90. Leiden: Brill, 2000.

Hardy, Edward R. *Christology of the Later Fathers*. Library of Christian Classics. Philadelphia: Westminster Press, 1954.

Harnack, Adolf von. *History of Dogma*. Translated by J. Millar. New York: Russell & Russell, 1958.

————. *Marcion: The Gospel of the Alien God*. Translated by John E. Steely and Lyle D. Bierma. Jamestown, NY: Labyrinth Press, 1990.

Hick, John, ed. *The Myth of God Incarnate*. London: SCM Press, 1977.

Hoffmann, Manfred. *Rhetoric and Theology: The Hermeneutic of Erasmus*. Erasmus Studies 12. Toronto: University of Toronto Press, 1994.

Holl, Karl. "Luthers Bedeutung für den Fortschritt der Auslegungskunst." In *Gesammelte Aufsätze zur Kirchengeschichte*. Volume 1: *Luther*, 414-50. Tübingen: J. C. B. Mohr [Paul Siebeck], 1921.

Hrabanus Maurus. *In honorem sanctae crucis*. Edited by Michel Perrin. Corpus Christianorum Continuatio Mediaevalis 100, 100A. Turnhout: Brepols, 1997.

Hugh of St. Victor. *Chronicon, vel de tribus maximis circumstantiis gestorum*. In *The Medieval Craft of Memory: An Anthology of Texts and Pictures*. Edited by Mary Carruthers and Jan Ziolkowski, 32-40. Philadelphia: University of Pennsylvania Press, 2002.

————. *The Didascalicon of Hugh of St. Victor: A Medieval Guide to the Arts*. Translated by Jerome Taylor. New York: Columbia University Press, 1961.

————. *On the Sacraments of the Christian Faith*. Translated by Roy J. Deferrari. Boston: Medieval Academy of America, 1951.

Illich, Ivan. *In the Vineyard of the Text: A Commentary to Hugh's Didascalicon*. Chicago: University of Chicago Press, 1993.

Jenson, Robert. "Can a Text Defend Itself? An Essay *De Inspiratione Scripturae*." *Dialogue* 28, no. 4 (1989): 251-53.

————. "How the World Lost Its Story." *First Things* 36 (1993): 19-24.

Johansen, Thomas K. "Aristotle on the Sense of Smell." *Phronesis: A Journal for Ancient Philosophy* 41 (1996): 1-19.

Kallas, Endel. "Martin Luther as Expositor of the Song of Songs." *Lutheran Quarterly* 2 (1988): 323-41.

Kates, Judith. "Entering the Holy of Holies: Rabbinic Midrash and the Language of Intimacy." In *Scrolls of Love: Ruth and the Song of Songs*. Edited by Peter Hawkins and Lesleigh Cushing, 201-13. New York: Fordham University Press, 2006.

Kavvadas, Nestor C. "Theodor von Mopsuestia zur Kanonizität des Hohenliedes." In *Studia Patristica*. Volume 52, 275-83. Edited by Allen Brent and Markus Vinzent. Louvain: Peeters, 2012.

Kelsey, David H. *The Uses of Scripture in Recent Theology*. Philadelphia: Fortress Press, 1975.

Köpf, Ulrich. *Religiöse Erfahrung in der Theologie Bernhards von Clairvaux*. Beiträge zur historischen Theologie 61. Tübingen: J. C. B. Mohr [Paul Siebeck], 1980.

Krey, Philip D. W. "The Apocalypse Commentary of 1329: Problems in Church History." In *Nicholas of Lyra: The Senses of Scripture*. Edited by Philip D. W. Krey and Lesley Smith, 267-89. Studies in the History of Christian Thought 90. Leiden: Brill, 2000.

Krey, Philip D. W., and Lesley Smith, eds. *Nicholas of Lyra: The Senses of Scripture*. Studies in the History of Christian Thought 90. Leiden: Brill, 2000.

Kuhn, Peter. "Hoheslied II: Auslegungsgeschichte im Judentum." In *Theologische Realenzyklopädie: Dritte Auflage*. Volume 15, 503-8. Berlin: Walter De Gruyter, 1986.

Lane, Anthony N. S. *Calvin and Bernard of Clairvaux*. Studies in Reformed Theology and History 1. Princeton, NJ: Princeton Theological Seminary, 1996.

Leclercq, Jean. *The Love of Learning and the Desire for God: A Study of Monastic Culture*. Translated by Catharine Misrahi. New York: Fordham University Press, 1961.

Lewis, C. S. *The Allegory of Love: A Study of a Medieval Tradition*. New York: Oxford University Press, 1985.

Liebing, Heinz. *Humanismus, Reformation, Konfession: Beiträge zur Kirchengeschichte*. Marburg: Elwert, 1986.

Liere, Frans A. van. "Andrew of St. Victor: Scholar between Cloister and School." In *Centres of Learning: Learning and Location in Premodern Europe and the Near East*. Edited by Hendrik Jan Willem Drijvers and Alasdair A. MacDonald, 187-95. Studies in Intellectual History 61. Leiden: Brill, 1997.

———. "The Literal Sense of the Books of Samuel and Kings: From Andrew of St. Victor to Nicholas of Lyra." In *Nicholas of Lyra: The Senses of Scripture*. Edited by Philip D. W. Krey and Lesley Smith, 59-82. Studies in the History of Christian Thought 90. Leiden: Brill, 2000.

Lubac, Henri de. *Exégèse médiévale: Les quatre sens de l'écriture*. 2 volumes. Paris: Aubier, 1959-1964.

———. *History and Spirit: The Understanding of Scripture According to Origen*. Translated by Anne Englund Nash. San Francisco: Ignatius Press, 2007.

———. *Medieval Exegesis: The Four Senses of Scripture*. 3 volumes. Translated by Mark Sebanc and E. M. Macierowski. Grand Rapids: Eerdmans, 1998-2009.

Luther, Martin. *Lectures on the Song of Solomon*. Translated by Ian Siggins. In *Luther's Works*. Volume 15: *Ecclesiastes, Song of Solomon, and the Last Words of David*. St. Louis: Concordia Publishing House, 1972.

Bibliography

————. *Luthers Werke. Kritische Gesamtausgabe. Tischreden.* Weimar: Böhlau, 1913.

————. *Sämtliche Werke.* Volume 4: *Predigten über die Evangelien.* Edited by J. G. Plochman. Erlangen: Carl Heyder, 1832.

Marrou, Henri-Irénée. *A History of Education in Antiquity.* Translated by George Lamb. New York: Sheed & Ward, 1956.

Matter, E. Ann. *The Voice of My Beloved: The Song of Songs in Western Medieval Christianity.* Philadelphia: University of Pennsylvania Press, 1990.

Mauritius de Sancto Victore. *Sermones.* Corpus Christianorum Continuatio Mediaevalis 30. Edited by Jean Châtillon. Turnhout: Brepols, 1975.

Mauser, Ulrich. *Der junge Luther und die Häresie.* Schriften des Vereins für Reformationsgeschichte 184. Gütersloh: Gütersloher Verlagshaus Gerd Mohn, 1968.

McVey, Kathleen. "The Use of Stoic Cosmogony in Theophilus of Antioch's *Hexaemeron.*" In *Biblical Hermeneutics in Historical Perspective: Studies in Honor of Karlfried Froehlich on His Sixtieth Birthday.* Edited by Mark S. Burrows and Paul Rorem, 32-58. Grand Rapids: Eerdmans, 1991.

Melanchthon, Philipp. *Elementa Rhetorices.* Edited by Karl Gottlieb Bretschneider. Philippi Melanthonis Opera 13. Corpus Reformatorum. Halle, 1846.

————. *Epistolarum Libri.* Philippi Melanthonis Opera 6. Corpus Reformatorum. Halle, 1839.

Merriam, Thomas. "Dissociation and the Literal Interpretation of the Bible." *Downside Review* 96 (1978): 79-84.

Minnis, A. J. *Medieval Theory of Authorship: Scholastic Literary Attitudes in the Later Middle Ages.* Second edition. Philadelphia: University of Pennsylvania Press, 2010.

Nautin, Pierre. "Hieronymus." In *Theologische Realenzyklopädie: Dritte Auflage.* Volume 15, 309-10. Berlin: Walter De Gruyter, 1986.

————. *Origène: Sa vie et son oeuvre.* Christianisme antique 1. Paris: Beauchesne, 1977.

Nordenfalk, Carl. "Les cinq sens dans l'art du moyen-âge." *Révue de l'art* 34 (1976): 17-28.

Nussbaum, Martha C., and Amélie Oksenberg Rorty. *Essays on Aristotle's De Anima.* Oxford: Clarendon Press, 1992.

Origen. *Commentary on the Gospel of John.* Translated by Ronald E. Heine. Fathers of the Church 80. Washington, DC: Catholic University of America Press, 1989.

————. *Homilies on Genesis and Exodus.* Translated by Ronald Heine. Fathers of the Church 71. Washington, DC: Catholic University Press, 1982.

————. *Homilies on Leviticus 1–16.* Translated by Gary Wayne Barkley. Fathers of the Church 83. Washington, DC: Catholic University of America Press, 1990.

————. *On First Principles.* Translated by G. W. Butterworth. New York: Harper & Row, 1966.

———. *The Song of Songs: Commentary and Homilies.* Translated by R. P. Lawson. Ancient Christian Writers 26. Westminster, MD: Newman Press, 1957.

Pagels, Elaine H. *The Gnostic Paul: Gnostic Exegesis of the Pauline Letters.* Philadelphia: Fortress Press, 1975.

———. *The Johannine Gospel in Gnostic Exegesis: Heracleon's Commentary on John.* Society of Biblical Literature Monograph Series 17. Nashville: Abingdon Press, 1973.

Parker, D. C. "Vulgate." In *The Anchor Bible Dictionary.* Edited by David Noel Freedman, 860-62. New York: Doubleday, 1992.

Pfeiffer, Rudolf. *History of Classical Scholarship from the Beginning to the End of the Hellenistic Age.* Oxford: Clarendon Press, 1968.

Pope, Marvin H. *The Song of Songs: A New Translation with Introduction and Commentary.* The Anchor Bible 7C. Garden City, NY: Doubleday, 1977.

Porter, Jean. "Responsibility, Passion, and Sin: A Reassessment of Abelard's Ethics." *The Journal of Religious Ethics* 28 (2000): 367-94.

Preus, James Samuel. *From Shadow to Promise: Old Testament Interpretation from Augustine to the Young Luther.* Cambridge, MA: Belknap Press, 1969.

Pseudo-Dionysius. *The Complete Works.* Translated by Colm Luibheid. Classics of Western Spirituality. Mahwah, NJ: Paulist Press, 1987.

Rorem, Paul. *Biblical and Liturgical Symbols within the Pseudo-Dionysian Synthesis.* Toronto: Pontifical Institute of Medieval Studies, 1984.

———. *Hugh of St. Victor.* New York: Oxford University Press, 2009.

———. *Pseudo-Dionysius: A Commentary on the Texts and an Introduction to Their Influence.* New York: Oxford University Press, 1993.

Ruether, Rosemary R. "Feminist Interpretation: A Method of Correlation." In *The Feminist Interpretation of the Bible.* Edited by Letty M. Russell, 111-24. Philadelphia: Westminster Press, 1985.

———. *Women-Church: Theology and Practice of Feminist Liturgical Communities.* San Francisco: Harper & Row, 1985.

———. *Womenguides: Readings Toward a Feminist Theology.* Boston: Beacon Press, 1985.

Russell, Letty M. "Authority and the Challenge of Feminist Interpretation." In *The Feminist Interpretation of the Bible.* Edited by Letty M. Russell, 136-46. Philadelphia: Westminster Press, 1985.

———. *Household of Freedom: Authority in Feminist Theology.* Philadelphia: Westminster Press, 1987.

Schmidt, Hans-Joachim. "Allegorie und Empirie: Interpretation und Normung sozialer Realität in Predigten des 13. Jahrhunderts." In *Die Deutsche Predigt im Mittelalter: Internationales Symposium am Fachbereich Germanistik der Freien*

Bibliography

Universität Berlin, vom 3.-6. Oktober 1989. Edited by Volker Mertens and Hans-Jochen Schiewer, 301-32. Tübingen: Max Niemeyer Verlag, 1992.

Schneemelcher, Wilhelm, ed. *New Testament Apocrypha.* Volume 2. Translated by R. McLeod Wilson. Louisville: Westminster John Knox Press, 1991.

Schüssler Fiorenza, Elisabeth. "The Will to Choose or Reject: Continuing Our Critical Work." In *The Feminist Interpretation of the Bible.* Edited by Letty M. Russell, 125-36. Philadelphia: Westminster Press, 1985.

Schwarz, Reinhard. "Mystischer Glaube — die Brautmystik Martin Luthers." *Zeitwende* 52 (1981): 193-227.

Smalley, Beryl. "Andrew of St. Victor, Abbot of Wigmore: A Twelfth-Century Hebraist." *Recherches de théologie ancienne et médiévale* 10 (1938): 358-73.

———. *The Study of the Bible in the Middle Ages.* Third edition. Oxford: Blackwell, 1983.

Sorabji, Richard. "Aristotle on Demarcating the Five Senses." *The Philosophical Review* 80 (1971): 55-79.

Steinmetz, David C. "The Superiority of Pre-Critical Exegesis." *Theology Today* 37, no. 1 (1980): 27-38.

———. *Taking the Long View: Christian Theology in Historical Perspective.* New York: Oxford University Press, 2011.

Stout, Jeffrey. *The Flight from Authority: Religion, Morality, and the Quest for Autonomy.* Notre Dame, IN: University of Notre Dame Press, 1981.

Suger of St.-Denis. *Abbot Suger on the Abbey Church of St.-Denis and Its Art Treasures.* Edited by Erwin Panofsky. Princeton, NJ: Princeton University Press, 1979.

Tamburello, Dennis, OFM. *Ordinary Mysticism.* Mahwah, NJ: Paulist Press, 1996.

———. *Union with Christ: John Calvin and the Mysticism of St. Bernard.* Louisville: Westminster John Knox Press, 1994.

Thomas de Chobham. *Summa de arte praedicandi.* Edited by Franco Morenzoni. Corpus Christianorum Continuatio Mediaevalis 82.1. Turnhout: Brepols, 1988.

Thommen, Rudolf. *Geschichte der Universität Basel, 1532-1632.* Basel: C. Dettloffs Buchhandlung, 1889.

Torjesen, Karen J. *Hermeneutical Procedure and Theological Method in Origen's Exegesis.* Patristische Texte und Studien 28. Berlin: Walter de Gruyter, 1985.

Tracy, David. *Plurality and Ambiguity: Hermeneutics, Religion, Hope.* Chicago: University of Chicago Press, 1994.

Turner, Denys. *Eros and Allegory: Medieval Exegesis of the Song of Songs.* Cistercian Studies Series 156. Kalamazoo, MI: Cistercian Publications, 1995.

Tyndale, William. *The Obedience of a Christian Man.* 1528. Edited by David Daniell. London: Penguin, 2000.

Vielhauer, Philipp. "Introduction to Part C. Apocalypses and Related Subjects." In

New Testament Apocrypha. Volume 2. Edited by Edgar Hennecke and Wilhelm Schneemelcher, translated by R. McLeod Wilson, 544-79. Louisville: Westminster John Knox Press, 1991.

Vinge, Louise. *The Five Senses: Studies in a Literary Tradition*. Acta Regiae Societatis Humaniorum Litterarum Lundensis 82. Lund: Liber Läromedel, 1975.

Vogel, Thomas, ed. *Über das Hören: Einem Phänomen auf der Spur*. Tübingen: Attempto Verlag, 1998.

Walz, Angelus. "Augustini de Dacia O.P.: 'Rotulus pugillaris' examinatus atque editus." *Angelicum* 6 (1929): 253-78.

Warfield, Benjamin B. "The Inerrancy of the Original Autographs." In *Selected Shorter Writings of B. B. Warfield*. Volume 2. Edited by John E. Meeter, 582-83. Nutley, NJ: Presbyterian and Reformed Publishing Company, 1973.

―――. *The Inspiration and Authority of the Bible*. Philadelphia: The Presbyterian and Reformed Publishing Company, 1948.

Wendel, François. *Calvin: The Origins and Development of His Religious Thought*. Translated by Philip Mairet. New York: Harper, 1963.

Willis-Watkins, David E. "The Unio Mystica and the Assurance of Faith According to Calvin." In *Calvin: Erbe und Auftrag. Festschrift für Wilhelm Heinrich Neuser zum 65. Geburtstag*. Edited by Willem van't Spijker, 77-84. Leuven: Peeters, 1991.

Zenger, Ernst. "'Gib deinem Knecht ein hörendes Herz!' Von der messianischen Kraft des rechten Hörens." In *Über das Hören: Einem Phänomen auf der Spur*. Edited by Thomas Vogel, 27-43. Tübingen: Attempto Verlag, 1998.

Zimmermann, Gunter. "Calvins Auseinandersetzung mit Osianders Rechtfertigungslehre." *Kerygma und Dogma* 35 (1990): 236-56.

Zwingli, Huldrych. *De vera et falsa religione*. Edited by Emil Egli and Georg Finsler. Zwingli: Sämtliche Werke 3. Corpus Reformatorum 90. Leipzig, 1914.

Index of Persons

Abelard, 36-37, 80
Abinadab, 6, 138, 141
Adam, 37, 53
Adam and Eve, 30, 37, 61, 112
Akiba, Rabbi, 99
Alan of Lille, 14, 22, 67, 75-76
Ambrose, Saint, 33, 35, 54
Aminadab, 5-6, 11, 141; Aminadab's Chariot, 5-7, 12, 14, 20, 22, 38, 47, 56, 61, 85, 86, 115, 137-39
Anderson, Bernhard W., 2
Andrew of St. Victor, 32
Anselm of Canterbury, 74
Aquinas, Thomas, 13, 39-41, 46, 100, 122-23
Aristarchos, 30, 32, 48
Aristotle, 12-13, 15-16, 22-23, 34, 40, 46, 59, 66-68, 87
Astell, Ann W., 101
Augustine, Saint, 31-37, 39, 53-56, 79, 89, 97, 116, 122n.19; *City of God*, 94; *Confessions*, 12, 33-34, 131; *On Christian Doctrine*, 19, 35-36, 55-56, 117, 127
Augustine of Dacia, 9n.16

Berendt, Joachim-Ernst, 68, 69
Bernard, Robert, 55
Bernard of Clairvaux, 80-81, 89, 96, 98, 101-14, 124-26, 129
Beza, Theodore, 110

Bonaventure, Saint, 96, 98

Calvin, John, 78, 99, 110-14
Campenhausen, Hans von, 28
Cassian, John, 17, 25, 72-73, 79, 93
Castellio, Sebastian, 99, 110
Chadwick, Henry, 33n.24
Charry, Ellen, 124
Chrysostom, John, 119, 127
Cicero, 31, 56, 73, 117
Clement of Alexandria, 28
Columbus, Christopher, 21

Daly, Mary, 129
Daube, David, 17
David (King), 4, 42, 120, 138
Dilthey, Wilhelm, 65
Diodor of Tarsus, 31
Dowey, Edward A., 112
Drewermann, Eugen, 43-44
Dulles, Avery Cardinal, 128

Ebeling, Gerhard, 8, 22, 118n.4, 132-33, 135
Eckhart, Meister, 106-7
Ehrman, Bart, 3
Erasmus of Rotterdam, 27, 77, 78
Eucherius of Lyon, 17
Eusebius of Caesarea, 32, 49

Fairbairn, Patrick, 61

Index of Subjects

127; Jewish faith, 20; Luther on, 82-83, 109

Feminist theology, 129-35

Fiction, 39, 61-62, 91, 123

fides ex auditu, 66n.2, 83

figura, 54, 56

Figure, 30, 47, 54-55, 90, 94, 119, 121; figuration, 20, 54-56, 78; figurative, 19, 20, 35, 59, 72, 86, 123

Fire, 46, 51, 69

Flesh, 12, 120, 136; Augustine on, 34, 56; Bernard of Clairvaux on, 106; Calvin on, 112; Origen on, 29, 50, 51

Flexibility (of the fourfold sense), 120-21

Food, 34, 50, 53, 71, 86, 88-90, 104, 125

Forgiveness of sin, 80, 109-10

Foundation, 38-39, 57, 73, 75, 126

Four, 11-12, 140; evangelists, 11, 140-42; horses, 6, 11-12, 56, 86; living creatures, 11, 96, 115, 142; rivers of paradise, 11, 115, 141; wheels, 11, 115, 138, 140. *See also* Gospel; Senses, scriptural

Freedom, 26, 33, 40, 97, 101, 106, 107, 125, 129, 134

Fundamentalism, 3-5, 43

Goal, 56, 74, 78, 86, 96, 126-28; of interpretation, 7, 18, 65, 98, 126

Gospel, 51, 70, 72, 74, 82, 110, 133, 135, 137, 138, 141; four Gospels, 11, 141

Grace, 56, 106, 109, 127, 130, 131, 137; throne of grace, 141

Grammar, 24, 36, 40, 43, 116, 117; grammatical, 31, 126; grammatical sense, 18, 23, 25-26, 42, 123

grammatikos, 18, 30, 48, 116, 117

Greek, 5-6, 13, 18, 30-32, 37, 47, 72-73, 79, 93, 94, 101, 116-17; ocularity of Greek culture, 66, 69-70

Hearing, 12, 14, 45-47, 63, 65-84, 88, 104, 133

Heart, 24-26, 63, 66, 76, 79-80, 96, 98, 102, 103, 109, 111, 124, 127, 130

Hebrew, 5-6, 31-32, 37, 69, 116-17, 129; "Hebrew truth" (Jerome), 31

Hermeneutics, 3, 9, 13, 27, 43, 49-50, 64, 65, 71, 72, 77, 85, 127, 133; existential, 82; hermeneutical circle, 127; hermeneutics of affection, 98; hermeneutics of ascent, 56, 59, 61, 90, 122; hermeneutics of suspicion, 134; post-modern, 2, 11, 24, 128n.35. *See also* Exegesis

historia, 30, 33, 35, 39, 42, 71, 121, 122

History, 9, 11, 21, 23, 29, 30-31, 60, 78, 80, 82, 94, 98, 121, 125; "history" as literal sense, 31, 38-39, 42, 94, 103, 122; of (biblical) interpretation, 7-9, 16-17, 19-20, 22, 116, 118-19, 136; of language, 37; of mentalities, 18; post-history, 23, 120; of salvation, 20, 57, 80-82, 88, 100, 141-42; of theology, 118; world history, 39

Holy Spirit, 26, 36, 51, 56, 109, 121; in Calvin, 112-13, 126-27

Honey, 34, 86-96, 105, 108

Horizon, 11, 27, 44, 119, 142; interpretive horizon, 49, 52, 65, 71, 77, 83, 107, 118

Humanism, 5, 27, 59, 77, 94, 99, 117

hypomnema, 30

hyponoia, 13, 48-49, 52-53, 62, 72. *See also* Sub-sense

Illumination, 57, 84, 113

Image, 25, 45-46, 55, 58, 62, 70, 73, 79, 91, 102, 106, 125, 136, 142; biblical images, 6-7, 11, 20, 50, 53, 80, 87, 88-89, 93, 96, 104, 139

Imagination, 7, 62, 116, 126, 137

Incarnation, 57, 136

"In Christ," 57, 82, 111, 113, 134, 137-38

Inspiration. *See* Scripture: inspiration of

Intensification, 87-89, 102, 105-6, 111, 121

Intention, 41, 79-80, 118; intention of the author, 23, 26, 39-42, 79-80, 99; intention of the author, Aquinas on, 40, 122-23; intention of the author, Augustine on, 36; intention of the author, Luther on, 26, 59

Interiority, 80, 89, 125; interiorize, 79, 80, 96, 105, 124

Interpret, 6, 20, 26, 48, 97, 115, 132; need to interpret, 6, 20, 79, 115

Index of Scripture References